Heavenly Bodies

...ORNIA FASHION INDUSTRY FRIENDS OF AIDS PROJECT LOS ANGELES PRESENTS

TODD OLDH

Heavenly Bodies

Remembering Hollywood and Fashion's Favorite AIDS Benefit

by Michael Anketell

Taylor Publishing Company

Dallas, Texas

Author's Note

WHODUNIT? Throughout this book, there are many incidences of embarrassing, hilarious, arrogant, obnoxious, and ill-considered behavior. The names of the individuals involved have been omitted to protect the innocent as well as the guilty. These blind items are written in such a way as to provide various clues to the identities of the celebrities and power players involved. As an extra clue, most of these people appear in at least one photograph somewhere in the pages of this book. It's a treasure hunt and you're meant to have a rollicking good time searching and guessing.

The proceeds from these ten events were donated to AIDS Project Los Angeles, an AIDS service organization that helps over 8,000 people living with HIV/AIDS. A percentage from the sale of this book is being donated to the AIDS ReSEARCH Alliance of America.

Photos by Michael Anketell, Brandon MacNeal, Allen Berliner, and Reggie Ing.

Designed by Hespenheide Design.

Published by Taylor Publishing Company
1550 West Mockingbird Lane
Dallas, Texas 75235
www.taylorpub.com

Library of Congress Cataloging-in-Publication Data:
Anketell, Michael.
    Heavenly bodies : remembering Hollywood and
fashion's favorite AIDS benefit / by Michael Anketell.
      p.   cm.
    ISBN 0-87833-247-2
    1. Fashion shows.   2. AIDS (Disease)—Social
aspects.   3. Benefit performances.   I. Title.
TT502.A55   1999
746.9'2—dc21   99-35239
                                                CIP

10 9 8 7 6 5 4 3 2 1
Printed in the United States of America

To the incandescent Lynne Koester and
to the memory of my beloved friend
Brandon MacNeal who made me promise
to write this book.

THE CALIFORNIA
FASHION INDUSTRY
FRIENDS OF
AIDS PROJECT
LOS ANGELES

CELEBRATE

GIANNI
VERSACE

Acknowledgments

With this my first book, I couldn't help but notice the changes that take place from the initial concept to the writing of the manuscript, the rethinking after writing until one day the correct form conveys what was intended.

There's no greater solace to a writer than to find the correct pair of hands in which to deliver your written words, an editor who is supportive, understanding, and brilliant in her work. I am forever thankful to Camille Cline, my editor at Taylor Publishing, for seeing my vision, embracing it, and walking me through the jigsaw puzzle of publishing a book. Her intellect and friendship will always be appreciated.

Other acknowledgments span more than a decade and must include the style, wit, and impeccable memory of Jim Watterson and the dedication of hundreds of volunteers to a cause that scared away many. You are all brave hearts.

Thank you to my friends who stuck by me though the good times and those "other times":

Chris Harvey ◆ Ali MacGraw ◆ Sharon O'Connor ◆ Barry Krost ◆ Harold I. Huttas ◆ Marilynn Lovell Matz ◆ Steve Marinko ◆

Arnold Steifel ◆ Bill Anketell ◆ Margaret Foutz ◆ Laura Dail ◆ Gerry Bremmer ◆ Dean Harris ◆ Kurt Schorr ◆ Steve Moore ◆ Isaac Mizrahi ◆ Shirley Wilson ◆ Kirk Gerou ◆ Brad West ◆ Tim Misuradze ◆ Linda Bruckheimer ◆ Marylou Luther ◆ Roddy McDowall ◆ Dana Delany ◆ Dusty Springfield ◆ Bruce Robertson ◆ DeeDee Phelps ◆ Joanna Dendel ◆ Mary Kay Stolz ◆ Roger MacFarland ◆ Allen Berliner ◆ George Christie ◆ Rita Airaghi ◆ Grace and Vernon Wells ◆ Annie Flanders ◆ Barbara Foley ◆ George Martin ◆ Barbara Austin ◆ Reggie Ing ◆ Becky Epperson ◆ Linda Kim ◆ Jeff Stanchina ◆ Katy Sweet ◆ J.C. ◆ Maxine Harris ◆ Debi Mazar ◆ Gianfranco Ferré ◆ Gianni Versace ◆ Elizabeth Taylor ◆ Thierry Mugler ◆ Katy ◆ Betty ◆ Big Boy

Kudos to my Steering Committee for a decade of hard work: Jim Watterson, Gerry Bremmer, Shirley Wilson, Lynne Koester, John Scott, Joanna Dendel, Mary Kay Stolz, Rudy Culebro, Michael Calderon, Barbara Foley, Ted Guefen, and Dori Bardavid.

And finally, XOXO's to my literary agent Alan Shafer and his terrific assistant Tony Westbrook.

Flamboyant actress Tallulah Bankhead was attending a Catholic funeral mass. As the priest comes up the center aisle swinging the incense carrier, Tallulah turns to him and says, "Daaarling, I love your dress, but your purse is on fire."

Introduction

Michael Anketell's *Heavenly Bodies: Remembering Hollywood and Fashion's Favorite AIDS Benefit* is a glorious scrapbook of photographs, anecdotes, and interviews from a series of benefits held annually in Los Angeles—over-the-top, fabulous nights when Hollywood turned out to applaud one particular fashion designer each year.

This combination of fashion and show business, fantasy and hype, Seventh Avenue and Hollywood made for some of the most spectacular fundraisers imaginable and raised huge amounts of money for people living with HIV and AIDS. *Heavenly Bodies* takes us backstage to show us all of that and to inspire and move us in much the same way that the "Hollywood Canteen" did during World War II.

My own small involvement came in the early years of this event, when my friend Michael asked me if I could help by emceeing the evening honoring the very brilliant Geoffrey Beene, in a retrospective of his work. As I no longer live in Los Angeles, I've not been able to attend each one of the ensuing extravaganzas, but the one honoring my friend Calvin Klein was certainly one of the best.

In fact my earliest jobs just after college were all in the fashion business—first as assistant to Diana Vreeland and later for the great photographer Melvin Sokolsky. My everyday work consisted of time spent with some of the great talents of our time—a list of designers and make up artists, hairdressers, photographers, and stylists too long to enumerate. I knew or met "everyone" in that business, but I guess that two of the most brilliant and most important to me, personally, were Way Bandy and Halston. There was a world we took altogether for granted, an explosion of originality and style, even theater.

And then one day the horror began, the slow decimation of a whole generation of friends and icons, as well as thousands upon thousands of innocent people all lost to this mysterious plague. Like everyone I know, I was devastated and felt powerless to help. But I have always believed what my mother told me, which was that each one of us makes a tremendous difference in the lives of others, in the quality of life on our planet, with even the tiniest contribution. I believe that we human beings and, in fact, all living creatures are an inter-connected community and that consciousness and caring and action really do make a difference.

The outrageous, glitzy, show-biz benefits produced by the California Fashion Industry Friends of APLA made a big difference. And to watch the combination of two of the worlds most devastated by the AIDS virus was inspiring, exhilarating, and profoundly moving. I witnessed the very best of the two industries in which I have worked all of my life—and I felt the power of their commitment as well as their grief.

It scares me that so many people think that the so-called AIDS cocktail has dramatically diminished the seriousness of the AIDS pandemic. I am haunted by the loss of so many of my friends, many of whom would have been celebrated at the very events in this book. At the end of the day for me, what are most important than anything else in life are health, love, and friendship. *Heavenly Bodies* somehow shows me in the most entertaining way just how much energy and passion have been generated for these values by two of the most outrageous and generous industries on earth: Fashion and Hollywood.

Ali MacGraw
June 9, 1999
Santa Fe, New Mexico

Contents

GIANFRANCO
FERRE

ADRIAN—I wanted one of everything!

GEOFFREY BEENE—New York produced Beene, a brilliant American designer.

BOB MACKIE—Hollywood glamour fit for Hollywood wives!

HOLLYWOOD COSTUMERS—To be sure, an interesting evening on all levels.

VERSACE—Hot, hot, hot! With plenty going on, on and off the runway!

THIERRY MUGLER—Punkish and scary sometimes. The only person he didn't have on the catwalk that night was me.

CALVIN KLEIN—Slinky, sexy, skinny, sexy, mod, sexy— bods with street appeal.

ISAAC MIZRAHI—Funny, personable, outrageous. A showman with Hollywood connections I'd like to have.

GIANFRANCO FERRÉ—Very of the moment and very architecturally sound.

TODD OLDHAM—Teenybopper goes to Cairo via Las Vegas.

JACKIE COLLINS REMEMBERS

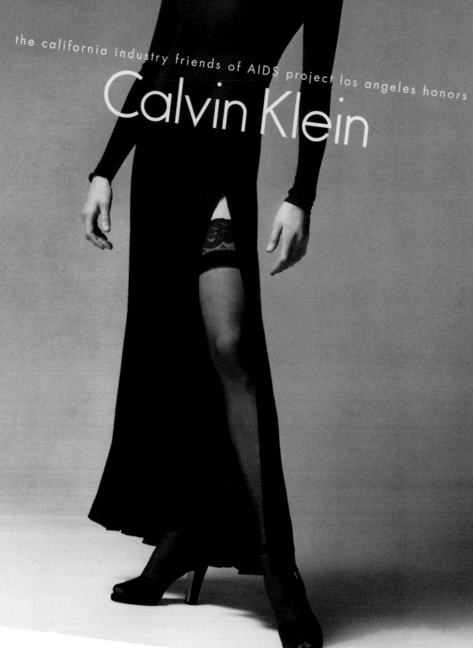

the california industry friends of AIDS project los angeles honors

Calvin Klein

California
Fashion Industry
Friends of
AIDS Project
Los Angeles
celebrates

Bob
Mackie
1989

Adrian
—Dead Designers Can't Say No

"When the rest of the world didn't want to get involved in this event, my friend Adrian, had he been alive, would have **jumped** at the **opportunity**. That's the kind of **man** he was."

— Roddy McDowall

The idea of the worlds of fashion, celebrity, and AIDS fund-raising coming together into a luminous event seemed a natural, particularly in Hollywood. It was a perfect way to integrate as many celebrities as possible in the fight against this dreaded disease and consequently attract the interest of mainstream America. We could raise money and raise consciousness, while spreading awareness of this dangerous new plague through the popular press. It was a brilliant and seemingly obvious idea.

When we started to try to put together this event in late 1985, however, we discovered the one, apparently fatal, flaw in our idea—none of the big names in fashion or in Hollywood wanted to be associated with the word *AIDS*. Though Perry Ellis had been one of the first in the fashion industry to die of AIDS, just a few months before our first requests went out, even his company chose not to lend his name. The disease was too new, too scary, and too stigmatized with minorities. At that time, in the public's mind, it was a disease that only affected homosexual men, Haitian refugees, heroin addicts, and hemophiliacs. It appeared that if you did not belong to a minority group beginning with the letter *H*, you were safe. A wonderfully dark joke that illustrates the double-stigmatization of being gay and having AIDS was circulating through the gay community at the time:

Q: What's the most difficult part of having AIDS?

A: Convincing your parents that you're Haitian.

It is easy now to forget the fear of AIDS in Hollywood before it was understood how AIDS was spread. Although there are many closets in Hollywood, there are fewer real secrets, and there were several notorious incidents at the time of female actresses refusing, while filming TV and movie scenes, to kiss actors they assumed to be gay. When Rock Hudson died in the fall of 1985, there was fear expressed (and exploited) in the media for Linda Evans, who had shared kisses with Hudson in the filming of the *Dynasty* TV series. (It speaks well of Evans that, whatever her personal fears, she did what she could to calm the budding panic of the time.) In 1985, it was only starting to become well known that AIDS is caused by a virus, and it was still not widely understood how the virus was being spread. Plus, AIDS was not an attractive disease with cute poster kids. The pictures in the public's eye were of young men looking old and sunken and often covered with purple lesions.

This was not a pretty combination of images for two industries built on marketing youth, glamour, sex appeal, and flawless beauty. Things would change drastically in just a year, but every major designer we approached for the premiere event in 1986 declined to lend their name to this cause. It is easy to forget when most celebrities on awards show telecasts now wear a red AIDS support ribbon that with a few dramatic exceptions, such as Elizabeth Taylor and Bette Midler, Hollywood was as squeamish about the whole issue of AIDS as was the rest of the country. Finally, because fashion and entertainment are so integrally a part of people's lives, it can also be easy to forget that, first and foremost, they are industries and, like most businesses, do not want to be associated with *any* issue that might offend *any* segment of their potential customer base.

The most dramatic earlier example of what can happen when Hollywood and the fashion industry rally around a cause occurred during World War II. On a February night in

Producer Doug Chapin and the late actress Elizabeth Montgomery. Elizabeth and actor Roddy McDowall were the first two Hollywood celebrities to lend their support to our event.

1942, the great Battle of Los Angeles was fought in the skies over the entertainment capital of the world as antiaircraft guns fired more than a thousand rounds of ammunition into the searchlight-swept skies. No enemy planes were downed, however, and it was later realized that the city had been "bombed" only by the same exploding anti-aircraft shells fired in panic into *empty* skies. America was *AT WAR!* and so was Hollywood. Just north of Los Angeles, a Japanese submarine had shelled a Santa Barbara oil field.

Carole Lombard had died in an airplane crash while returning from a Buy War Bonds tour and was nearly canonized by the nation as her grieving husband, Clark Gable, enlisted in the service. Also enlisting were many of Hollywood's other major male stars, such as Tyrone Power, Mickey Rooney, and Jimmy Stewart, who had to beef up his skinny body to make the minimum weight requirement for the Air Force. And in the movies themselves, everyone left behind was busy fighting the Axis powers—even Tarzan fought the Nazis. Trumpeting Hollywood's morale-boosting skills, the *Hollywood Reporter* on the first-year anniversary of the Pearl Harbor attack ran a slightly ludicrous headline that read:

Eisenhower and Generals in Greatest Praise for Hollywood's Pictures, Second Only to Actual Fighting!

Hollywood's female stars were also busy supporting the war effort and were invaluable in raising money by selling war bonds. Hedy Lamarr offered to kiss any man who would buy $25,000 worth of war bonds and sold $17 million in bonds in one day. It is estimated that Dorothy Lamour sold more than $350 million worth during the war. Other stars were lending their aid, faces, and bodies to wartime rationing efforts and scrap drives.

To help entertain the many servicemen without money or companionship who wanted to see Hollywood before departing for combat in the Pacific, Bette Davis and John Garfield, with the donated labor of studio workmen, converted a barn at 1451 Cahuenga Boulevard, near Sunset Boulevard, into a virtual nightclub. In October 1942, the Hollywood Canteen opened to welcome up to 3,000 servicemen a night—500 entering at a time. Hollywood's biggest stars donated their time serving food, washing dishes, entertaining, socializing, and dancing with the troops. An evening might find Fred MacMurray emceeing, with Bing Crosby and Judy Garland singing, while Marlene Dietrich baked cakes, young Roddy McDowall bused tables, and Barbara Stanwyck and Rita Hayworth jitterbugged on the dance floor. Though the Canteen cost $3,000 a day to operate, nobody was ever charged a penny, and it's estimated that the Hollywood Canteen entertained more than three million servicemen during the war. The millionth GI to visit the Canteen was Sergeant Carl Boll, and he got to spend four days in the company

Designed for Joan Crawford, this black-and-white evening gown was purchased from her private collection by Joseph Simms.

These gingham sundresses were made in the 1930s and still look modern today.

Original Adrian costumes. He made gingham sexy and fashionable.

BETTE DAVIS
DARK VICTORY
WB
ORRY-KELLY

NEEDS NEW SKIRT
NEEDS: NEW BEANIE

Original sketches for the
Bette Davis tribute.

Lake complied and her career took a nosedive. Lorraine Day and Claudette Colbert adopted feathercuts like those given women joining the Waves and Wacs. Most working women left their hair long, however, and kept it safely out of the way with hairnets, kerchiefs, and crocheted snoods inspired by those Vivien Leigh and Olivia de Havilland had worn in 1939's *Gone with the Wind*.

There were many other fashion changes brought about by the war. Because of wartime cloth rationing, cuffs, vests, wide lapels, extra pockets, and a second pair of pants disappeared from men's suits while women's skirts had reduced hems, narrowed and raised above the knees. Short coats were de rigueur for both men and women. Wool was mostly unavailable and was replaced by rayon. Unable to get silk or nylon stockings, women began using leg makeup, some even acrobatically painting stocking seams up the back of their legs with eyebrow pencils. The problem of leg makeup for men was, according to the words of a popular song, "It decants on your pants." Though women might wear pants and over-alls to work, they also had more money than ever before to buy makeup, such as Elizabeth Arden's *Victory Red* lipstick, and to indulge in new fashions inspired by the movies. High Cuban platform shoes, popularized by Carmen Miranda, were the rage, as were upswept hairdos employing wire rollers or rats that built the hair high in the front.

The one truly distinctive fashion style most associated with the war years, though, was the thickly padded shoulders of women's suits and dresses. In contrast to the more relaxed, ornate look of the previous decade, women's styles became more stark and mascu-line, reflecting not only the wartime rationing and the entry of women into the labor force but the purposefulness of a country at war. The person most responsible for creating this wartime style was the legendary MGM cos-tume designer Adrian. It is interesting that at this time, the start of war, Adrian's amazingly influential and prolific career with MGM was coming to an end.

So we arrive at Adrian, the honored designer of our first annual gala to raise money to assist people living with HIV and

of Hollywood's royalty. This event provided the basic story framework around which Warner Brothers created a star-studded 1944 movie called *Hollywood Canteen*, a movie notable for the introduction of the Cole Porter tune "Don't Fence Me In," sung by Roy Rogers as his horse Trigger danced on his hind legs.

Talk about war effort—Veronica Lake, famous for her long silky blond tresses drap-ing seductively over one eye, was asked by the War Department to trim her hair because the now-working women were getting their hair entangled in the defense-plant machinery.

AIDS in Los Angeles. (The organization we chose to support was at the time the second largest AIDS service organization in the world.) Adrian fulfilled one crucial requirement for us, he was dead and couldn't say no. Yet, in retrospect, the guiding hand of necessity had pushed us to make the most perfect choice possible had we been wiser in the first place. Who better to represent the glamour of fashion and Hollywood than Adrian? He was the man responsible for the most glamorous costumes of the most glamorous studio during Hollywood's most glamorous decade. During the 1930s, MGM claimed, with pre-Hubble-telescope hyperbole, to have "more stars than there are in the heavens," and it was Adrian who dressed them and who created the signature looks that will be forever associated with them—including Jean Harlow, Norma Shearer, Katharine Hepburn, Garbo, and, especially, Joan Crawford. Crawford later graciously admitted that her reputation as a fashion trendsetter was a consequence of the genius of Adrian. The first costume designer to enjoy a long, continuous career in American film, Adrian is regarded by many as the father of American fashion.

Adrian was born Adrian Adolph Greenburg in Naugatuck, Connecticut, in 1903. Fashion was in his blood—his parents' successful millinery shop had been founded by his maternal grandmother. Adrian studied design at New York's School for Fine and Applied Arts. When in Paris continuing his studies, Adrian met composer Irving Berlin while both were attending a costume ball at the Paris Opera House. Berlin was taken with a costume that Adrian had created for a classmate and swept him back to New York to design costumes for Berlin's *Music Box Review*. Later, after Adrian created costumes for many New York productions, Rudolph Valentino and his wife, Natacha Rambova, a costumer and set designer herself, brought him to Hollywood to design costumes for two Valentino films, *Cobra* and *The Eagle*, both released in 1925.

Adrian was next hired by Cecil B. DeMille's art director, Mitchell Leisen (who would himself later direct films such as *Death Takes a Holiday* and two Preston Sturges scripts, *Easy Living* and *Remember the Night)*.

DeMille's grand style of epic moviemaking allowed Adrian to indulge his taste for the elegant, opulent, fantastic, and downright mind-boggling, including the legendary camp classic *Madame Satan*. (*Madame Satan* includes a mad costume party in a zeppelin that is being ripped to shreds by a storm. As the incredibly costumed cream of New York society parachute out of the zeppelin, the hero gives the last parachute to his wife, then dives out of the zeppelin without a parachute—only to land safely in the lake in New York's Central Park.) DeMille's instructions were, "Don't design anything you could possibly buy in a store," and Adrian was happy to oblige him. Adrian was also learning showmanship and the value of self-promotion from DeMille as he developed a personal style appropriate for early monochrome film stock—the skillful use of black and white fabrics incorporating satins, silks, sequins, rhinestones, beads, and bows for shimmering highlights and contrast.

Then, in 1928, Louis B. Mayer signed Adrian to a contract as chief costume designer at MGM. Adrian was just 25 years old and he had already made it to the top of his profession. At MGM, Adrian would sketch up to 50 designs a day, for everyone from star to extra. He designed the costumes for 200 films at MGM, while he annually spent more than a million dollars on clothes and earned as much as President Roosevelt.

All designed for Bette Davis, we recreated these costumes from original sketches. The clothes are on display today at Warner Bros., which touts them as the real thing.

It's said that Garbo, with her lack of curves and her angularity and tragic exoticism, was Adrian's favorite star for whom to design. He designed her costumes for such classics as *Mata Hari, Queen Christina, Anna Karenina,* and *Camille.* The looks he created for Garbo were imitated by women around the world—especially the hats: the cloche, the turban, the slouch, and the pillbox. For Norma Shearer, the wife of the studio's head of production, Irving Thalberg, Adrian fashioned a look of tailored softness with high waists to flatter her long waist with short legs. In such films as *Dinner at Eight* and *Hold Your Man,* Adrian created Jean Harlow's blond bombshell signature look of clinging negligees and gowns of white satin set off with feathers and furs. For Myrna Loy's highly nuanced persona, he created a more subtle, soft, and understated well-tailored look. Adrian also dressed Katharine Hepburn in *The Philadelphia Story* and *Woman of the Year.* He simultaneously clothed most of MGM's women stars in just one picture, *The Women.* But it was perhaps Adrian's designs for Joan Crawford that were the most memorable and influential on American fashion. With Crawford's broad shoulders, long waist, and strong facial features, Adrian felt she overwhelmed most clothes. To match Crawford's physical dominance and to make her hips appear smaller, Adrian added even more width to her shoulders. The design worked well for Crawford and she used variations on it throughout her career. The look

Adrian created for Crawford, often referred to as the American Silhouette, was a sensation with the American dress-buying public and is still a dependable perennial of the worldwide fashion industry.

After a decade with MGM, Adrian got to truly stretch his playful side and work in color when he designed the costumes for *The Wizard of Oz.* One problem was how to make Judy Garland appear younger than she really was at the time. (Questionable Hollywood lore has it that Shirley Temple had originally been sought for the role.) Adrian finally settled on the now-famous gingham-blue dress. Among the other materials he employed were real straw for the Scarecrow, buckram and silver-painted leather for the Tin Woodsman, two real lion skins for the Cowardly Lion (a fifty-pound costume that Bert Lahr said was like "acting inside a mattress"), and miles of felt for the Munchkins. To be sure, Adrian also designed Dorothy's legendary Ruby Slippers. (There were actually at least five pair of Ruby Slippers: two for Judy Garland in the film; one for her stand-in, who had a different shoe size; one, a test pair not used in the movie, now owned by Debbie Reynolds; and a pair that was given away as a 1939 contest prize. This last pair sold at Christie's auction house in New York City in 1988 for $150,000. At MGM's studio wardrobe auction in 1970, the first pair of Ruby Slippers ever auctioned went for *just* $15,000—and is now in the Smithsonian Institution.)

When America entered the war, studios cut their budgets and designers were forced to use cheaper designs and materials. These changes frustrated Adrian, who decided in 1942 not to renew his MGM contract. He and his actress wife, Janet Gaynor (a leading lady of the 1920s and 1930s and winner of the first Best Actress Oscar in 1927), left Hollywood and moved to New York, where Adrian opened his own successful couture. He would occasionally come out of retirement to do a movie such as 1948's Hitchcock film, *Rope.* In 1952, after suffering a heart attack, Adrian, Janet Gaynor, and their son Robin moved to a ranch in Brazil. When Adrian returned to New York in 1959 to design the costumes for the Lerner and Loewe musical *Camelot,* he died suddenly of a heart attack at age 56. Because of the worldwide impact of the movies in which he created the clothes, Adrian may well have been the most influential fashion designer in history.

In 1985, having exhausted a long list of designers that included such famous names as Calvin Klein, Donna Karan, Jessica McClintock, and Ralph Lauren, we knew we needed to become more resourceful in our search. After all, we were idealistic, young professionals with countless contacts in both the entertainment and fashion industries. Sure enough, the solution to our seeming dead end came from a member of our very own steering committee—Jim Watterson, Senior Vice President of Public Relations at the May Company department stores and one of Los Angeles's most socially prominent philanthropists. Jim had worked with every Blue Ribbon Group from San Marino to Beverly Hills to Malibu, and he knew and lunched with Betsy Bloomingdale and the Bistro Garden Lunch Brigade. Jim was present in 1986, when, in our effort to form a committee to bring this first event to fruition, 100 of Los Angeles's fashion, entertainment, and retail movers and shakers were invited to lunch in downtown's Hilton Hotel.

After presenting our plan and our plea over lunch, we heard excuses, apologies, or outright dismissals of our idea from those assembled that day. The dismissal that sticks most in my mind to this day was from a well-known producer of a morning TV show who said:

No one has ever been successful in producing a fashion show in Los Angeles that anyone would pay to see. And besides, gays were "in"

A black cocktail dress worn by Rosalind Russell in *The Women.*

From the movie *Lovely to Look At,* this costume would be one of Adrian's last efforts for film.

Adrian's famous "yin and yang" dress was designed for Joan Crawford.

Jean Harlow's wedding gown was designed and made by Adrian.

in the late 1970s and early 1980s. They were a must-have at any dinner party. But they are all sick now—no longer desirable. Normal people are afraid they'll catch AIDS if they're in the same room with them. Forget it—it'll never happen.

Upon finishing her prophecy of doom, this oracular producer got up, grabbed her Louis Vuitton handbag, and walked out the door. She was soon followed by most of the other invited guests, who departed with wish-

Bette Davis
a 'Margot'
All About Eve
20th-Fox 195
Edith Head
RECREATION

es of "Good luck" and final rebuffs of "Thanks, but no thanks." By 1991, just six years after that futile lunch, *Women's Wear Daily* (the bible of the fashion industry, now called *WWD*) would declare our event "the most important fashion event in Los Angeles and the largest fund-raising effort of its kind in the world … Breathtaking." But on that downhearted day, only nine men and women remained seated. If we were going to have a fashion fund-raiser, it was now exceedingly clear that it would only happen through the pigheaded commitment of these nine. It is interesting that eleven years later, this small committed core group were all still there, working hard to make this event happen.

Our fortunes took a dramatic turn for the better in the summer of 1986 when Jim Watterson took a trip to New York and met with his friend Lenore Benson, head of the Costume Institute of the New York Metropolitan Museum. He confirmed with Lenore a lead he had about a large collection of Adrian dresses in Philadelphia. The magical Goddess of Necessity who led us to select Adrian was also accompanied by her half-sister Good Luck, who led us to the largest private collection of Adrian suits and gowns—the collection of Joseph Simms, a schoolteacher in Philadelphia who, for much of his life, had been collecting Adrian dresses. As Jim and Lenore boarded a train to Philadelphia from New York's Penn Station, they didn't know what they might find in a collection accumulated over the years by a man they knew little about, Joseph Simms, a public high school teacher. As their cab pulled up to Simms's address, they were surprised to find a modest apartment building in a middle-class blue-collar neighborhood. In his apartment, Simms displayed several original Adrian sketches. But when Jim and Lenore descended into the basement of the apartment building, it was the fashion-lover's equivalent of the first opening of King Tut's Tomb. In the basement were rack after rack after rack covered with sheets. When Simms pulled back the sheets, *voila*, there were 400 glorious Adrians!

How Simms had managed to amass this amazing collection is still a bit of a mystery.

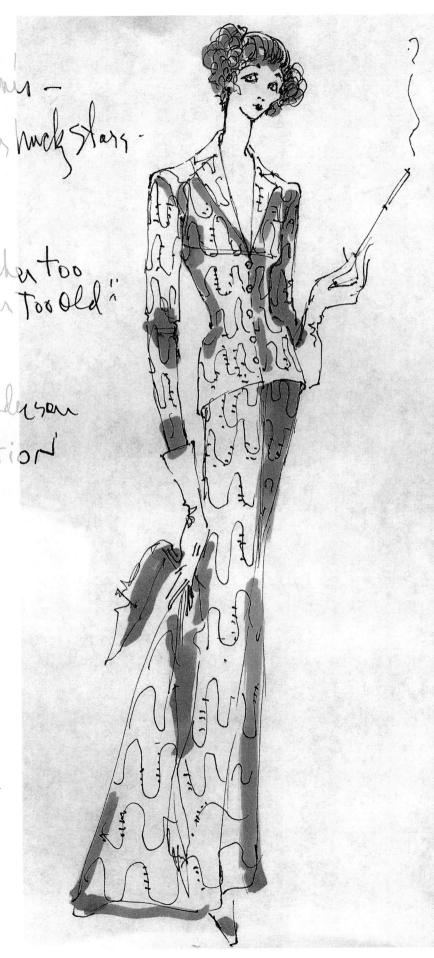

Some gowns were no doubt purchased at the famous MGM wardrobe sale in 1970, but others were apparently acquired by traveling from town to town asking women if they would donate their Adrians—and they did. Many of the clothes in Simms's collection were from Adrian's glory days at MGM, but the majority were from the 1940s when Adrian had a Beverly Hills couture salon on Beverly Drive. The Adrian salon had the neo-classic "Beverly Hills Georgian" look popular in the 1940s and was decorated with a unicorn backdrop painted by renowned artist and designer Tony Duquette. (Duquette later worked with Adrian on his last film project, *Lovely to Look At*, and, following Adrian's fatal heart attack, Duquette completed Adrian's work on the Broadway musical *Camelot,* which starred Richard Burton and Julie Andrews.) For Adrian's shows, where only ice water was served, he would take one outfit from that collection and dress it on his pet monkey, who would perch on Adrian's shoulder during the show.

Then and there, with the help of Lenore and Joseph, Jim began excitedly Polaroiding and putting together the lineup for the Adrian show. As Jim says now about this wondrous moment, "It was easy; it felt so natural, nothing had to be pushed ... as if Adrian was living inside my head. I thought Adrian had somehow invaded my psyche as we just invented the scenes right on the spot." The

Another actress who was not intimidated by lending her name to AIDS causes was Brenda Vaccaro and her husband, Guy.

very show that came together so magically in Simms's basement was the same one we later presented on our stage.

- The first scene would be suits from the 1940s that Adrian had designed with Pola Stout, who did incredible fabrics. Stout had a real genius for engineering silhouettes and also for mating fabrics. These dresses were all wools.
- The second scene would be beautiful print dresses and some of Adrian's more casual, special-occasion clothes. There were delightful dresses such as "Washington Crossing the Delaware," "Snow in Vermont," and Joan Crawford's "Rooster Dress." They were all storytelling dresses, mostly made of rayon, with huge, voluminous skirts. Other dresses showed that Adrian could even make gingham look elegant. And they'd all be presented to the recording of Carol Burnett singing the song "I'm Still Here" from the Broadway musical *Follies*—because they were still here. These amazing dresses would later cause the audience to erupt with applause.
- On his many travels, Adrian had gone to Spain and met the Duchess of Alba. Our third scene would be a series of Spain, with bullfighting-inspired clothes Adrian had created in red and black and all black. With incredible detailing, some of these dresses were so diabolically engineered and complicated that it would later take a lot of time to just figure out how to put them on. This scene would be both opened and closed by Donna Wood, the prima ballerina of the Alvin Ailey Dance Company, who donated her performance, dancing to the music from the opera *Carmen*. The scene would end with "The Toreador," Janet Gaynor's famous $3,000 beaded jacket with a cardinal's cape over it.
- The final scene would be Hollywood glamour clothes and the legendary star gowns. There would be the famous Joan Crawford "yin and yang" white and black-beaded crepe dress, a Norma Shearer dress from 1939's *Idiot's Delight*, and a black velvet dress with an incredibly tiny waist that Zsa Zsa Gabor had worn in *Lovely to Look At*, from which we would use lots of clothes. Adrian's last film, 1952's *Lovely to Look At*, was the second film adaptation of Jerome Kern's musical *Roberta* and starred Red Skelton, Howard Keel, and the very narrow-waisted, big-bosomed Kathryn Grayson. The big fashion show sequence at the end of the movie featured Adrian gowns in a Tony Duquette décor.

"There were so many wonders to choose among, it was hard to edit his collection," Jim Watterson recalls. "Every piece had a history, a story behind it. It was like trying to choose between diamonds and rubies." Jim decided that the fashion show would be accented with movie scenes selected, with the knowledgeable guidance of film historian David Chierchetti, from MGM classics that would best show off Adrian's genius.

- The first clip would be from 1938's *Marie Antoinette* in which Marie in white confronts Madame DuBarry in black. Although the script was distorted in an effort to make Marie into a sympathetically suitable role for Norma Shearer (as Irving Thalberg's widow, the studio's anointed First Lady as well as a large MGM stockholder), the film was resplendent with 1,250 of the most elaborate costumes ever made in Hollywood, including Adrian's costumes for two French poodles.

Although *Marie Antoinette* was ultimately shot in black and white, Adrian had originally designed the costumes for Technicolor.

- The second classic film segment would be Judy Garland's lavish South American musical number from *Ziegfeld Girl*. This 1941 musical-drama chronicled the efforts of Judy Garland, Hedy Lamarr, and Lana Turner to attain the lofty status of Ziegfeld Girl.
- The wonderful confrontation scene from 1936's *Camille*, where Robert Taylor throws money at Greta Garbo's feet, would be the third movie clip. Alexandre Dumas's classic weepie was directed by George Cukor, who helped Garbo make death from tuberculosis look romantic and glamorous.
- One of the most gloriously gowned and brilliantly scripted seven minutes in the history of cinema, the powder room scene from 1939's *The Women*, would be our final clip. Based on a play by Clare Booth Luce (the wife of Henry Luce, the founder of *Time, Life, Fortune,* and *Sports Illustrated* magazines), this wise-cracking monument to female cattiness included hilarious lessons on how to destroy other women's reputations while defending your own and keeping your man. It also had a wonderful Technicolor fashion show of dazzling Adrian gowns.

With Jim and Lenore's astonishing discovery, our first show was born. There were still major obstacles ahead, many of which would seem insurmountable at the time, but they were, one by one, overcome. In retrospect, it was almost as if the bejeweled and Adrian-gowned Glinda, the Good Witch of Oz, had waved her magic wand and granted each of our wishes, always with the assistance of one or another unsung angel.

One unexpected problem, relatively small but pesky, was finding models who could fit into the Adrian dresses. To our surprise, the female stars of the 1930s and 1940s, Crawford, Garbo, Hepburn, Shearer, and Harlow, although bigger than life on the silver screen,

were, actually, very short women—not at all like today's statuesque models who stand at 5'10" or taller. In 1940, the actresses averaged between 5' and 5'5" with dress sizes of 1 and 2. But the typical runway model today has a dress size that starts at size 6 and runs as large as size 10! Finding models in 1987 who could work a runway and at the same time wear a size 1 or 2 looked, at first, to be impossible. But a fortuitous recurring fashion trend saved us. Luckily, the first versions of high platform heels (popular also in the 1970s and again in the late 1990s) became a fashion rage in the late 1930s and early 1940s, popularized by that tiny sensation from Brazil, Carmen Miranda. With the added height of these shoes, a 1940 "five-foot-two, eyes of blue" actress was actually wearing a dress designed for a much taller woman.

Still, where could we get the models, with almost no money? Then, two more angels came to our rescue. One was Nina Blanchard, who, at the time, owned the largest modeling agency in Los Angeles, was partnered with the Ford Agency in New York, and represented supermodels Rene Russo, Janice Dickenson, and Cheryl Tiegs. The second angel was Mary Webb Davis, who had the other premiere modeling agency in the city. The compassion of these two women and their generous world-class models, who donated their talents to our show, made the casting of our first show another small miracle.

A much more daunting obstacle to success, however, was how we were going to even get noticed amid the usual relentless swirl of Hollywood events. Getting Hollywood's attention for this first-time fashion show looked as impossible as it had been finding a live designer to honor. Had it not been for the valiant efforts of a few of Hollywood's favorite stars and their managers, Barry Krost and Doug Chapin, who encouraged them, neither Hollywood nor the fashion world would have taken any but passing notice of our efforts. Without stars, there would have been little press coverage and our message would not get out. But on the night of the Adrian show, the stars did come. Actress Carol Kane, an Emmy-winner as the endearingly nutty Simka on TV's *Taxi* and an Oscar-nominee for playing the

Our hero, producer Barry Krost, and author Jackie Collins attended all ten events.

Jewish-immigrant Gitl in *Hester Street*, came that evening, as did Brenda Vaccaro, an Oscar-nominee for *Once Is Not Enough* who first gained wide recognition when she employed Jon Voight as a sex toy in 1969's classic film *Midnight Cowboy*. Bess Armstrong, the beautiful star of series TV and movies such as *The Four Seasons* and *The High Road to China* with Tom Selleck, was in our audience along with JoBeth Williams, who streaked onto the big screen with a nude appearance in *Kramer vs.*

Kramer and later, even more memorably, as a mom saving her child from the perils of late-night TV viewing in *Poltergeist*. The glamorous novelist Jackie Collins was there, no doubt taking mental notes to use in her next best-selling tome chronicling the lives of Hollywood's denizens. Jackie is the sister of actress Joan Collins, famed *Dynasty* troublemaker and sparring partner of Linda Evans. Possibly our most popular star that evening was Elizabeth Montgomery, the beloved Samantha of

Bewitched. Elizabeth was the daughter of film star Robert Montgomery and the wife of actors Gig Young and then Robert Foxworth. She had starred in a couple of dozen TV movies in which she was often a victimized woman who would find her personal strength—though she also portrayed Western bandit Belle Starr and parent-hacker Lizzie Borden.

A good friend and personal manager of the late Elizabeth Montgomery, movie producer Barry Krost, discussed with us Miss Montgomery's personal involvement in bringing awareness to AIDS and other causes:

> *Elizabeth became very political and very caring and yet, at the same time, always was strangely shy for a lady who had all her life been around press and Hollywood. She protected her private life and she found the spotlight, at times, very uncomfortable, unless it was about a specific project—a movie or a cause she believed in. She was one of the first public people to get involved in the very early days of the fight against HIV. I think Elizabeth was on the side of anybody, any group of people that she thought was being treated inappropriately. But she was still shy. I remember when we arrived that first year at the Adrian event. There was a press line outside and she suggested we stop the car, get out, and go in the side entrance. I said, "It sort of defeats the point of your being here." And she said, "Oh yes, you're right," and she went in the front way, through the press.*

These giving, compassionate ladies graced our premiere event with their radiance and posed for the pictures that assured that we *would* be noticed. According to Barry Krost, who personally asked each of these stars to support our first event, "They all knew why they were coming, where they were going, and they all answered yes without flinching." It was an unexpected delight that evening to watch these not-easily-impressed women marvel at Adrian's gowns with their timeless elegance and attention to detail. Adrian had won over a whole new generation of Hollywood stars!

During the fashion show that evening, California's biggest sportswear designer at that time sat boldly at a runway table. She was accompanied not by the typical table of friends and important clients and celebrities, but by a table full of her design staff who were madly sketching and Polaroiding everything Adrian—including hats, shoes, wraps, and accessories. For the next several seasons, we saw a definite Adrian influence in her collections. From similar fabric designs and colors to silhouettes, it was unmistakably Adrian. Her faux-Adrian designs sold very well and got her collections prominent space in the major department stores. Because of that success, she was subsequently able to quite profitably take her company public.

Another memorable scene during the fashion show that evening occurred when a famous, husky-voiced actress became downright overcome with emotion as the Adrian gowns started down the runway. Her love of drink as well as her acting genes no doubt contributed to her histrionics that night, but it was the beauty of the original costumes for Norma Shearer and Rosalind Russell making their way down the catwalk that set her to screaming, "Norma Shearer! My God … Norma Shearer wore that!" "Bette Davis!" "Judy Garland!" she went on, tears streaming down her cheeks. "I've got to touch them for luck!" she told her husband. And, with that, she climbed onto the top of the table and crawled across our 72-inch round, knocking over water and wine glasses. She pulled herself onto the runway and stopped traffic as she touched, as if it were a religious relic, a gown worn by Joan Crawford in *The Women.* Her husband quickly grabbed one of her legs as her manager grabbed the other and they dragged her off the runway and back across the table. Her performance had been a magical moment, and the audience laughed and applauded their approval. Her comedic timing had been flawless, even though it had not been scripted.

The first big star to agree to lend his name and talent to our show was Roddy McDowall, a friend of Adrian's for many years and one of the few openly gay actors in Hollywood. Roddy was already a child movie star in England before he and his family evacuated to the United States during the Battle of Britain. Roddy soon landed

Talking With Roddy McDowall, August 1998:

• **You were the first star to lend his name to our first AIDS benefit in 1987. Why did you help us? Didn't you consider it a threat to your career as so many others did?** Heavens no, I never thought about it. It does surprise me [that I was the first]; usually Hollywood is quick to help the underdog. I had already lost several close friends to the disease. The government seemed unengaged and unconcerned, so I said, "Fine." Elizabeth [Taylor] was already on her way to becoming an activist. She certainly had my ear and my admiration.

Actor Roddy McDowall was a personal friend of Adrian and our first Master of Ceremonies in 1987.

We wanted to do something. It was just hard to decide what and how. • **When did you meet Adrian?** I believe it was through his wife, Janet Gaynor. Certainly every working actor in those days knew who he was. He'd done hundreds of films by the time I met him. He was an extraordinary talent. There's not been a costume designer since with such sophistication, style, and genius. • **Were you close friends?** Yes and no. Not long after we met, Adrian and his family moved to Brazil. Adrian was tired of Hollywood; he needed to recharge. I would see him and Janet sporadically, when they happened to be in New York or Los Angeles. • **What was Janet Gaynor like?** A beautiful thing. She was short, four feet eleven inches or something like that. But such fun to be around. • **What about her legendary friendship with Mary Martin; what was that all about? I've heard they were lovers.** I wouldn't know. Yes, they were the best of friends, but why would that make them lovers? That's a silly question. • **I'm going to throw out some famous names and I'd like you to respond to them.** Okay. Sounds like fun. • **Joan Crawford?** The quintessential movie star. She was smart, shrewd, and very tough. I liked her. • **Lauren Bacall?** Someone who should work more. • **Claudette Colbert?** Style, grace, and a wonderful, wicked sense of humor. • **Katharine Hepburn?** What has always troubled me about Kate is her lack of spiritual faith. She believes that we're born, we live, we die—like a bug. I find it hard to believe that we die like bugs, like we never existed. • **Joan Hackett?** A strange woman. She was always confusing me with Tony Perkins. • **Joan Collins?** Pass. • **Rosalind Russell?** One of my favorite actors. A friend and brilliant comedienne. • **Diana Ross?** The Supremes. • **Lassie?** (He laughs.) A great actor by Hollywood standards. • **Elizabeth Taylor?** My best friend. I fell in love with Elizabeth the first day we met. I'd never seen such a beautiful girl. We became best friends immediately and remain so today. Like brother and sister, we're that close. • **Why do you think Elizabeth Taylor became so passionate in her fight against AIDS?** It was, of course, the death of Rock Hudson that brought her to the forefront. And I feel that as long as people are dying of AIDS, Elizabeth will be there battling this disease and bringing awareness to the people whose lives it's affecting. • **Why do you think AIDS is no longer the popular cause it once was in Hollywood?** Like anything else in life, people tire of it. They move on; they find other causes. Right now, it's breast cancer, right? Next year, it will be something else. Hopefully, AIDS will eventually disappear from our lives. • **Jane Withers told me once that you're the celebrity's celebrity, meaning everyone in Hollywood loves you. Even after five decades of being a celebrity, you have no enemies. You're sort of the male version of Audrey Hepburn.** How flattering. I'm just a man who has been blessed with a wonderful life and dear friends. I've been surrounded by extraordinarily interesting people. I came from a generation that worked hard and understood what it was like to have nothing. It made us strong, built character, and gave us values.

the juvenile lead in John Ford's 1941 classic, *How Green Was My Valley*, and also landed a long contract with Fox. After sixty years of acting on stage, film, and TV, McDowall may end up being best remembered for his work with animals: a dog in *Lassie Come Home*, a horse in *My Friend Flicka*, and monkeys in *Planet of the Apes*. McDowall was also an acclaimed photog-

rapher and shortly before his death, the Academy of Motion Picture Arts and Sciences named its photo archive after him.

Roddy not only emceed our first event but graciously introduced the Adrian Collection. In an interview with Roddy McDowall in August of 1998, just two months before his death from cancer, we sat down over tea and talked about Adrian, AIDS, and his friendships with some of the biggest stars in Hollywood history.

So, in 1986, with an entire working budget of just $14,000, which covered lighting, sound, food for guests, printing, set design, and everything else, our first event was launched. Just seven years later, our budget would grow to more than $800,000, most of it then underwritten by corporate America. That first year, Joseph Simms had not only lent us his entire collection of Adrian gowns but paid for all expenses to transport it from Philadelphia to Los Angeles and back again. The May Company department stores, alone among the industry corporations, bought up many of our tables and lent their support and name to the event. And the only "garmento" brave enough to be associated with our event that first year was designer George Rudes

(who had done very well in the 1980s with tailored jumpsuits that flatteringly showed off women's waists, rears, and as much cleavage as they were willing to unzip). When others were ducking for cover, George Rudes not only donated his money but lent his name as executive chairman of our event.

It was this kind of unselfish, gracious generosity (which became less common as the event later grew in size and prestige) that allowed us raise more than $120,000 to help people living with AIDS. We hadn't seen ourselves as courageous—it was an adventure. We were all dedicated and emboldened because we'd all lost people by that time. With no track record and against all odds, we had dreamed of and created, with little more than spit and polish, something wonderful that would last for many years and raise millions of dollars.

2

Geoffrey
Beene
—Cutting on the Bias

"I don't **fly** anything but MGM Grand Air and neither do my **collections.**"

— Geoffrey Beene

By any standard of measure, our Adrian show had far exceeded any realistic, or even unrealistic, expectations we might have had for its success. To our delight and amazement, everything we had tried to create had actually worked! The show had been beautiful, the fashions stunning, and the evening great fun for all. We had sold 600 tickets, made some impressive money for the charity, and had created one of the first successful AIDS fundraisers in Los Angeles. We had also inadvertently created, while flying by the seat of our pants, a model for using fashion and celebrities to create a glamorous fund-raiser that would serve as a template for other such events in future years in Los Angeles, around the country, and even in Europe. The coverage of our newborn gala in the *Los Angeles Times*, *Women's Wear Daily* (*WWD*), *The Apparel News*, and other news and fashion periodicals had been supportive and even downright flattering. In Los Angeles, we had cracked the 11 o'clock news programs on all the local network affiliates.

Dear Elizabeth. She would attend every one of our events up until the time of her death. Here with AIDS activist and producer Barry Krost. It was Barry who got Hollywood to get involved.

On the day after our show (certainly not an annual event, it was just *our* show at this point), I returned phone calls to reporters. I had been too overwhelmed to answer their calls earlier. They wanted to know how much we'd raised, followed by their other big question—"What designer are you going to do next year?" Were they crazy? We'd barely survived the first show and I wasn't sure I wanted to try to do a second. There were so many components to producing an event like this

and, in some ways, I felt that we were lucky that everything had worked out so well in the end. Did we really know what we were doing or had we just escaped the imminent catastrophe we always seemed to face while putting together the Adrian show? I was dog tired and so were the other members of our steering committee. It had been almost two years of work to do this first show. I was weary of feeling like a beggar. The first event had only happened because people did us favors or repaid favors. I had spent days on the phone asking friends and business associates to support us. Maybe I'd used up all my chips and had no more to cash in for a second show.

After all, hadn't it taken a minor miracle for us to stumble onto an entire collection of Adrian dresses? And wasn't it another miracle that the man who owned this unlikely collection, Joseph Simms, would not only lend it to us, people whom he'd never heard of before, but would also pay for shipping it to Los Angeles? Maybe we shouldn't press our luck. The fact remained, too, that every living designer we had approached up to this point had said no to us. If there was going to be a second year, the designer we featured would have to be a big name and would have to be alive. Otherwise we would appear to be just working our way through the fashion collection of a museum. If we couldn't find a living, big-name designer to say yes, then we shouldn't try a Year Two. After such a surprising success with Adrian, did I really want to face another six months of "No, thank you" and "We gave at the office"? We'd had a low-budget surprise box-office hit and now everyone was demanding to know the story line of the sequel. Maybe it was best to quit on a high note.

My outlook changed dramatically a couple of months later, toward the end of spring 1987. My best friend, Brandon, and I had a retail store that we owned and ran together in the Los Angeles seaside community of Santa Monica. Stems Village Store was a happy shop filled with fresh flowers, colorful dishes, glassware, flatware, tablecloths, and napkins. We had a diverse clientele, wealthy westsiders from Santa Monica, Brentwood, Pacific Palisades, and even Malibu, and funky, artistic, New-Agers and ex-hippies from the

Venice community to the south. We also
got a surprising number of clients from the
Hollywood star community, including
Madonna and Sean Penn, Cher, Barbra
Streisand (always asking for a 33 percent
designer's discount), Bruce and Patty
Springsteen, Nicole and O.J. Simpson (in
happier times), Arnold Schwarzenegger
(whose offices were one block from our store)
and his wife, Maria Shriver, Diana Ross (fur-
nishing her Malibu beach house), Bette
Midler, Dana Delany, Whitney Houston,
Melanie Griffith and her husband for the
second time, Don Johnson, Phyllis Diller,
Diane Keaton, and Nancy Reagan preparing
her post–White House abode in Bel Air. You
get the picture. Even with all the expensive
Italian dishes in our shop, we remained kid-
and dog-friendly, and Hollywood seemed
to like that ambiance. Plus everyone loved
Brandon. He could charm a snake or even the

most spoiled and difficult celebrities. They'd
be on a first-name basis before they left
the shop.

I also had a freelance job working as a
wardrobe consultant on tons of shows at all of
the TV networks. I was dressing divas, starlets, and game show hosts. One day Brandon
called me on the set and told me we had to
meet. He had something important to tell me.
We met right after work at a restaurant then
owned by the artist formerly known as "the
artist formerly known as Prince" who is now
known as merely "the Artist."

When I joined Brandon at his table and
looked into his eyes, I was worried. Something
was very wrong. His blue eyes were red and
full of tears. "I've got AIDS," he told me. That
knocked the wind out of me. "Are you sure?" I
finally asked. "I got the results this morning,"
he said as he choked up and looked away. That
was the moment when it was clear to me that

Geoffrey Beene's 25-year
retrospective 1988.

Inspired by his many trips
abroad, Beene's collections
remain some of the greatest
clothes ever made.

I had to move forward and create a second event. What else could I do?

Not much had changed in Hollywood or the fashion industry since we first met with rejection while putting together the Adrian show. Both were still gun-shy of any connection to anything associated with AIDS. The Rocco King of Showbiz, Liberace, had died of AIDS in Palm Springs only days before our Adrian show. There was worldwide attention and mourning, but those close to him still denied that AIDS was the cause of his death. There was still too much shame and bias attached to the word *AIDS*. Many in Hollywood knew that ventriloquist-comedian Wayland Flowers was very ill from AIDS and would soon take Madame and Crazy Mary away with him. In New York, actor, playwright, and founder in 1967 of the legendary off-Broadway Ridiculous Theater Company Charles Ludlam had just died of AIDS. With Ludlam as artistic director and playwright-in-residence, the group had developed a style of ensemble playing that synthesized wit, parody, vaudeville, farce, melodrama, and satire. AIDS continued to take a heavy toll in the creative communities on both coasts—but it was still far from being the popular red-ribbon cause it would become. President Reagan, nearing the

end of his eight years in office, had finally mentioned the word *AIDS*, but just barely.

If we were going to attract a name designer, we would need help. We had done a retrospective of a dead Hollywood costume designer. Even if we ignored the aversion to the word *AIDS*, why should any living designer jeopardize his or her reputation by putting on a fashion show with a bunch of amateurs in Hollywood? We needed someone with credibility to vouch for us. The only person I could think of who might be able and willing to help us is a woman who has been a patron to our event, always extremely generous to us and always a great connection to many of the designers we would work with in future years—Marylou Luther. Marylou had been the *Los Angeles Times* fashion editor for more than a decade and since has been a columnist for the Los Angeles Times Syndicate. She personally knows all the important designers and has been instrumental in helping launch many famous careers, including those of Gianni Versace, Thierry Mugler, Bill Blass, Isaac Mizrahi, Ralph Lauren, and Yves Saint Laurent. Marylou has often written the introduction to the designer and his work for our programs. Even after she stepped down as editor at the *Times*, Marylou is still always given a front-row seat at big shows, next to the editors of the *New York Times, Vogue, Bazaar,* and the *Chicago Tribune.* In fact, Marylou is so well connected and well liked that she often has a better seat at the press shows in New York, Milan, and Paris than the current fashion editor of the *Los Angeles Times* does. This has caused hard feelings and an occasional kitty fight.

I called Marylou at her Park Avenue apartment in Manhattan and asked if she could help us in some way. "How about Geoffrey Beene?" she asked. "Great," said I, picking myself up off the floor. "As long as he's breathing and can make a personal appearance." Marylou made the call to extend the invitation—and Beene accepted!

Why had a big designer like Beene agreed to be our honoree when so many others—all others—had said no? Clearly, Beene's acceptance was mostly a very big favor to Marylou Luther. We were fortunate also that 1988

Geoffrey Beene was the first living designer to do a show for us.
This evening dress was hand-
beaded.

This silk and faux leopard print
evening gown grabbed everyone's attention at the fashion-
starved L.A. fund-raising event.

marked the twenty-fifth anniversary of
Geoffrey Beene on Seventh Avenue, and he
may also have been looking for an appropriate
venue to do a retrospective of his work since
1963. Probably Beene had lost people he knew
in the fashion industry, maybe members of his
staff, and had a true empathy for the AIDS
cause. But Geoffrey Beene has always run
against the current. He doesn't care what's
happening in Paris or Milan or on the streets.
He's a man who has always had his own sense
of what fashion should be and that's what he
has always done. Doing an AIDS benefit
wouldn't have bothered him personally nor
would he have worried about any effect it
might have on his business. Geoffrey Beene is
one of the most important American designers
of this century and we were lucky to have him.

Cutting on the bias—or the diagonal
grain of a fabric—ensures a smooth fit, a fluid
movement, and "you can eliminate darts and
seams" is how Beene explains the cutting tech-
nique that is key to so many of his stylish and

deceptively simple designs. Beene has been
ahead of the herd from the 1960s until today
in his progression toward ever more comfortable, fluid, and clean designs. He is like a
mathematician who trusts that the correct
equation will be simple and elegant. According
to Beene, simplicity is not easy: "Arriving at
simplicity is a complicated process. It's about
trial and error and discipline. You have to work
at it. It's a tedious process, but I love doing it.
Taking off excess is a modern way of dressing.
In the end, the sheer simplicity of comple-
menting a figure and the person wearing
clothes that don't require much care is the
essence of modernity." While his silhouettes
have become cleaner, his designs have not
become austere. They've become even sexier
and more graceful.

Geoffrey Beene is known as a man of the
cloth, with an eye for textiles. His signature
fabric is wool jersey, which he borrowed from
menswear. Beene finding wool jersey was like
the sculptor Alexander Calder finding wire—

This feathered tutu by Geoffrey
Beene helped us build an audience that in the end would raise
more than $9 million for people
living with HIV/AIDS.

each had found a material that would open up a world of creative ideas. Beene has said, "Wool jersey is ideal because it will define the body and, at the same time, be kind to it. Not many fabrics will do that. Its versatility is incredible." The fabric allowed him to design simple, comfortable, yet elegant, clothing for the modern woman and enabled him to bring casual clothes with a seductive edge into the ballroom. With wool jersey, Beene was able to create the seemingly oxymoronic—opulent understatement.

Beene attributes the surgical precision of his designs to his years as a premed student at Tulane University in New Orleans (he was born in Louisiana in 1927). Although he

Morgan Fairchild in 1988 at the Geoffrey Beene event with her publicist. Fairchild became active in many AIDS causes in the 1990s.

abandoned his medical studies after two years, he claims that his time was well spent: "I left medicine because I had no manner in which to express my creative vision, but realize that was the best time I ever spent in the learning process. Knowledge of the human body and its proportions has been a tremendous asset. What I once hated, I am now so grateful I studied." After a brief period in Los Angeles doing window display for I. Magnin department store, Beene studied design in New York and Paris. He returned to New York in 1951 and held several design jobs—one for 10 years with Teal Taina—until he opened his own atelier in 1963. The following year, Beene won the first of his eight Coty Awards, the fashion industry's highest honor.

As fresh and inventive today in his seventies as when he began, Beene says he learns a lot from the women who frequent his shop at the Sherry Netherland Hotel on New York's Fifth Avenue. He also enjoys being a champion of American fashion abroad. He was the first American to present a collection in Milan and says, "I think I have helped elevate the image of American fashion, which is the greatest influence on the world today. The world is into American sports clothes like wildfire. For years, Americans have gone to Paris for their clothes. I don't think they need go anymore." This man who brings old world classicism to the modern woman also finds his relaxation in a classic old world hobby—he tends his more than 2,000 orchids. "I've been a flower freak since I was a kid. Gardening is how I get my exercise. When things are growing, you're always busy."

A Geoffrey Beene retrospective might also be a refreshingly classic antidote to, or at least a brief respite from, the go-go garishness and greed of the 1980s culture. It was a time when money was flowing—uphill, but flowing. It was a time of Donald and Ivana Trump and the Billionaire Boys Club, when *noblesse oblige* was out and trickle-down theory was in. We had Michael Milken in 1986 and in 1987, Oliver Stone's movie, *Wall Street*, had Michael Douglas portraying Gordon Gekko, a money-obsessed high-roller preaching "Greed is good!" and audiences weren't sure if he was supposed to be the good guy or the bad guy.

The look of the time was high glamour, but also brassy, and everything was big—big hair, big shoulder pads, clunky earrings, set off by too much bad makeup. The ultimate fashion role model for the 1980s, whether you took her seriously or as a camp critique, was the Nolan Miller–dressed Joan Collins in her *Dynasty* TV series portrayal of Alexis Morrell Carrington Colby Dexter Rowan. Geoffrey Beene was the opposite of what was happening in our culture. He had always marched to his own drummer and it wouldn't be until the 1990s that the parade would catch up with him again. It would be interesting to present him to a Hollywood that was over the top, out of control, with frizzy hair and garish gowns to prove it.

It was interesting that we faced a lot of criticism from the California fashion industry for choosing a New York designer. What made this painfully ridiculous was that, to date, with two notable exceptions, none of these members of the Californian fashion community had been willing to even lend his or her name to our event or, for that matter, to any other AIDS fund-raiser. The exceptions notable for their generosity and courage were George Rudes, owner of the California sportswear line Saint Germain, who served as our first-year Fashion Industry Chairman, and California sportswear designer Carole Little, who was our second-year Industry Chair. Soon all of the others would be begging to participate, after it took no real nerve to do so and after we really didn't need their help.

Jim Watterson, the member of our steering committee most responsible for working with the designers on our early shows, and George Martin, our set designer, both happened to be in New York City at the same time on other business. They called to set up a meeting with Geoffrey Beene in his showroom. Beene was very clear that he wanted a set with no stairs, extremely clean with a white back wall. That was it. No other demands. The Century Plaza Ballroom had voluminous red draperies and we had to pay to have them taken down. George designed a set that used the turntable in the ballroom's stage and five enormous 18-foot tall columns. Three columns sat on the turntable and one

column sat stationary on each side of the turntable. When the turn-table rotated, the whole set changed. The set was built by volunteers and staff from George's set design company, Patina V, who donated their labor and talent. The end result was a beautifully elegant, functional, and minimalist set that perfectly suited the Beene designs.

The Beene Machine did not travel to Los Angeles until just a few days before the show. Although we were constantly in touch, the House of Beene left many decisions to us. It was a real collaboration, which would not always be the case with later designers who were more omnipresent and obsessive. To understand what goes on to prepare a major fashion show in Los Angeles, one must think of a Broadway production or a low-budget movie. Careful consideration must be made to have an appropriate venue, and in Los Angeles, there are not a lot of choices. Take notice of the Oscar shows, which alternate between the Shrine Auditorium and the Dorothy Chandler Pavilion at the Music Center. If the show is held at the Chandler, then not all the bigwigs in Hollywood can get a ticket and they complain. Then it's moved to the Shrine, which seats 6,500 (twice as many as at the Chandler), and people complain that it's not special or exclusive enough. If we'd held the Adrian show at the Shrine, we would have had 5,900 empty seats … not a pretty picture. As it was, at the Century Plaza, we were able to close off part of the ballroom to make it look full.

Another simple factor was the cost of the location. If the site were a union house, such as the Hollywood Bowl that we would later use, then our volunteers would not be able to touch a light or move a bench—almost everything had to be done by union members and our production costs would skyrocket. There were other practical factors to consider. For instance, we needed to put up a $1,000 deposit to reserve the Century Plaza Ballroom and for every event, we had a midnight to midnight, 24-hour insurance policy that gave us $1 million dollars worth of injury and damage liability coverage for the day of the show.

An advantage in using the Century Plaza location is that they offered us the ballroom for free. Our cost was factored into the charges for the liquor, including wine, and dinner. Keeping the cost of the dinner below $40 per person was always one of our greatest challenges. But by sitting down with the hotel's Director of Catering (who became a great friend of ours over the years) and cleverly planning our menus, we managed to keep our meals interesting and reasonable—and free of the dreaded banquet chicken. My only food rule in 10 years of producing the events was *No veal*. We opted for game hens instead of chicken, for fish instead of beef. And rather than lamb, we had pasta. In 1996, our menu would be totally vegetarian, a menu that our 1988 audience would have rejected. Most of our designers took an active part in choosing the menu for their show. Adrian, of course, had nothing to say about the food, and Geoffrey Beene left that issue up to us. He also left it up to us to design the look of the tables, invitations, and commemorative program and advertisements.

The first two years, with so little money in our budget, we went to Los Angeles's fashion community and asked for fabric to make tablecloths and napkins, for cutters to cut the fabric, for stitchers to sew the hems on the napkins and tablecloths, and for pattern makers to design chair covers. It was all done by bartering: "I'll give you a full-page ad in our ad journal and two tickets if you donate fabric." Many times the larger manufacturers in Los Angeles, such as Carole Little, Guess?, and Karen Kane, would have the fabric left over in inventory and would just give it to us, asking nothing in return. Things would change in later years. In 1994, 60,000 yards of silk were Fed-Exed to us from China! Each year the event would grow and grow and the old adage "You can't go home again" would become more apropos.

But in 1988, we were still small-time. We were still amateurs, grassroots fund-raisers, almost virgins. We could still naively assume that the only reason a designer might agree to do our event was from an altruistic urge to help people who were hurting. We would wise up, but not for a few years yet. For the first three events, Brandon and I would get up at 3 A.M. and head to the wholesale Flower Mart

in downtown L.A. Because we owned a store that sold fresh flowers, we had regular vendors who knew us well and counted on our regular business. So, once a year, we would hit them up for donations of flowers. Then we'd transport the flowers to the ballroom in our blue Chevy pickup. For the Beene dinner tables, we'd pick up 900 gardenias and bushels of

Geoffrey Beene and his bevy of beauties.

fresh lemon leaf. We floated the gardenias in leaf-shaped serving dishes that we borrowed from the California based Metlox Pottery Company. The lemon leaf added another color to the white flowers in the lilac, rose, canary, and jade colored serving dishes that we had transformed into low, floating vases. The china, crystal stemware, and silverware for

each place setting were provided by the hotel. It was an exciting time for us, making something spectacular out of almost nothing. It reminded me of my college days when I could stretch $25 into a week's worth of movie tickets, beer, candy bars, coffee (remember those college days of hyperglycemic diets?) and tokens to ride the BART from San Francisco

1960s starlet Yvette Mimeaux shown here with her business-man husband were big Beene fans and even bigger contributors in 1988.

not. The problem was that this MGM airline expense alone could eat up close to one-fifth of our entire budget. Still, this was Mr. Beene's only difficult request and it did seem doable even if we had to pay for it—which fortunately we did not. A travel agent friend of our event was able to get two round-trip MGM Grand tickets donated in trade for a free ad in our journal and a couple of good seats. The other Beene staff members were flown out coach on United Airlines, which also donated the seats. Hotel rooms for all were donated to us. Still, this problem had illustrated a lesson that we would all too painfully learn in subsequent years—designers who are not dead tend to have real egos and expensive preferences.

For any event in Los Angeles to be truly successful, it had to be greased by that special Hollywood lubricant—stars! I knew Barry Krost, who'd helped us so much our first year, would do his best to show up again with his bevy of upstanding television beauties: Elizabeth Montgomery, JoBeth Williams, Bess Armstrong, Carol Kane, and author Jackie Collins. Having a living designer had one big plus, he also had his own regular clients who were celebrities. We asked Mr. Beene and his staff to invite some of his well-known clients. In attendance were Old Navy's Morgan Fairchild, *Dynasty*'s Linda Evans, costume designer Nolan Miller, Belinda Carlisle, pursuing a solo singing career after leaving the Go-Go's in 1984, *Knots Landing* star Joan Van Ark, and a woman who would subsequently be a con-stant supporter of our event, both in the audience and on stage, comedienne Sandra Bernhard. There were times, too, that I would snag a celebrity or two myself, whom-ever I might run into or work with at the time. That's how I recruited actors Sally Struthers, Dixie Carter, Holly Hunter, and Richard Dysart. It was a glamour turnout that kept our audience star-gazing, the paparazzi reloading, and lent our still-fledgling event a real Hollywood cachet.

The year I first met Ali MacGraw was 1987. She hurried into our store, Stems, one day to buy a set of pale green dinnerware for

across the Bay to Berkeley. Somehow I made it all work and had a great time in the process. It would be an interesting paradox of our decade of events that as the budgets got big-ger the process became less fun.

Because of our success with the Adrian event, our budget for the second year was tripled. So we had three times as much of almost nothing. This provided a worrisome problem when Geoffrey Beene informed us that he would fly to Los Angeles only on MGM Grand Air. "I don't fly anything but MGM Grand Air and neither do my collec-tions," he said rather sternly on the phone one day. "I'll be traveling with my personal assis-tant. Everyone else can fly on—I don't care." (An interesting aside, Mr. Beene's assistant at that time was Gene Meyer, now an acclaimed designer in his own right.) MGM was the Rolls-Royce of airlines in 1988 and only flew between Los Angeles and New York. It catered to the very rich, celebrities, and busi-ness moguls. Inside, it was truly grand, look-ing more like the sitting room at the old money, posh downtown L.A. Jonathan Club than an airplane. Southwest Airlines, it was

her son, Josh, who had just moved into his first apartment on his own. Ali immediately fell in love with our Dalmatians, Alex and Katy, and thought that Brandon and I were unusually brave (or foolhardy) for letting them have the run of a shop that was crammed with expensive pottery and Italian glassware. She loved the way our dogs greeted the customers and played with children. Dog lovers all, we became instant friends. Ali even offered to dog-sit the two spots if Brandon and I ever needed someone to watch them for us. In a flash, I thought of Ali as the perfect celebrity to introduce Geoffrey Beene on the night of his show. With as much courage as I could muster, I began telling Ali about the event. She knew Geoffrey Beene from the 1960s when she was a stylist for Diana Vreeland at *Vogue* and when she became a top New York fashion model and cover girl. By the early 1970s, she had become a movie star in *Love Story*, one of the most successful tearjerkers of all time, and had married Paramount Studios chief Robert Evans, the father of her son, Josh. Ali thought for a second and then, to my amazement, said yes. I felt a bit embarrassed to ask such a big favor of a new friend, so I gave Ali an Effie Marie chocolate cake, the best cake in the world, as a thank-you. To this day, Ali still raves about that chocolate cake, sends kisses to Alex and Katy, and never forgets me at Christmas. I love Ali and so did Brandon.

In January, I phoned Ali to arrange a visit to the Beene studio for a fitting on her upcoming trip to New York. On the night of the gala, Ali did introduce Beene and dazzled our audience, looking every inch the movie star and former model in her black Geoffrey Beene original. It was one of Ali's very rare public appearances, and her attendance helped make the evening even more special. With her hair pulled back and a touch of gray (she did this on purpose) at each temple, she was Hollywood royalty and she wooed everyone with her intellect, beauty, fame, and courage.

Geoffrey Beene and his staff arrived in Los Angeles a few days before the gala. Beene is a short man, a bit heavy set, with snow-white hair and black horn-rimmed glasses. He always wore a dark suit and tie except on show night, when he wore a black tuxedo. He is extremely intelligent, even brilliant, a little remote, though not unfriendly. There was a palpable sense of dignity about him, a sense of who he is and what he has to offer. Unlike some designers we'd work with later, Beene doesn't need flattery or star hype. He was actually very easy to work with.

We were using all Los Angeles models in the show, who had all donated their services. Eventually, it became a real thrill to be in our show, so models would seek us out. It was impressive on their resumes. Later, when the designers started flying in super divas from New York, the competition to be in our show became tough. We had done the casting before the Beene staff arrived. Mr. Beene fit the clothes according to his precise concepts. He taught the models the way he wanted them to walk. It was an arch style, almost a parody of old-fashioned modeling. The models took little poses, but with irony. He used modern music, with dissonances and sound effects. There was also music from Bach and from *The Untouchables*. And it was the first time most of us had ever heard "Music of the Night" from the Andrew Lloyd Webber *Phantom of the Opera.* He would take tulle and wrap it around the head of a model in a simple sheath dress. There were whimsical dresses from the 1960s such as a series of sequined Felix the Cat ball gowns in various colors and silhouettes. Beene's aesthetics as well as his training of the models really held up well throughout the show. His vision was so truthful that he made the show the way he wanted it. Not in a demanding way, but like a real pro. It was a 25-year retrospective, but not in chronological order, so the audience didn't know the year they were looking at. But Beene's designs are so timeless, so modern, they could have all been done that year. If we put the same gowns on the runway today, they would still look absolutely contemporary. His clothes had some of the highest aesthetic of any collection we presented in the 10 years. Mr. Beene also seemed pleased with the show.

One glaring absentee for the evening was *WWD*, which had sent a photographer and

Dynasty star Linda Evans at the
Geoffrey Beene event in 1988.

the old war horse editor of *Architectural Digest,* that she could photograph the house. John Fairchild, the granddaddy of *W,* became enraged and expelled Geoffrey Beene from the pages of *W* or any other Fairchild publication. I was sure that Fairchild would make an exception because our event was to raise awareness and money for AIDS care. But I was wrong and the excommunication of Geoffrey Beene held. Not a word about our event appeared in *WWD* or *W.* In subsequent years (all eight of them), the Fairchild papers were back in force: *WWD, W,* and *Daily News Record,* with their top brass, John Fairchild, Michael Coady, and Patrick McCarthy all flying in from New York. They came to rub elbows with Hollywood, to schmooze with California designers and court their advertising, and to be represented among the more than 200 members of the press who started covering our events beginning with our breakout Bob Mackie show the following year. Recently, another similar Beene feud story made the rounds. Apparently, when *Vogue* editor Anna Wintour quit covering Geoffrey Beene, he banned *Vogue* from his shows. "The taste level is very low," says the elegant curmudgeon about *Vogue.* "Even the ads used to be quite beautiful. Now it's merch, merch, merch." So much for life in the big city. In Hollywood, people fake niceness even to those they hate because they don't know who'll be hot next week or who might be able help them make money. They tend to avoid offending each other—at least when they're sober. Still, I guess it says a lot for Beene personally that he would stick to his previous promise to *Architectural Digest,* even though it was clear he would anger John Fairchild, one of the most powerful men in fashion publishing.

There was one celebrity present for the Geoffrey evening who broke my heart. Her determination to keep her commitment to us despite her own broken heart touched me that evening. On this night, she sat at my table, covering her face every so often to hide her tears. There was no applause from her that night, nor any whistles or cheers as there had been the previous year. I wouldn't know until

reporter to our Adrian event. They had loved the Adrian show, which they had raved about to their readers, so they were expected again for our second gala. But by that time, we had also heard the fashion lore about the famous feud between Geoffrey Beene and Fairchild Publications. As the story goes, *W,* (the big sister of *WWD*—and the pretty one) had wanted to photograph the New York home of Geoffrey Beene (some stories claim it was Beene's townhouse in the city, others his house in the Hamptons) as he is nearly as famous for his brilliant interior design. John Fairchild himself had asked Beene for permission to do a full-color spread. Beene, however, had already promised Paige Rense,

later that Carol Kane and her boyfriend, actor Woody Harrelson, had broken up that very day. Instead of canceling out on us, however, Carol pulled herself together, arrived in time to pose and smile for photographers and to sign autographs for fans. She reminded me that the personal tragedies we all experience pale in comparison to other tragedies that many around us are facing. I admired Carol's bravery, her selflessness, and her class.

The Geoffrey Beene show was not my personal favorite. Many would argue that, aesthetically, he was the most brilliant of the contemporary designers we would honor. But for me, the mood of the show seemed too somber, dark, and moody—very New York black. The Beene audience appreciated the beauty of his designs, but they never smiled or laughed or cheered, and they certainly never got rowdy. Unlike most of our other shows, a sense of celebration was missing. From the stark but beautiful set design to the mysterious and foreboding music, the show felt almost like sitting in a church. It was tinged by a gentle sadness, like a memor-

ial service for a friend, and you never forgot why you were there. Maybe during years of so much sadness, one desperately needs some escape, even some silliness—and there was nothing silly in a Beene show. Maybe it was just me. Still, I couldn't wait for the show to be over so I could have a drink—make that two.

Nevertheless, I am grateful to Geoffrey Beene for lending his name and talent to our show. Beene had nothing to gain from doing our event. He was already a legend, rich and successful. He wasn't trying to build his image or drum up clients in Hollywood. He did it from his heart, as had Ali and the 100 or more volunteers who sewed, escorted people to their seats, cleaned up the ballroom afterwards, and repacked the clothes for their first-class trip back to New York on MGM Grand Air. We had made even more money for the charity than the year before, and we had struck another blow to end the bias and fear that surrounded AIDS—and after all the floors had been swept up, isn't that just what we were trying to do?

Bob
Mackie
—The *Seinfeld* of Sequins

"The Gambinos were wonderful, lovely, absolutely terrific people ... I adored them."

— Bob Mackie on the Gambino crime family of New York

It was the summer of 1988 and we still needed a designer to honor for our 1989 show. These events require lead time to find openings on the calendars of our potential honoree, the hoped-for guests, and the professional models and production technicians who will be donating their time and services. Of course we also had to pick an exact date in late winter of 1989 so we could promote the event, book the venue and the models, and solicit airline tickets and hotel accommodations. Our first two events had returned more than $300,000 to the AIDS charity and had begun to establish an annual occasion of note in a town where there is a lot of competition for notice. It was still early, however, in the evolution of our gala, and many people continued to be skittish about connecting their names with anything connected with AIDS. We were hearing from the California fashion industry that we ought to next honor a California designer. Although the California fashion industry—distinct from the Hollywood costume industry—was known worldwide for its trend-setting swimwear and casual sportswear, I and the others on the event steering

committee worried that there wasn't any California designer whose name could sell enough tickets to fill a ballroom. We decided that if there were a California designer who could pull a crowd, it would have to be couturier James Galanos. Galanos, at that time, had won every major fashion award during his then four-decade career and was considered by many to be the equal of his European peers. Although well-known in the fashion world, Galanos was a far cry from being considered a hot designer. The last time he'd created any sensation was when Nancy Reagan wore his floor-length, one-shouldered cream satin gown with a sheer, beaded overdress to her husband's 1981 presidential inaugural ball. (As unlikely as it may seem, now that the most infamous dress associated with the White House is blue and DNA-stained, some felt it unseemly for the size 4 First Lady to bare one mature shoulder.) And Galanos didn't have any Hollywood film costumes with which to attract celebrities except a single lonely credit for Susan Oliver's wardrobe in the deservedly forgotten 1973 Sissy Spacek film, *Ginger in the Morning*. Although Galanos had been quietly gay for much of his career, his clients were old-monied society women who were rich California Republicans. It now seems exceedingly unlikely that a blue-blood, Republican-based fund-raiser for AIDS would have been successful in early 1989—just weeks after George Bush's Presidential inauguration. And what might our supporters have thought about our decision to honor a designer known to the general public, if at all, mostly for his association with the wife of Ronald Reagan, a president with an abysmal record on gay rights and AIDS care? Maybe Galanos realized these problems better than we did, or maybe he'd just been honored so many times already that he knew the work involved for him and his career didn't need it. In retrospect, we were definitely fortunate that James Galanos immediately declined our invitation to be honored. Later in the 1990s, after the Democrats had regained the White House, Galanos and his longtime companion became regular attendees at our yearly galas.

South Pacific's Mitzi Gaynor and *Hello Dolly*'s Carol Channing raise eyebrows and awareness for AIDS at the Bob Mackie show in 1989.

There were no other couture designers based in California who we felt could create enough buzz and excitement in Hollywood to fill up the Century Plaza ballroom. It was already late in the summer and the other committee members and I were feeling the pressure to get a commitment from someone soon. Remember that in our first two years, we'd collided with wall after wall of rejections—"Thanks, but no thanks." It would be a couple of years yet before it would get easy to attract big-name designers. The answer to our urgent question—Who?—would materialize in, of all places, a strangely vivid dream that I had one sweltering August night. Sure, it sounds too Southern California New Age flaky that the solution came to me in a dream, but it's true.

In my dream, Cher is onstage wearing a bright yellow–beaded Bob Mackie gown. Her long black hair drapes over her bare shoulders as she sings Stephen Sondheim's only hit single, "Send in the Clowns." It's the early 1970s, and I'm a CBS Television City page (and I looked damned cute in my CBS blazer!) working in the audience during a taping of a *Sonny and Cher* TV show. Cher is surrounded by a chorus of sad-faced clowns who are dressed in costumes of bright and happy red, blue, yellow, and orange sequins. Suddenly I know the clowns. They're friends I've lost to AIDS and others whom I love who are infected but still doing okay—my best friend, Brandon; Las Vegas impersonator of Cher and Bette Midler, Kenny Sasha; Broadway dancer Gary Wales; and famed interior designer Pasquale Vazanna. In a deep sweat and gasping for breath, I shook myself awake. As I composed myself and realized that it had only been a dream, I also somehow knew with an odd certainty that Bob Mackie would be our next honoree.

That literally is how we came to ask Bob Mackie to be the honoree of our third annual fashion gala. When hidden hands guide you, strange coincidences happen. When I brought the idea to the others, they all thought Mackie, the contemporary designer most linked with Hollywood glitz and glamour, would be a perfect choice. In fact, so perfect,

why hadn't we thought of him before? Then one of our committee members, Gerry Bremer, had an amazing surprise for us. I knew Gerry as the PR Director for L.A.'s highly regarded Fashion Institute of Design and Merchandising, and I even knew that early in her career, she'd been the private secretary to MGM's megamogul, Louis B. Mayer. What I hadn't known about Gerry was that she was also a writer and had ghostwritten Bob Mackie's 1979 book, *Dressing for Glamour.* What are the odds? This choice seemed fated.

So Gerry asked Bob Mackie for us and he said yes. The timing of our request to Mackie also proved fortuitous. Mackie was about to initiate his first retail line of clothing for the everyday woman. It would be a New York–based line of ready-to-wear clothes, and Mackie felt our show would be the perfect platform to help him launch it. The show would also be a twenty-fifth anniversary retrospective of Mackie's career. Later, Mackie's clothing line would fail, and the friends who appeared as clowns in my enigmatic dream would succumb to AIDS, but in 1989, our Bob Mackie tribute would prove to be an advantageous match both for us and and for him.

Bob Mackie is an internationally famous costume and fashion designer whose work in film, TV, theater, Las Vegas, and occasionally even opera has been applauded and rewarded

Designed for Diana Ross's Las Vegas Show in the 1980s, this beaded Bob Mackie gown remains supreme.

Designed for Cher. Most of her wardrobe is in Mackie's personal collection.

Mackie designed for the 1980s Supremes sans Diana, whom he dressed separately.

A Mackie design for the original *Sonny and Cher Show.*

with seven Emmy Awards (including the first Emmy ever awarded for costume design) and three Oscar nominations (*Funny Girl, Lady Sings the Blues,* and *Pennies from Heaven*). A rare Hollywood celebrity who is actually a Southern California native, Mackie was born in 1940 in Monterey Park (a small city six miles east of downtown Los Angeles, which since 1970 has become an upscale, suburban Chinatown glowingly marketed to immigrants from Taiwan and Hong Kong as "the Chinese Beverly Hills"). Mackie won a scholarship to Chouinard Art Institute in L.A. (now California Institute of the Arts). He married in 1959 and quickly became a father of a son, Robin. The marriage did not last long. Robin Mackie died of AIDS-related complications in 1993. Mackie graduated from Chouinard and was soon working as a sketch artist for the legendary film costume designer Jean Louis. After working on several films with Jean Louis, Mackie left to apprentice with the even more famous costume designer Edith Head, who was then at Paramount Studios. In 1963, veteran costume designer Ray Aghayan

selected Mackie to assist him on the short-lived but fabled *The Judy Garland Show* on CBS. Aghayan, who had been raised in Iran where his mother had been a seamstress to the family of the Shah, is probably best known to the general public today for his perennial—and seemingly perpetual—appearances as costume designer for the Oscar telecasts. Aghayan became Mackie's mentor and then his lover. Aghayan and Mackie moved in together, became design partners, and started a design business called Elizabeth Courtney Costumes. They have remained personal and business partners to this day.

Based on clothes Mackie designed for Mitzi Gaynor's nightclub act, TV producer Joe Hamilton (the ex-husband of Carol Burnett) placed Mackie under contract in 1967 to design the wardrobe for the first *Carol Burnett Show.* Mackie remained the show's costume designer for the 11 years it aired. His close association with Carol Burnett continues to this day. He did costumes for her 1995 Broadway production of *Moon over Buffalo,* and she has been quoted as saying about Mackie:

The key to Bob's success is that he has a producer's mind. He doesn't just think of his department alone. He looks at every show as a whole. His true genius lies in his zeal for detail and his sense of humor.

Beginning in 1971, Mackie's fame exploded because of his designs for Cher on her two variety shows with Sonny Bono and her solo TV show. Not since World War II had "navel maneuvers" received such consistent and detailed scrutiny from the press and public. Other Mackie TV work includes designs for Diana Ross, Julie Andrews, Raquel Welch, Angela Lansbury, and Bette Midler in *Gypsy*. Mackie has designed costumes for such Broadway productions as *The Best Little Whorehouse Goes Public*, *Lorelei* with Carol Channing, and *On the Town with Bernadette Peters*, and for the traveling revival of *Ain't Misbehavin'* with the Pointer Sisters. Mackie created costumes for the San Francisco Opera's production of Alban Berg's *Lulu* and did both sets and costumes for the Elvis-inspired ballet *Blue Suede Shoes*. He's also worked in Las Vegas, creating 1,000 costumes for the *Hallelujah Hollywood* show and has wardrobed the famed Vegas acts of performers such as Diahann Carroll, Juliet Prowse, and Joan Rivers. On the Internet these days, Bob Mackie is probably best known for his creation of collectible Barbie dolls and for the $50–$65 hand-painted scarves and other "Wearable Art by Bob Mackie" being pitched on QVC.

Throughout Bob Mackie's prolific career, his trademark has been imaginative show-stopping glamour. He has the ability to impress, delight, and surprise, which has made him the world's most famous living designer of entertainment costumes. How many designers could claim performers as diverse as the septuagenarian girl-next-door singer Rosemary Clooney and drag disco diva RuPaul for their client Rolodex?

The huge Los Angeles Ballroom of the Century Plaza Hotel, in the middle of Beverly Hills–adjacent Century City, would once again be our venue for the gala. Early on, the diva of all media, Cher, agreed to be in the show. The explosion of Cher's career and fame as a solo

Joan Collins, Bob Mackie, and Jackie Collins. Joan's publicist insisted that she not be photographed in front of any sign that had the word "AIDS" on it. A difficult request at an AIDS benefit.

artist coincided with her association with Mackie and his resultant fame. In the 1970s and early 1980s, the two names were integrally linked in their public images—for years, it was hard to think of one without the other's name coming to mind. Mackie still owns most of the one-of-a-kind costumes he has designed for Cher through the years. Unless Cher wanted to buy a particular costume, they were all returned to Mackie and his private collection. This accumulation of Cher costumes enabled Mackie to plan an entire Cher sequence for the gala. There would be about three dozen of his costumes for her, spanning two decades, with the sequence capped by the appearance of Cher herself in one of her most famous and notorious Mackie costumes, her near-naked 1988 Academy Awards gown. Bob personally asked Cher to be in the show and she readily agreed. It was going to be a lot of fun and a real crowd-pleaser.

What actually happened the night of the show, however, might be deduced by the photo and headline that ran in the *Los Angeles Times* the day after the event. Under a headline—a play on the title of the 1969 film about wife-swapping, *Bob & Carol & Ted & Alice*—"Bob & Carol & Carol & Carroll" was

Bob Mackie designed this beaded cool cat costume for the late Juliet Prowse.

Pia Zadora provided entertainment and drama. Here she mugs for the camera with daughter Kady in matching Mackies.

The clothes were magnificent and our audience loved them so much that they came back for seven more years and raised more than $9 million for people living with HIV/AIDS.

a photograph of Bob Mackie with Carol Burnett, Carol Channing, and Diahann Carroll. Extremely conspicuous in her absence was Mackie's good friend and star client Cher. Oh sure, Cher was there that night, but she hadn't shown up for the rehearsal nor did she appear on stage as planned. In fact, in what had to have been an intentional insult to Mackie, Cher didn't even show up in a Mackie outfit. She didn't even show up in a dress. Cher arrived in the audience just before the Cher sequence began, dressed in torn blue jeans, a white Jockey V-neck T-shirt, and a black leather motorcycle jacket with biker boots. She found an empty seat at a table with rocker Rod Stewart, watched the Cher sequence, then quickly disappeared before the show ended. I couldn't see any reason for Cher showing up looking as if she'd dressed out of lesbian daughter Chastity's closet as opposed to wearing her Mackie duds unless it was to stick it to Bob. Mackie has said that, "When Cher wears pink, peach, or nude, she's usually in love." We can safely assume, then, that on this evening, Cher was not in love with Bob. But I didn't know, and have never found out, what was going on between her

and Mackie that made her drop out of the show. A 1993 *Vanity Fair* article wrote that a $100,000 loan that Cher had made to Mackie's ready-to-wear company, which he did not repay according to their agreement, had ruined their friendship. I don't know if that was the source of their conflict in 1989. Trying to understand the motivations of Cher—or Bob Mackie, for that matter—is, at best, a spectator sport.

Luckily for the show, Bob was able to enlist another good friend, the effervescent comedy icon Carol Burnett to substitute as the surprise guest at the end of the Cher sequence. As the lights in the house went down, a lone figure, with a very familiar silhouette, appeared pushing a wheeled bucket with a mop handle. When the spotlight finally hit her, it was Carol Burnett dressed as the beloved cleaning lady character we all knew from her long-running variety show. The audience burst into delighted applause. Then, at the moment when it seemed the applause couldn't get any louder, Carol, in one motion, ripped off the cleaning lady outfit, which had been held together by Velcro, and there she stood, beautiful and glamorous in a beaded Mackie gown. The audience went mad. I remember thinking, "See, Cher, all this love could have been for you."

Besides the Cher shipwreck, the preparations for the show had gone amazingly—and deceptively—smoothly. Mackie seemed very agreeable and easy to work with. He wasn't very hands-on, but was involved in and signed off on most plans and decisions. The opening music would be the dramatic overture from Leonard Bernstein's musical *Candide*, and a sequence of chiffon evening gowns would be accompanied by the evocative music from the 1986 movie *The Mission*. Mitzi Gaynor would do the introduction of Bob Mackie, and Diahann Carroll would introduce one of the show's segments. At the finale of the show, Bob Mackie would come out with a model in a Mackie wedding gown, accompanied by the song "Masquerade" from *Phantom of the Opera*.

Everything was going great—until the rehearsal on the day of the show. We usually began our loading in, set construction, and

Bob and Carroll and Carol and Carol.

lighting and sound setup at just after mid-night on the day of the show. That's when the ballroom was ours. Then we would have a full dress rehearsal in the afternoon. So the set had been constructed, the lighting had been hung and cued, the music tracks had been laid down, and the dining tables had been set and pin-spotted for dramatic effect. At 3 P.M., Bob Mackie arrived for the dress rehearsal and immediately went into a full-blown, out-of-control, overly dramatic panic! He became angry and bossy, swearing and ordering people around like a drill sergeant. It was a gross and rude scene, which prompted the irreplaceable hub of our steering committee, Jim Watterson, to say, "Never again!" (Fortunately for us, Jim

later changed his mind and continued to work on all our subsequent shows.)

For some reason, Bob had clearly not understood the magnitude of our event until he walked into the ballroom that day. Maybe Mackie's mind had been preoccupied with the loan made to his New York fashion house by a trucking company owned by the infamous Gambino crime family. It certainly takes a facility for a high degree of denial to say to *Vanity Fair* in 1993, "The Gambinos were wonderful, lovely, absolutely terrific people … I adored them." Whatever distracted Mackie, he seemed to have thought our show was to be no more than a slightly larger-scale varia-tion of a department store tearoom fashion

Bob Mackie's tribute to Cher, who arrived in torn jeans, a V-neck T-shirt, black leather jacket and motorcycle boots. Instead of wearing Mackie, she opted for something from daughter Chastity's closet.

Mackie had the entire Cher collection in 1989—but no Cher.

show in which models walk from table to table as the women look on, sipping tea and eating finger sandwiches. Surprise! The grandeur of the set with his name projected on the scrim, the 65-foot-long runway, one hundred fifty 90-inch round dinner tables set with white linen, white bone china, and huge bouquets of white tulips clearly overwhelmed him. When Mackie entered the ballroom that day, his face said it all—he immediately went pale, his upper lip under his perfect nose began to perspire, and easygoing Bob turned into a raging Cecil B. DeMackie.

As the day progressed, Mackie grew more agitated, upset, short-tempered, and rude. From everything I've heard, Mackie is typically known for being calm, even sweet-tempered. It's his partner Ray Aghayan who has the reputation for tantrums and yelling. At one point, Mackie screamed in exasperation, "This rehearsal is a train wreck!" It's possible that because Mackie's background had been in Hollywood, he was not as familiar with the pressures and extraordinary demands of putting on a spectacular fashion show as were

some of our other designers. Still, there were some moments of lightness that afternoon in the ballroom sealed off to all outsiders. As Bob ran through the show's lineup with the models, he would grab the appropriate gown, hold it up in front of himself and walk the catwalk while vogueing, posing, exaggerating his hip movements, and admiring himself on the monitors. He would instruct each model on her timing, her walk, her facial expressions, and her time on stage. What amazed me, as I looked on, was his great sense of timing and movement. Cher's hair toss and lip lick were clearly not her own—they were pure Mackie.

Close to show time, there was yet another critical moment. A woman had been hired to "call the show." Her job was to watch from a booth out front and overhead and communicate with Mackie backstage on headphones. She would keep him abreast of the progress of each model on the runway, since each entrance had to be precisely timed for a model to enter to the right music and lighting for her costume. This woman made an unpardonable mistake when she walked into the green

No one does it better for evening than Bob Mackie, who helped us raise awareness and attention in the fashion and entertainment press.

were, as always, tables reserved for the last-minute celebrity—celebrities were the currency with which we could attract press and paying guests and raise money. This year, we had more press and more celebrities, decked out in their Mackie originals, than ever. Especially fetching that evening was the legendary dancer, the late Juliet Prowse, beautiful with her red hair clipped boyishly short. Little did any of us know then that she was battling breast cancer and had lost her hair to chemotherapy.

That evening, as our guests dined on poached salmon and fresh winter vegetables, a loud commotion erupted at the table next to mine. Seated at the table with Juliet Prowse were two bickering B-grade celebrities, the pint-sized actress and singer Pia Zadora and a hairdresser to the stars also known as an infomercial hawker of his hair care products. The hairdresser, appearing as *the* hair expert on morning TV shows and donating makeovers for dowdy housewives on afternoon TV shows, had parlayed his skill for self-promotion into a chain of high-priced hair salons in Beverly Hills, Las Vegas, Rancho Mirage, and anywhere else people have too much money and too little hair. Considering his heavy Latin accent and fussy ways, the hairdresser's ever-present cowboy hat, decorated with male peacock feathers, has always seemed a bit incongruous. We were about to discover why it was ever present, and why he'd ignored his mother's instructions to always remove your hat at the dinner table.

Pia Zadora, originally from Hoboken, New Jersey, began her film career in 1964 at the age of 9. She played Girmar, a Martian kid, in the first of her classically bad films, *Santa Claus Conquers the Martians*. Seventeen years later, she made her adult film debut in *Butterfly,* an overdone melodramatic adaptation of a James M. Cain novel, with costumes by Bob Mackie. Zadora played a sex-kitten who attempts to seduce her supposed biological father, played by Stacy Keach. Between these two archetypal guilty-pleasure bombs, Zadora made one good career move when she married multimillionaire Israeli immigrant Meshulam Riklis. The innuendo around Hollywood during the early 1980s was that

Like an old Loretta Young rerun—Mackie ended his show with (yawn) a wedding gown finale.

room backstage and interrupted Mackie as he was applying some sort of instant face-lift adhesive strips to the back of his head, under his hair. These adhesive strips were apparently used to pull his skin back tighter and make him look younger by smoothing out his wrinkles. This woman was a veteran of the fashion world and couldn't have cared less what Mackie was doing to make himself look better, but, she recalls, "He got livid, screamed at me, and ordered me out of the room." She was a tough broad herself and the two of them started hurling insults at each other. It was one helluva scene. But they were both pros, so the fight ended with no broken fingernails or blood drawn. But I imagine the headset communication between the two that night was not too chatty.

The night of the event was so star-studded that the hotel had to bring in extra security forces to help restrain the press and the fans, both trying to get close to the arriving celebrities. The ballroom had been sold out for weeks, with a waiting list of people willing to pay anything for a ticket. There

Designed for Cher in the 1980s.

Mackie's homage to *Star Trek*.

Riklis was trying to buy Zadora's way into stardom, and the images conjured up were of the William Randolph Hearst–inspired character played by Orson Welles in *Citizen Kane* who tries to make an opera star out of his talentless paramour, comparisons made all the more irresistible by Welles's bit part in *Butterfly*. Riklis and Zadora seemed to go out of their way to reinforce everyone's suspicions. After Zadora had won a Golden Globe as Best New Star of the Year for the universally panned *Butterfly*, it was discovered that Riklis had sweetened up the members of the Hollywood Foreign Press Association with an expensive junket to Las Vegas. Zadora's film career died a quick death, though it lingered with her occasional camp appearances in films such as John Waters's *Hairspray* (starring Cher's ex, Sonny Bono) and O. J. Simpson's last film, so far, *Naked Gun 33 1/3: The Final Insult.* Later, Zadora and Riklis further endeared themselves to the Hollywood community by buying Pickfair, the legendary Beverly Hills estate of silent film stars Mary Pickford and Douglas Fairbanks, then razing the fabled home to make way for a new Moroccan fortress–inspired palace. Zadora has had some success as a big-voiced belter of song standards and toured in 1990 with Frank Sinatra and Don Rickles.

So these were the two personalities, famous mostly for being famous, who would provide the evening's high drama/low comedy dinner entertainment. As the wine flowed at their table, so did the words between Zadora and the hairdresser. I never knew what their fight was about, but it kept building and building. Abruptly, Zadora excused herself from the table, stood up, and headed off to the powder room with her young daughter Kady, named for Zadora's character in *Butterfly*. After several minutes, Pia and Kady reappeared in the ballroom in their identical beguiling Bob Mackie black velvet cocktail dresses jeweled in the front with rhinestones. Pia stealthily sneaked up on the hairdresser from behind. She suddenly yanked his straw hat off his head, flung it to the floor, and stomped on it with her tiny stiletto pumps. Zadora then picked up the flattened hat and tossed it across the ballroom. It sailed like a

Frisbee over the well-coiffed heads of many of the hairdresser's rich and famous clients, who could now verify what they no doubt long suspected—he had the same hairdo as Benjamin Franklin. Apparently, his product called Secret Hair must grow hair in some location other than the top of the head. The hairdresser instantly tried to cover his bald top with his hand. Adding injury to insult, his handsome and attentive young male date whisked the napkin off his lap and covered the hairdresser's hand and head with it. To my astonishment, the hairdresser, looking like some veiled drag queen on his way to confession, left the napkin sitting there on top of his head—an odd decision for a man who sells his stylistic judgments. Pia, having modeled party decorum for her young daughter, scurried out of the ballroom with Kady, trailed by echoes of her taunting hysterical laughter. Eventually, the cowboy hat came sailing back from the other side of the ballroom and landed nearby on the floor. The attentive date quickly retrieved what now looked like a Buster Keaton prop and substituted it for the napkin on the hairdresser's head. The nearby tables roared and applauded. Hollywood loves a colorful feud almost as much as Washington, D.C.

Among our other celebrity guests that evening were the glamorous Collins sisters: novelist and screenwriter Jackie Collins and her actress sister Joan Collins. Best known for her villainous *Dynasty* role, Joan had also starred in the film versions of two of sister Jackie's novels, *The Bitch* and *The Stud*, both produced in 1978 by Joan's then–husband Ron Kass. And Joan herself has authored an autobiography, *Past Imperfect*, which suggests she dallied with every male actor in London and Hollywood except Sir Ian McKellen and Benji. It's interesting that however much they love each other, glamorous sisters always seem to be competitive. One thinks also of the sisters Jackie Onassis and Lee Radziwill. The Collins sisters sat at different tables that evening. Joan sat at Bob Mackie's personal table, and Jackie sat with her manager and best friend of our events, Barry Krost. Late in the evening, the two sisters did briefly come together once for a photo-op, with Bob

The late dancer/entertainer Juliet Prowse wearing Bob Mackie.

Mackie between them. In a long black beaded Mackie gown, Joan was showing so much cleavage that it prompted one catty young female fashion editor to later write, "So that's what 60-year-old tits look like." It was interesting also to watch Joan Collins's publicist, a gay man, trying to guide his client around so she wouldn't have her picture taken in front of the banner proclaiming the name of the AIDS charity.

Another celebrity guest that evening, one of the biggest Broadway musical stars ever, made a startling impression on me when she arrived looking so, well … orange. Her appearance was shocking to the other guests and the media as well. Decked out as she was in a white Mackie gown with a matching white fox jacket and her platinum white hair, the contrast with her bright orange skin was frightening. Had she bathed in some of that old orange quick-tanning lotion? Was she jaundiced from liver cancer? She certainly didn't look well. Whispers zoomed among the guests, was this national treasure dying of cancer? When I shook her hand backstage, it didn't ease my worries. Her hand was thin, frail, and cold. Finally, I asked her if she'd been out in the sun. "No, deeeeaaar," she corrected, "I'm on an all-carrot diet." Instantly, I recalled reading about teenage boys during World War II who'd eaten so many carrots, trying to improve their night vision to become

combat pilots when they came of age, that they would turn orange. Our orange diva wasn't trying to improve her night vision; she was just trying to stay thin. I guess it was a variation of other food fad diets, such as all-grapefruit or all-papaya, that circulate every so often. To my knowledge though, this was a diet that only one person was trying. She ended our conversation by asking me to remind the hotel staff to serve her only carrots. The chef that evening sent her, with compliments, pureed carrot soup, steamed carrots with fresh dill, raw carrots for a crunch, and a slice of carrot cake instead of the baked Alaska enjoyed by the rest of the guests. I found it strangely funny that the star who'd made famous the song "Diamonds Are a Girl's Best Friend," who had thrown out handfuls of large rhinestone rings at the end of her stage show, and who wore a rock the size of Rhode Island on her very orange finger was now filled to the brim with *karats*.

Over the years, each event would have its own striking moments of drama, pathos, and slapstick and each would develop its own character and mood. Each designer would bring out a different cast of clients, vendors, celebrities, and fashion groupies. The Mackie evening had its own distinct flavor—like *Seinfeld,* it was a show about nothing. A Las

After the Cher tribute this California wedding dress looked more like a Beverly Hills nightshirt.

Mr. and Mrs. Michael York were just a few of the stars that turned out to see and support our show.

Vegas–type extravaganza whose audience was primarily TV and film industry people who came of age in the 1960s and 1970s, Mackie's costumes brought a warm and nostalgic delight to the audience, who remembered seeing so many of them through the years in well-loved TV shows, movies, musicals, and stage acts, and on famous people. A glittering parade of feel-good nostalgia. Our show included Mackie costumes for:

- The stage acts of Diana Ross, Barbra Streisand, Liza Minnelli, and Joan Rivers
- The Broadway shows of Angela Lansbury and Juliet Prowse
- The Las Vegas shows of Tina Turner, Ann-Margret, and Carol Channing
- Elton John's 1987 world tour
- Bernadette Peters in *Pennies from Heaven* and Brooke Shields in *Brenda Starr*
- Goldie Hawn as a pirate and Barbara Eden in *Kismet*
- Linda Gray on *Dallas*
- Lucille Ball and Cyd Charisse in the 1960s

- All the Carol Burnett characters on her TV show, including the cleaning lady and Eunice, plus her green velvet-drapery dress with the drapery rod still running through the shoulders from her hysterical *Gone with the Wind* parody ("I saw it hanging in the window and I just couldn't resist it").

By now we had a large Hollywood following, and our core group of supporters—Carol Kane, Jackie Collins, JoBeth Williams, Elizabeth Montgomery, Robert Foxworth, Cindy and Michael Landon, Bernadette Peters, and others—were all out front as the first "Oooh!" and "Ahhh!" arose from the audience. But before the show would end that evening, Bob Mackie did one more very odd thing that seemed self-defeating. Without warning me, or anyone else for that matter, when the show was over and the last model in the lineup made her way backstage, Mackie sent out another model, then another, and another. And on and on for an extra 20 minutes, creating a music and lighting quagmire. I'm not sure if anyone out front noticed anything wrong, but you should have heard the four-letter words flying back and forth among Mackie, the lighting tech, the music engineer, and me! This last tacked-on segment of Mackie's ready-to-wear collection was such a letdown after the previous glamorous costumes that guests started leaving in droves. By the time Sam Harris, famous for his string of wins on Ed McMahon's *Star Search* and for being a white singer signed by Motown Records, went on stage and sang "Somewhere Over the Rainbow," nobody was listening. And Harris has a huge voice.

The Mackie show was a breakthrough for our event. It put us on the map as far as the press was concerned. The show had had a lot of star power, with consequent swarms of paparazzi. Even though showing the Mackie retail line after his glittering star costumes was anticlimactic and made the show drag on too long, it was definitely a very glamorous evening and a smashing success. The show also marked an evolution for us; it was our year of humility. We had to realize that it was their show, the designer's show, and not

Joan Rivers, Mitzi Gaynor, and Bob Mackie in 1989. A team effort.

ours any longer. Our control was lost from the moment we selected a designer who said yes. After that, we could collaborate on the design of the show and event only to the degree that the chosen designer would allow us. Dealing with Mackie, and even more so dealing with some of our future honored designers, would remind me of a line from Ecclesiastes:

Vanity of vanities, saith the Preacher, vanity of vanities; all is vanity.

4

Hollywood Costumers

—A Scavenger Hunt through Hollywood Closets

"You have a hit TV series; you're a much bigger **star** than she is. If she wants to meet you, she has to **come over** here— you're not going over there!"

—Stage mother to her daughter who wanted to ask Cyd Charisse for an autograph

By 1990, our event had achieved an annual event status in Los Angeles. Because of the star power of Bob Mackie and the New York bravado of Geoffrey Beene, our evening was now considered a hot ticket in Hollywood. And AIDS had become—for the moment, anyway—a force for those celebrities who lend their support to worthy causes. Within the fashion industry, AIDS finally had a face, or rather several faces: male super model Matt Collins, designer Halston, and one of the most beautiful models of the decade, Gia. AIDS had continued to take its toll in Hollywood. Besides the headlined deaths of Rock Hudson and Liberace, there had been recent deaths of puppeteer Wayland Flowers (famous for his appearances with Madame on *Hollywood Squares*), beloved writer and director Colin Higgins (writer of *Harold and Maude* and writer-director of *Nine to Five* and *The Best Little Whorehouse in Texas*), actor

Timothy Patrick Murphy (known for his TV work on *Search for Tomorrow* and *Dallas*), and the daughter, Ariel, of *Starsky and Hutch* star Paul Michael Glaser. Glaser and his wife, Elizabeth, who was also infected (as was their second child), were becoming tireless AIDS awareness activists in Hollywood and in Washington.

Hollywood was abuzz with studios, agents, managers, and stars speculating on who else might be infected with HIV. Rumors were rampant. If an actor lost weight too quickly, he must have AIDS. If one disappeared from sight for too long, people assumed he was either too ill to work or had gone away to die in peace. One has only to remember that even a major star like Burt Reynolds felt he had to go on *The Tonight Show* to deny the raging rumors that he had AIDS. Mere rumors could be enough to make an actor unemployable—not just because of the yet ill-informed, often bizarre ideas on how HIV was spread, but because in order to work in a movie, an actor has to be okayed by the company insuring the completion of that film. If the insurance company, worried about an actor's health, says no we won't insure him, the actor cannot be hired. Katharine Hepburn and director Stanley Kramer had to put up their own salaries as collateral for the movie *Guess Who's Coming to Dinner* because the insurance company would not insure the ailing Spencer Tracy. Tracy, who never knew what Hepburn and Kramer had done, died one week after the filming ended and garnered a posthumous Oscar nomination for his moving performance.

So it was against this backdrop of AIDS as celebrity cause and destructive rumor that we planned our fourth annual fashion gala for February 23, 1990, honoring some of the most notable costume designers in Hollywood past and present. But first, we had to find a show to put on. With tremendous persistence, we began to research the best of the best in costume designers—the Academy Award winners and nominees. Some were alive, well, and actively working on current projects. Others had died long ago, memorialized on celluloid and in historical books about the Hollywood crafts. One by one, we approached each of the

Heartthrob of the 1950s, singer Eddie Fisher at the *Fashion in Film* event.

Diana Ross's wardrobe from
Lady Sings the Blues.

Our volunteer models for
Dangerous Liaisons.

The original costume that
Valentino wore in *The Sheik*.

Our model for the *The Last Emperor* stole the show. Academy Award–winning costume designer James Acheson hand-delivered the costume to Los Angeles from London.

major studios asking them to open their costume vaults to us. Some gladly obliged us, while others were hesitant—the word *AIDS* still threatening. Among the studios that opened their arms, their hearts, and their vaults were Universal, Warner Bros., and the Burbank Studios. Also helpful were Lorimar and the legendary repository of Hollywood costumes, Western Costume Company.

Our goal in our fourth year was to celebrate Hollywood costume designers from the 1920s to the present. It was a daunting task, but not impossible. Unlike our experience with the Adrian show, where the entire collection had been painstakingly acquired, documented, and preserved for decades by a single man, finding the costumes needed for our *Fashion in Film* show was more like a scavenger hunt. But our hunt was full of delightful surprises as we located classic costumes spanning seven decades of legendary filmmaking, from the 1921 Valentino bodice-ripper, *The Sheik* (which included 7-year-old Loretta Young as an Arab child), to 1988's *Dangerous Liaisons*.

Western Costume was the first place we went on our hunt. Jim Watterson, a member of our steering committee and himself a veteran producer of fashion shows, still refers to his visit to Western Costume as "the visit of no more wire hangers," because he saw so many beautiful, famed clothes with wire hangers, some rusty, sticking through the shoulders of costumes. At that time, Western Costume was still in its ancient building on Melrose Boulevard near Paramount Studios. Jim had

to take a creaky old elevator up to what they called the star section, which was locked behind a chain-link fence, with light streaking in through the dust-covered windows. It was there that we found the legendary Valentino *Sheik* costume and two Walter Plunkett dresses for *Gone with the Wind*—Scarlett's barbecue dress and the famous green velvet dress made from draperies that Carol Burnett hilariously parodied on her TV series. It's amazing that

(top) *Somewhere in Time* mixed present day with 18th-century England.

(center) Bill Travilla's hot pink costume from *Gentlemen Prefer Blondes* was one of the highlights of the evening.

(bottom) Marlon Brando's costume as Napoleon from the film *Desirée*. Many of these costumes have since been sold into private collections.

(top) *Dangerous Liaisons*

(center) Backstage at *Fashion in Film*. Many of these costumes are priceless.

(bottom) Cindy and Michael Landon at the *Fashion in Film* AIDS fund-raiser in 1990. Cindy was one of our biggest supporters.

Walter Plunkett, who began his four-decade career at the FBO Studios of Joseph P. Kennedy (father of President Kennedy), didn't win an Oscar for our four-hour search through the *Gone with the Wind* clothes—but 1939 may well have been the greatest year for classic films in Hollywood history.

There were also wonderful clothes from the 1950s, including some Ethel Merman dresses. Western Costume lent us the amazing Marlon Brando Napoleon coronation outfit from 1954's *Desiree*. Designed by Rene Hubert and Charles LeMaire, it included a velvet-and-ermine cloak, satin slippers, and a gold laurel crown. Unfortunately, there were many important old costumes in incredibly bad condition, as Hollywood was only then beginning to understand the value of its heritage and starting to protect it. Previously, film masters had been allowed to deteriorate, and props and costumes were either destroyed or sold off for pennies. Though there is still

much to be done to preserve Hollywood's old treasures, at least the awareness of the problem has increased dramatically.

Next we went around to hunt through the studio collections. The biggest thrill at Sony was finding the Oscar-winning collection of *Dangerous Liaisons* costumes, which had been designed just a few years earlier by James Acheson. Considered by many to be one of the most brilliant costume designers working today, Acheson had taken antique laces and brocades and incorporated them into the costumes. There was the famous Glenn Close yellow and black outfit, and there were all the accessories to the costumes—lace knit gloves, hats, shoes, belts. These clothes required such a huge cast that we had to use the International Ballroom of the Beverly Hilton Hotel because we needed the smaller ballroom for a dressing room.

At Warner Bros., we found Cecil Beaton's legendary *My Fair Lady* costumes, including the wonderful hats, which were protected in glass cases. Unfortunately, the memorable high-necked gown that Audrey Hepburn had worn to the ball in the film had once been loaned to a Warner Bros. producer's wife. The dress had been placed in a large black plastic garbage bag and was accidentally thrown out—gone forever. Sir Cecil Beaton—knighted by the Queen in 1972—was most famous for his photographic portraits of British royalty and international stars such as Garbo. Beaton had also worked as an author and illustrator of books and a set designer for theatrical productions, operas, and ballets. He won both Best Costume and Best Art Direction Oscars for 1964's *My Fair Lady* and had previously won a Best Costume Oscar for *Gigi* in 1958. He died in 1980.

One of our biggest thrills was when we went to the Paramount studio lot. At first, Paramount told us that they didn't have anything and, then, that they didn't want us to look. Finally, with our persistence, Paramount relented and let us search through their closets. Again the costumes were all jammed together in a room. But in long boxes against the back wall of the room, we found some wondrous treasures of the costume art. Our most startling discovery that day was

Claudette Colbert's stunning Queen of the Nile costume from the original 1934 Cecil B. DeMille *Cleopatra*. Colbert's costume had been designed by Travis Banton. We also found one of the most celebrated costumes in movie musical history, Ginger Rogers's sequin-and-mink Edith Head–designed dress from 1944's *The Lady in the Dark*—originally a Moss Hart, Kurt Weill, and Ira Gershwin Broadway musical. There were some beaded dresses of Mae West and of the "It Girl" of the Roaring 20s, Clara Bow. We found Edith Head costumes from DeMille's remake of his silent *The Ten Commandments* and also some of the Theoni V. Aldredge's clothes from Robert Redford's remake of *The Great Gatsby*, but they were not in good condition—another "no more wire hangers" story. There was Grace Kelly's *To Catch a Thief* gold lamé dress by Edith Head, but it had disintegrated along its fold marks. When Paramount realized what they had lying around, they pulled most of the costumes and didn't let us use them. We were able to use some of the *Gatsby* clothes and a couple others. As for the truly amazing treasures, including the Cleopatra dress, the beaded dresses, and the Ginger Rogers's outfit, they all went to Sotheby's and were auctioned off. Once again, a studio sold away its heritage for a few grubby bucks.

In hindsight, it is surprising that our biggest obstacle in trying to put the show together was not a giant studio but instead a diminutive movie star who was also an avid collector of film costumes—Debbie Reynolds. A multimillionaire herself, with her own Hollywood memorabilia museum in Las Vegas, she said no to us as many times as we would ask her, Please. A singer, dancer, Oscar-nominated actress, and Hollywood icon "girl next door," she continually rebuffed our entreaties, despite requests from actors Roddy McDowall, Jane Withers, and Loretta Young, designers Donfeld and Jean Louis, and anyone else we could enlist. Reynolds's bizarre reason

Rosemary Stack (Mrs. Robert). Her husband refused to be photographed. His reasons are still an unsolved mystery.

for not wanting to lend us even a single dress was because "it's an AIDS fund-raiser and my costumes will end up on drag queens. Drag queens are too big to fit into anything I own and I don't want my costumes altered." Of course there were no drag queens in our show, only the top models from Nina Blanchard, Elite, L.A. Models, Prima, and the Ford Agency in New York. We never could get Miss Reynolds to lend us a single costume, though the "Princess Leia" actress and *Postcards from the Edge* author-daughter, Carrie Fisher, was in attendance the evening of the event. Fisher was accompanied by her then-husband, a powerful Hollywood talent agent who would shortly smear himself and Carrie all over the tabloids by running off with the gay boyfriend of one of Hollywood's most powerful entertainment managers and producers.

This year we again used film clips to interpose the fashion segments of the show. Besides providing spice to the show, the film sequences gave us badly needed time to make some amazingly elaborate costume changes. We used film from Cecil B. DeMille's original *Cleopatra*. This 1934 version attempted to make its history lesson palatable for its Depression-era audience by reshaping Cleo's

Cyd Charisse and her husband, Tony Martin, members of Hollywood's old guard, turned out to see friends and support our event.

story into a gold-digger-makes-good scenario, by giving the architecture of Rome and Egypt a decidedly art deco flavor and by using delightfully modern dialogue, such as Caesar barking to a scribe, "Take a message … to Mark Antony … Rome," or Mark Antony, after his Caesar eulogy, being chided for "all that 'friends, Romans, countrymen' business." Despite its lavish look, this 1934 version had a budget only one fortieth that of the 1963 Elizabeth Taylor *Cleopatra* remake. We showed a scene from Adrian's last film, *Lovely to Look At*, from which we also modeled some Adrian evening clothes. We featured Adrian gowns again as we ran a scene from 1933's *Dinner at Eight*, directed by George Cukor. It was the film's hilarious last scene in which Marie Dressler says to Jean Harlow, "Oh dear, you should come over some night and we'll talk about the Civil War," and then the doors close, The End.

We had a live orchestra that year and they played music from the films of the modeled clothes. For the finale of our show, we decided to recreate some of Bette Davis's famous lost costumes. We got volunteer

designers to sew the iconic *All About Eve* evening gown by the Oscar-winning Edith Head and Charles LeMaire and to recreate Orry-Kelly's designs for Bette Davis outfits from *Jezebel*, *Now Voyager*, *Mrs. Skeffington*, and *Little Foxes*. Edith Head was born in San Bernardino, California, a place we in Southern California refer to, with insufficient irony, as the Inland Empire. She became the only costume designer whose name is well known by the general public. And no wonder, for during her five decades at Paramount and Universal, Edith Head received 35 Oscar nominations and won eight of the statuettes. One year she was nominated for four different pictures! Australian-born Orry-Kelly designed costumes for 33 years and was proclaimed "the greatest of all Hollywood designers" by his equally legendary colleague Walter Plunkett. Orry-Kelly, who won the last of his three Oscars for putting Jack Lemmon, Tony Curtis, and Marilyn Monroe in dresses in 1959's *Some Like It Hot*, summed up his career with, "Hell must be filled with beautiful women and no mirrors." We discovered that Bette Davis had an unusual physique—she was extremely tiny, big-bosomed and high-waisted. After providing the finale of our show, these Bette Davis replicas were donated to Warner Bros., where they are today sometimes touted, so we hear, as being the original costumes.

For the opening of the show, we had wanted to use the opening scene from *Mommie Dearest* in which Faye Dunaway is awakened by an alarm, gets up and plunges her face into a bowl of ice water, is chauffeured through dark streets to the studio, and gets into a makeup chair, which turns around and—it's Joan Crawford. To use the clip, we had to get the permission of the star as well as the copyright holder. We called and spoke to a person who we thought to be Miss Dunaway's agent, but she turned out to be Faye Dunaway herself. She said, "No, I will not give my permission. That's not how I want to be remembered." Then, *slam!*—down went the phone. So, no *Mommie Dearest* clip. We ended up using the beginning sequence from *Dangerous Liaisons* to open our show. It was a similar concept, with crosscutting of Glenn Close and

John Malkovich made-up and dressed and eventually coming from opposite ends of Paris to meet as the salon doors open. We of course did get the okay of Glenn Close and John Malkovich to use the film clips, and the designer of the glorious costumes, James Acheson, was himself in the audience that night. He had flown in from London with a shopping bag on his lap containing the little boy emperor's costume from *The Last Emperor*. When the adorable little kid who modeled the golden costume scampered out onto the stage, he stole the show.

The other highlight of the show was the Marilyn Monroe scene. A Marilyn look-alike wore Monroe's famous *Gentlemen Prefer Blondes* Lorelei Lee pink satin gown with long gloves and tons of jewelry as she sang "Diamonds Are a Girl's Best Friend," surrounded by eight men in white tie and tails as her chorus boys. The gown had been designed by the legendary Bill Travilla, whose film costume career spans five decades. The number was a delicious surprise for the audience, who loved the moment because it was just so campy, wonderful, and out-there.

In the ballroom of Merv Griffin's Beverly Hilton Hotel on the night of the gala, Hollywood's luminaries turned out in greater numbers than ever before. Fred Astaire and Gene Kelly's most talented dance partner, Cyd Charisse, was there with her legendary crooner husband, Tony Martin, who had early in his career been featured in the Adrian-designed *Ziegfeld Girl*. There was Myrna Loy, the famous Nora Charles of the *Thin Man* movies, who, though in a wheelchair, had flown in from Texas to visit with old friends and see some of her favorite designers honored. And there was Hollywood's most popular female star of the 1930s, Claudette Colbert, looking very fit and lively in cranberry trousers with a tailored gray jacket. With his wife, Rosemary, was TV's Eliot Ness and *Unsolved Mysteries* tour guide Robert Stack. Few people realize that Stack's movie career began in 1939's *First Love*, a role for which he received much publicity as "the first boy to kiss Deanna Durbin"—Universal's 17-year-old singing starlet. Michael Landon showed up, accompanied by his wife, Cindy. After his first

Belinda Carlisle of the Go-Go's offered to sing, but the 1980s pop icon somehow did not fit the evening's format. Here she is with her husband, Morgan Mason, son of actor James Mason.

starring role in 1957 as a *Teenage Werewolf*, Landon went on to star in three hugely successful TV series. Little more than a year after this evening, as Landon was preparing his fourth series for television, *US*, he would learn that he too had a terminal illness. Comedian and cult hero of *Shakes the Clown*, Bobcat Goldthwait was in attendance as was the first woman to ever become president of a major Hollywood studio, Sherry Lansing. Because of Lansing's hugely successful career in film production, it is easy to overlook her role with John Wayne in legendary director Howard Hawks's last film, *Rio Lobo*. Lansing played the beautiful secondary heroine, Armelita, who gets facially disfigured by the villains. Maybe that's why it was her last film as an actress. Jane Withers, who began her career as an obnoxious child brat opposite Shirley Temple and who later achieved fame as Josephine the Plumber in a series of commercials for Comet cleanser, also came that evening.

A former First Lady had clearly planned on coming to our earlier gala honoring Geoffrey Beene. She was in town at the time,

Rita Hayworth's costume from *Gilda* was in amazing condition.

she liked Beene's designs, and many of her longtime friends were planning to attend the event. The Secret Service even paid a visit to the Century Plaza ballroom to access security issues. But her husband had just left office, and she may have worried that her personal appearance at an AIDS fund-raiser would appear to put the Reagan political stamp of approval on AIDS care issues—a definite no-no in Republican circles in the late 1980s.

From the film *The Golden Child.*

Still, I'm not sure—though I have a strong opinion—if it was the realization that the Beene tribute was also an AIDS fund-raiser or another reason that changed the former First Lady's plans, but she did not attend the Beene show. Two years later, though, the former First Lady was apparently less conflicted about being associated with AIDS issues and probably felt more comfortable being a civilian enjoying an evening out with old friends without it seeming to have political significance. Anyway, the former First Lady and also former actress Nancy Davis did come, accompanied by a phalanx of Secret Service agents, to our *Fashion in Film* event. However, the former First Lady, still a politician to the bone, arrived after the dinner, left immediately after the show, and did not allow a single photograph of herself to be taken at the event.

It was a night of Hollywood legends rubbing elbows with the elite of new Hollywood. It was a night of celestial bodies schmoozing with streaking comets. It was a guest list from Mount Olympus. One member of Hollywood's old guard, a famous 1950s pop singer and teen heartthrob, better known today for his infamous marriages than his amazing string of gold records, approached us through his now-famous daughters with an offer to sing at our *Fashion in Film* gala. It

seemed a perfect match as we were celebrating many of those very years of bygone Hollywood. We heartily accepted his offer and looked forward to this legendary crooner's performance as much as we knew our audience would. On the night of the event, though, our delight faded when we saw our featured performer backstage, so intoxicated that he had to be propped up by his two actress daughters (from his third marriage to a well-known singer, actress, and TV cricket). When our famous singer was announced, his daughters continued to flank him as they carefully shepherded him out onto the stage.

When the three reached the microphone, our singer didn't warble, he babbled … on and on. Not about AIDS or Hollywood or costumes but about how wonderful his new wife, a wealthy Asian woman, was to him, financially and otherwise. Clearly, he was not able to sing. So to save him from further *National Enquirer* revelations to the assembled, we had the orchestra strike up some exit music, and his daughters took the cue to help him off the stage. There is always a slightly perverse curiosity about how our old favorite stars are holding up these days, as illustrated by the success of the *Airport* movies, the *Love Boat*

One of Adrian's last films was represented with this gown from *Lovely to Look At.*

Audrey Hepburn's gown from *Sabrina* brought wild applause from our Hollywood audience.

No one could believe we had original costumes from *Gone With the Wind*.

Depression would tolerate to keep their young breadwinners working.

At my table that evening were seated, as usual, an eclectic mix of guests—stars, journalists, agents, managers, and people living with HIV. One refreshingly funny young lady, then costarring in America's number one sit-com, was seated on my right. Her mother, who was also her manager, and her stepfather, a well-known Hollywood publicist, accompanied her. The young actress informed her mother that she wanted to go over to get Cyd Charisse's autograph. Her mother quickly corrected this intended breach of Hollywood etiquette by informing her daughter that since she was in a hit TV show, she was a much bigger star than Cyd Charisse and she should stay seated and let others come to her.

Later, when the Cornish game hens stuffed with wild rice were presented under glass to the $2,500-a-person, black-tie table, our funny girl's mother starting pulling six plastic Tupperware containers out of her black Chanel shoulder bag. The unfolding scene grew weirder as the mother served two plastic containers each, one pasta and one green salad, to herself, our sit-com actress, and her famous stepfather. As Mom waved away the waiters' attempts to serve our elegantly prepared repast, out of that magic Chanel bag next came her own silverware, crystal glassware, napkins, and bottled water. The other guests at the table were transfixed, not believing their eyes. It was the equivalent of wearing a chest protector to a breast-cancer fund-raiser.

When I finally asked our funny girl what her mother was doing, she said, "Mom just wants to make sure none of us catch anything." Almost laughing and trying not to cry, I said, "You can't catch anything from eating this dinner." "Don't all these people have AIDS?" she asked. "Well, sure, some of them do, but the food and the silverware isn't contaminated," I tried to reassure her and her ill-informed mother.

Suddenly another voice, from a movie star who was represented by the young lady's stepfather, shouted from across our table, "Put the goddamn Tupperware away or I'm leaving! Are you people out of your fucking minds?" With that, some of our HIV-positive table-

TV series, and the tabloids. So, even though this interlude was sad, it was also undeniably memorable for all in attendance.

There was one actress that evening who held her tablemates spellbound with tale after tale from her child star years at MGM during that studio's golden age. One story is particularly memorable because it involved an apparently not-uncommon unchaperoned private meeting with studio head Louis B. Mayer in his office. Actually, the reason the story sticks in my mind is that it included the words "sitting on his lap" and "boner" in the same sentence. Besides the incongruous choice of the word "boner," which had us all convulsed with laughter, the story gave us an unsettling insight into what stage mothers during the

mates called further attention to our table by shouting across the ballroom to their friends—"Hey, Steve, get over here! You've got to see this!"

Soon most of the 1,200 guests in that filled-to-capacity ballroom were aware of the Tupperware spectacle. Shortly, a parade of Hollywood's biggest stars traipsed past our table for a look, supposedly on their way to the bathrooms—which were out the doors on the opposite side of the ballroom. One popular stand-up comic even inquired, "Where's the candid camera?" But our young starlet, naive and oblivious, had a good time greeting and waving to her favorite stars of film, television, and music as they passed by. Maybe her mother had been correct about her staying seated after all. Later she slipped away from her domineering mother, sneaked a glass of champagne, posed for pictures, and spoke maturely to the press about AIDS.

Yet, this bizarre sequence was not played out. At the end of the evening, as the young actress's mother made her way out the door and down the red-carpeted, paparazzi-lined, celebrity Diamond Lane, she passed a group of protesters from PETA (People for the Ethical Treatment of Animals), who had been protesting the use of fur in our show—which, in all honesty, had been dead for almost 50 years at this point. Well, when the PETA group spotted the white fox fur coat the mother was wearing, they pelted her coat with red food coloring. With this, she shrieked, "I've been exposed to AIDS!" She rushed to her waiting limo and hurried off into the night, never to be seen again at another AIDS fund-raiser. The following day, I sent a note to our sitcom starlet and her mother. I apologized for the incident and assured them that it was only food coloring and not blood. All in all, though, in their own inimitable way, those two had done wonders to increase awareness about how the AIDS virus is not spread.

Although our tribute to outstanding Hollywood designers was not, in many ways, our best show, it was the most fun to prepare and present. It was great seeing all those costumes we'd known for years. And we had shown Western Costume and the studios that what they owned was still something valuable

and if they didn't sell it off, worth taking better care of in the future. The show was also an incredible save because the designer who we thought had committed to be that year's honoree but later informed us that he hadn't really made a commitment would just three years later beg us to honor him. Without the Hollywood show, there wouldn't have been any show that year, which would have dissipated the building momentum of the event. That year was a huge step in establishing us as a Hollywood heavyweight among fundraisers. With such a star-studded guest list, our gala was now garnering worldwide media attention. It played well on MTV and drew reviews in such institutions as *W, Vanity Fair, New York Times, Vogue,* and *Bazaar.* In four short years, we had created *the* venue for fashion designers who understood the value of publicity and contacts in Hollywood.

We had started as a grain of sand that was merely irritating to the international fashion community, but after being coated with layer upon layer of stardust, we had been transformed into a lustrous pearl. With the noble purposes and boundless enthusiasm of volunteers, we had, almost inadvertently, created the premiere platform for a designer's big moment in the media—an event that could help a designer become a household name. Other occasions at that time were mere by-products of the designers' own publicity machines. But our very success would sow the seeds of our undoing. During the upcoming years, and only with belated understanding, we would watch our volunteerism be progressively overwhelmed by those very designer publicity machines.

5

Gianni Versace
—Waltzing with the Maestro

"I love my **friend** Gianni."

— Sylvester Stallone

"At that moment, the most expensive clothes in the world by the most famous designers in the world—all French except for Versace and Valentino—were shown on the same runway. Of course there was the appropriate applause for the grand couturiers, but then, suddenly, there was a real moment of magic when Versace's sexy, opulent, and daringly modern clothes hit the catwalk. First there was silence—a serious silence not paid the other designers. Then, suddenly, a stunning kind of acclamation New York fashion people (retail executives, editors, and socialites) do not often bestow." By the end of the show, recalls Los Angeles Times Syndicate columnist Marylou Luther, "it was clear that the old guard looked just that—old—and that Gianni Versace was onto something new." In 1990, at the Fashion Group's haute couture show at the Plaza Hotel in New York City, Gianni Versace had broken into the pantheon of fashion icons as had Balenciaga, Chanel, Dior, Pucci, Courreges, Cardin, Gernreich, and St. Laurent before him.

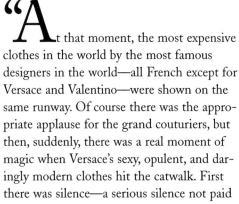

Actor Richard Gere looked on as then-wife Cindy Crawford modeled in the Versace show. From the runway, she flashed him the "Peace" sign. He flashed it back...hmmm!

Gianni (Johnny) Versace launched his first signature line and opened his first boutique in Milan in 1978. But it wasn't until the 1980s that his clothing lines took off, and in the 1990s, they skyrocketed—with more than 200 boutiques worldwide yearly selling $1 billion worth of Versace products. Versace had long been known as a designer to the stars. He'd designed the famous red leather jacket for Michael Jackson's *Thriller* video and costumes and set designs for Elton John. Other rock-and-roll clients included George Michael, Bruce Springsteen, Sting, David Bowie, Phil Collins, Tina Turner, Paul McCartney, and Cher. Movie stars such as Sylvester Stallone, Barbra Streisand, Sophia Loren, Jane Fonda, and Faye Dunaway were among his regular clients. He also made clothes for Princess Diana of England and Princess Caroline of Monaco and made costumes for the theater, opera, ballet, and the *Miami Vice* TV series. As Versace proudly described his creations in May 1995, "I've always said that I would like to mix rock and simplicity because this is fashion; they're the extremes, chic and shock. That's why Lady Diana and Madonna—two of the most important women of the moment—wear Versace and I think I'm satisfied by this. Even if it took me twenty years, I've got to where I wanted to go."

The Versace look could be young, aggressive, and sexy, with metallic fabrics, skintight and brightly colored, with low cuts and high slits. It was a look that might be merely exhibitionist or simply vulgar in lesser hands. Or Versace could surprise all with designs that were amazingly restrained, classic, simple, and elegant. Designer Carla Fendi, in July 1997, described Versace's strengths: "He found his unique style in fashion, using the traditions that come from his land, from the traditional and the classic. But he added freedom to this … the courage to do what he believed in and the creativity that pushed him to dare. Result: young fashion, rock, beauty that passed from tradition to shameless modernism. In this he was a magician."

Steven Seagal and actress Kelly LeBrock had a tiff backstage over her very short haircut. He sported a ponytail.

In 1990, Gianni Versace was the hottest designer on the scene. With the magnitude of our now famous event solidified with four successful outings, it was a natural that Versace be our next honoree. We made an overture to Gianni Versace with the help of a *WWD* editor and Carolyn Mahboubi.

Our offer to the Versace family was met with a resounding Yes. It was set—the hottest designer in the world, and we had him. Our first choice, and it had been easy. We were not used to this. But on February 13, 1991, *Gianni Versace—The Man and His Art* would

At the time, Carolyn Mahboubi was the 20-year-old owner of the world's highest grossing Versace boutique, on Rodeo Drive in Beverly Hills. The Saturday after our Versace event, the boutique grossed $250,000. Carolyn's father, Dar Mahboubi, had escaped from Iran during the revolution with his fortune intact and invested heavily in Beverly Hills commercial real estate just before property values exploded in the 1980s. He is also owner of Bijan.

be our fifth fashion gala and it would catapult our event into the international arena under a worldwide spotlight. With Carolyn Mahboubi's Beverly Hills boutique, Versace had had a presence in Los Angeles during the booming economic times of the late 1980s. Still, few people could pronounce his name and fewer still could afford his clothes. But his sexy advertising in *Vanity Fair, Vogue,* and *GQ* and his designs for rock and movie stars had finally garnered him notice from the young of Hollywood and the trend-setting gay community.

The Versace empire is a family business. Gianni had founded his company in 1977 with his brother, Santo, who ran the business affairs. Eventually, their sister, Donatella, joined the company as creative muse and counsel to Gianni and later as a designer in her own right. (Gianni had 45 percent of the company, Santo had 35 percent, and Donatella had 20 percent.) Donatella's husband, Paul Beck (an American and former New York model who had met Donatella while he was looking for modeling work in Milan), handled the company's publicity and advertising wing. In the fall of 1990, Paul Beck flew into Los Angeles from the Versace villa in Milan to scout prospective venues for the show. Paul, a tall, blond, handsome, well-put-together man, looked very Northern Italian that day in his all-black suit and white undershirt, with a black leather backpack. Paul was very smart and approachable and easy to work with. We showed Paul our preferred location, the Los Angeles Ballroom at the Century Plaza Hotel. Built on what used to be the 20th Century Fox studio back lot, the hotel is probably best known to the world as the place where U.S. Presidents from Johnson to Bush stayed when they were in Los Angeles. With a presidential suite that could accommodate Secret Service and a president's telecommunications needs and with a heliport on the roof, the hotel was the perfect place for a quick presidential visit to Los Angeles. There is also an underground entrance that could accommodate a presidential motorcade. The president would then be escorted through the kitchen and up a service elevator to his suite. The hotel's Los Angeles Ballroom was the site of both of Ronald Reagan's presidential election victory parties. Even though the ballroom had a 1,600-guest seating capacity and a modern stage with state-of-the-art lighting and sound systems, Paul Beck made it clear it was not his or Gianni's first choice. After all, it was only a hotel ballroom, not the sort of grand theatrical venue the Versace clan was used to working with. But because it was an AIDS benefit and using the Century Plaza Ballroom would allow us to control expenses more effectively, Gianni graciously put his grander ideas aside and agreed to use our preferred site.

Versace fan Rosanna Arquette in Versace.

When I first met Gianni, only days before the show, he told me that Los Angeles was one of his favorite cities because of the movie and music stars and the Hollywood glamour. His favorite place to stay in L.A. was in a bungalow at the landmark Beverly Hills Hotel. The coral-pink Mission Revival–style hotel had been built on 12 acres of lima bean fields in 1912. It has 194 luxury suites, including bungalows, with gardens, pools, and restaurants such as the fabled Hollywood watering hole the Polo Lounge. The Beverly Hills Hotel has always catered to Hollywood's most glamorous and powerful—Howard Hughes had rented Bungalow Three for $350,000 a year. One year after our Versace event, the Hotel was closed down for a $100 million remodel by its current owner, Muda Hassanal Bolkiah, the Sultan of Brunei, one of the richest men in the world. Versace liked to sit by the pool at the Beverly Hills Hotel, sketching, and holding court for Hollywood royalty. He said he never grew tired of this group because he would make a new friend each time a new star was born. Versace also felt right at home with the L.A. weather. "It is a city with a climate much like the Mediterranean," he told me.

This illustrates two often-opposing goals of our events. We want to raise as much money as possible for charity, yet the designer wants to present his work and his image with meticulous attention to detail. It is under-standable that a designer would be fanatical about his image. After all, image is what he is selling, which has usually taken years and millions of dollars to create. And no one could be more meticulous than Gianni Versace. The wonderful difference with Gianni is that he felt that all these expensive extras to create the perfect presentation of his clothes and image were expenses that should be borne by his company and not by the charity. The Versaces not only paid for the creation and transport of all their elaborate décor and expensive clothes, but also paid for the travel and hotel expenses of everyone they brought in to work on the show, including all the Versace family's expenses. Some of the other designers we worked with seemed to feel that we were just so damned lucky to have them accept our honor—ignoring all the free publicity and goodwill the event was generating for them—that the charity should pay the often outra-geous expenses for their elaborate table settings, centerpieces, and menus, their costly décor, and their high-priced personnel flown in from around the world. As a result, less money would be left over after the event for the charity. After our first event, the Adrian

Sally Struthers and the late actor George Peppard.

show, 80 percent of every dollar raised went directly to help people living with HIV. After our last event, the Todd Oldham show, little more than a third of the money raised was left to help anyone. By contrast, this upcoming Versace event would, in the end, raise more than half a million dollars to benefit people with AIDS. The day after our Versace gala, I would meet with Gianni's brother, Santo, to go over the expenses for the event. Santo handled the business end of the company but kept in the background so I hadn't met him before. He didn't look at all like his brother—he was short, stocky, round faced, with short-cropped black hair, wearing a Versace suit of course. Santo said that he'd cut us a check for all of the Versace company expenses as soon as he got back to Italy. And that's exactly what he did. This is one of the many reasons that working with the Versace family—and with the other designers who put the charity's needs first—was such a delightful and refreshing experience.

I would later gain a more personal insight into Gianni Versace's commitment to raising money for people living with HIV. Several of the Versace staffers and I were having a

Artist David Hockney, singer/actress Lainie Kazan, who dressed in the limo on the way to the hotel, and L.A. philanthropist Harold I. Huttas.

lunchtime meeting poolside at a fashionable West Hollywood boutique hotel. As we munched on our tuna sandwiches and French fries and sipped our mint iced teas, we reviewed the budget and verified our timetables for mailing invitations, advertising, and physically preparing the show. In a moment that seemed to drift in to remind us of what all these details were really about, our conversation changed to a discussion of the dramatic effect AIDS had had on the fashion industry. After learning the HIV status of much of Seventh Avenue, it was almost casually dropped that Gianni himself was HIV positive. No wonder, unlike some of our other honorees, Gianni never lost sight of the purpose of the show—to raise as much money as possible to help others infected with the virus. I was asked to keep Gianni's HIV status to myself, and of course I did. If Gianni didn't want to share his personal health issues with the whole world, I understood perfectly. And that went also for all the other

Richard Gere, Donatella Versace, and photographer Herb Ritts at the Versace event.

celebrities whose HIV status I knew about from them or from mutual friends. I feel comfortable discussing it now because it has been made public knowledge in a recent book about Versace's killer, Andrew Cunanan, but mostly because it tells us a lot about the courage, grace, and generosity of Gianni Versace himself. He was a very classy man.

Donatella Versace, Elizabeth Taylor, and Gianni Versace backstage. Gianni gave her armfuls of clothes.

With our honoree, date, and venue set, we immediately began planning the February event. We notified the fashion press and other media that Gianni Versace was now officially on board. Within hours after the *Los Angeles Times* published our report announcing the show, the date, and location, I received a call from Billy Sammath, who at the time was Cher's manager. Billy was offering Cher's guarantee of her participation in our Versace show. Funny, we hadn't even

Sylvester Stallone would fill in at the last minute for fickle Cher.

asked. This really was getting easy. We referred Sammath to Versace's public relations representatives, the New York–based PR firm Keeble, Cavaco, and Duka (KCD). It was quickly decided that Cher (the fashion trend-setter who popularized hip-hugging bell-bottoms in the 1960s, ironed hair and glittered eye makeup in the 1970s, ribless midriffs and semi-nude Oscar outfits in the '80s, and who hawked cosmetics in the '90s) would be the perfect celebrity to present Gianni his Crystal Apple Award for AIDS service. (Later, Mayor Tom Bradley and the Los Angeles City Council would also proclaim the day of the event Gianni Versace Day.) The following Friday, a picture of Cher appeared in the *Los Angeles Times* touting her scheduled appearance at our event. We were off and running. Still that word *scheduled* in reference to Cher left me with a nagging uneasiness. This was, after all, the same Cher who, two years earlier, had also promised to appear in the Cher sequence of gowns that her good friend Bob Mackie had created for her over the years. She not only let Mackie and us down—without any notice—but showed up at the event not on stage but in the audience and not in sequins but in badly torn jeans and a black Harley-Davidson leather jacket. To call Cher unpredictable would be generous. I was worried. I suggested to the Versace production team that it would be prudent to round up a fall-back celebrity as award presenter in case Cher flaked out on us again. "Don't worry, she'll be there," they kept reassuring me. "Gianni gives her tons of clothes every time she calls him." Perhaps they were right. Perhaps she wanted to make amends for letting us down in 1989. Wasn't she pushing 50 after all? Perhaps she had become more dependable. Perhaps.

In November 1990, our steering committee, other volunteers, and the Versace production team from Milan jumped into the preparation of the event with unusual ease and joy. It was a comfortable and productive real collaboration with the set builders, the dressers, and the lighting and music people. Versace's longtime producer Sergio Salerni instinctively knew what Versace would want. Everything in the room would be transformed into the

Versace aesthetic—the tablecloths, the napkins, the lampshades, the flowers, the set, the music, the lighting. Thousands of yards of specially designed fabric arrived from Europe and our "friends of the event" straight away began to cut, sew, and hem tablecloths, napkins, and even a cummerbund designed for me (as chairman I would be expected to say a few words on the night of the event). The Versace-designed lampshades for the 150 fourteen-inch-high nightclub table lamps presented a special problem—no one in all of Southern California could produce them in our short time frame. We ended up shipping the lampshade fabric to a small shop up in Fresno, California. I wondered, at the time, what the Fresno workers living in the Raisin Capital of the World must have thought of the expensive Versace fabric, with wildly mixed bright, bold colors in harlequin, check, and paisley designs. But for us, these shades fabulously said *Versace!*

Back at the Los Angeles Ballroom of the Century Plaza Hotel, preparations continued, now in high gear. The Italian set designers measured the room and sketched out plans for the stage and runway. To our surprise and delight, Versace had arranged for a backdrop created by him for the La Scala Opera House in Milan to be flown over to Los Angeles. The huge canvas was painted to look like lush theater curtains held back by ropes of gold. It would replace the ballroom's own gaudy, red velvet theater curtains, which we removed.

In the beginning of February, Sergio Salerni returned with a cast of characters from KCD, Versace's longtime PR and special events firm. Sadly, two of KCD's founding partners, the married couple Keeble and Duka, had themselves died of AIDS by this time. The new guard was represented by the lively Midwesterner Julie Mannion (now a partner), who led the KCD team. Julie, originally from Kansas City, Missouri, was a rail-thin, perfectly coiffed dynamo, who always dressed in black pants with a white shirt and appeared to eat only French fries and only once a day. According to designer Isaac Mizrahi, Julie is "a gal who really has her shit together." Julie also gave one the distinct impression that she took inordinate pleasure

The superluxury airline MGM Grand (with lounge areas, sleeping compartments, an actual bar, and an onboard chef) flew our New York models into town at no charge. MGM Grand promoted their generosity by announcing to the press that they were tripling their usual flight insurance because of their superpassenger cargo, dubbing the trip "Angels' Flight." The arrival of the models into MGM Grand's small private terminal just south of LAX was heavily covered by the press and because the models deplaned down a staircase directly onto the tarmac, their glamorous descent from the jet was reminiscent of celebrity plane arrivals in the 1940s.

Dr. Quinn, Medicine Woman Jane Seymour borrowed her Versace cocktail dress and had to give it back the next day. She hates when that happens.

The whole humongous Super Model phenomenon was only a couple years old at that time. During earlier decades, there had always been a female fashion model or two who would break through to become well-known to the general public, such as Christie Brinkley, or Lauren Hutton before her. Occasionally, one would even move on to a successful acting career, such as Ali MacGraw or Candice Bergen. But by the beginning of the 1990s, helped by celebrity magazines and celebrity news TV programs, the worldwide fame of the most successful female models had zoomed into the ionosphere. I would learn early on in securing film, TV, and music

celebrities for our Versace event, and also in arranging seating plans, that it was our girls from New York whom the Hollywood celebrities were most eager to meet. Forget about the chance to meet Stallone, Cher, or maybe even the reclusive Audrey Hepburn, who made one of her rare public appearances to honor her friend Gianni. (In reality, no one created more excitement on the night of the gala than Audrey Hepburn as she arrived.) Our local celebs wanted to meet the Super Models of the World and to watch them strut their magnificence down the runway. "The reason I'm here tonight is to meet that Naomi babe," shared a very married with children rock star perched at his front and center table. "Can you please arrange that?" he kept asking his manager, loudly enough for me and anyone else nearby to hear. The Versace event was our most star-studded evening yet. As one big star after another descended down the escalator into the salon of the Century Plaza, the paparazzi went frenetic. But it was the presence of the Super Models that evening that made our gala the hottest ticket in town. Because of the Super Models, our event received seemingly ubiquitous press coverage during the subsequent months. Before that evening, Gianni Versace had been a well-known name in the fashion world; but after that evening, he was a well-known name to the public at large—even if they still couldn't pronounce it.

in ordering around the world's most glamorous super models.

When the valuable Versace collection arrived at the hotel, the racks had to be protected around the clock by armed guards. The incredible luxury of the clothes was truly awe-inspiring. The fabrics were remarkable, with everything lined in silk. The accessories—shoes, handbags, jewelry, hats, everything Versace used—looked as though they had been created for King Midas. Next to arrive from Italy were the great Versace seamstresses. These brilliant needleworkers were soon meticulously taking out seams, hemming up, letting down, and nipping and tucking as each new model was cast for the show.

This show marked the first time that our cast would include the crowned Fab Five supermodels of the fashion world: Cindy Crawford, Naomi Campbell, Christy Turlington, Linda Evangelista, and Claudia Schiffer. Our gala would also be the first time for Claudia Schiffer to work live as a runway

model, though she was world famous for her many cover girl appearances on *Vogue* and *Bazaar* and for her provocative pulchritudinous print poses for Guess? jeans. All the models that evening, including the Fab Five, were unbelievably generous in donating their time.

On Sunday, February 10, Gianni was due to arrive on Al Italia accompanied by his longtime lover, Antonio d'Amico. The fashionable Four Seasons Hotel in Beverly Hills had donated their presidential suite to accommodate them for this auspicious visit. Everyone at the Century Plaza was busy taking care of last-minute details, anticipating Versace's imminent arrival at LAX. The table preparations were complete. Each table would be adorned with a Versace tablecloth and lampshade and a floral centerpiece of roses in uncommon shades of pink and red. Each place setting would have white china rimmed with 18-karat gold, leaded crystal goblets, sterling silverware, and a Versace napkin. The

Paula Abdul kept being mistaken for Oprah.

Actor Pierce Brosnan and his wife, who passed away from breast cancer just a short time later.

menu for the evening was set, Italian of course—pasta, fish, and a memorable tiramisu, a creamy coffee, cocoa, and rum dessert. The focal point of the room would be the stage and runway. With the breathtakingly beautiful La Scala backdrop now in position, everything else in the room, although spectacular, paled in comparison. The lighting had been hung and computer programmed for the light cues. The music was prepared on alternating reel-to-reel tracks, so complex that it took a full 24 hours to lay down the music for the show, which would be a fascinatingly eclectic mixture, jumping from Pavarotti doing "Nessun Dorma," from Puccini's aria from *Turnadot,* to a 1990 update of "I Heard It Through the Grapevine." The runway was completed and all of the tickets had been sold weeks before. We were ready for the maestro.

Oh well, I guess it really wouldn't feel like one of our events without some last-minute terror. As I was working on the map-sized seating chart of the Los Angeles Ballroom that Sunday afternoon, my telephone rang.

A member of Versace's staff informed me that Gianni would not only not be arriving that afternoon, but he would not be attending the gala in his honor on Wednesday evening either. Versace's reason? I guess I could blame it on President Bush, or maybe on Saddam Hussein—Versace's reason for not coming was the Persian Gulf War. The coalition forces were bombing and shelling Iraq and a land invasion was imminent. All flights into and out of Italy were on high alert for possible terrorist retaliatory attacks. Gianni hated to fly under the best of circumstances and didn't want to take a chance, however small, of being blown out of the sky by a terrorist bomb or missile. His sister, Donatella, and her husband, Paul Beck, were safely ensconced in a three-bedroom bungalow at the Beverly Hills Hotel with their children, Allegra and Daniel, and the Versace production team and seamstresses were already living at the Century Plaza. According to Gianni, the event could go forward fine without him. Sure, just like a coronation without the king!

Hyperventilating, I telephoned the patron saint of our events—Marylou Luther, fashion columnist for the Los Angeles Times Syndicate. Marylou, who had already arrived in Los Angeles, had helped us out many times before—starting with the Adrian show.

Claudia Schiffer, in her debut as
a runway model.

Claudia Schiffer brightens up the
Versace runway.

A crowd pleaser and
teaser…Cindy Crawford.

Naomi Campbell was the only
model who insisted on paying
for her dinner at the posh 1991
black tie event.

Marylou immediately told me to call Anna
Wintour, editor-in-chief at *Vogue*. Anna completely understood the disastrous effects of a
Gianni no-show, not only on our event, but
also on his reputation and career. Did he want
to get a reputation for being capricious and
undependable like Yves St. Laurent? Would
he seem to be saying that AIDS wasn't an
important enough cause for him? Hollywood
was turning out and they expected to see the
maestro. If he didn't come, the event would
have to be canceled, the ticket money refund-
ed, and the charity sustain huge losses. It
would be the end of the event as an annual
fund-raiser. Wouldn't he feel even safer if he
flew on an American flight instead of on Al
Italia? Whatever Anna Wintour said to
Versace, it worked. Gianni and Antonio
would be on the next scheduled American

flight to Los Angeles. Thank you, Marylou
Luther and Anna Wintour!

So after all these months of preparations,
Gianni Versace was finally, and safely, in Los
Angeles accompanied by Antonio d'Amico.
Gianni and Antonio had been lovers since
1983. Antonio was handsome, tall, and very
continental looking with wavy black hair and
green eyes, dressed youthfully in black leather
pants with a tight T-shirt. Antonio was very
attentive to Gianni, but then everyone was.
During the final day's preparations, Antonio
and Paul Beck were assigned the task of taking care of the many celebrities who were
coming into town to honor Gianni. They were
off entertaining the likes of Jeff Bridges and
his wife, and Sylvester Stallone and model
Jennifer Flavin (later Mrs. Stallone), who had
flown in from Miami.

Super model agent and right-handed pitcher Nina Blanchard, George Peppard, and Shari Belafonte.

We had sequestered an entire ballroom adjoining the Los Angeles Ballroom to hold the tables of expensive accessories and jewelry, the racks of bravura clothes, and the mirrors with chairs for makeup and hair preparation. There were table after table of seamstresses busy sewing. In the middle of all this purposeful commotion, Gianni Versace was taking care of detail after detail, overseeing all. In black pants, a black and copper embroidered vest, and an open-collared white shirt with his sleeves rolled up, Gianni was reviewing final fittings and the lineup and numbering of accessories. The show had been scripted and timed as precisely as a Broadway musical, and Gianni was making final adjustments to the order in which the show would be called. Gianni's eyes darted constantly, taking in everything. For months, others had had control of the preparations, and here was the maestro stepping in at the last moment, like a great conductor taking charge to make sure the complex orchestrations would produce a harmonious symphony. He was much shorter than I expected, as is often the case when one meets a larger-than-life person. Gianni was very thin, almost frail-looking, with graying hair and beard, perfectly groomed, as were his hands and nails. He was not a particularly

handsome man, average looking really, though I found myself wondering what he might look like without his beard. He was calm, quiet, serious, with an old-world reserve, a grounded part of him that was not for the public. To those who worked under him, he was unfailingly polite and gentle, but to the point. Gianni's presence recalled a feeling I'd experienced once before when I met jewelry designer Paloma Picasso, the daughter of artist Pablo Picasso and stepdaughter of Jonas Salk, the discoverer of the first polio vaccine. I felt not only close to greatness, but touched by a historic epoch. Sure, Gianni Versace was a fashion designer, not one of the great artists of Western civilization or the man who rid childhood of a horrifying scourge. But there was something about him, some connection that felt like it ran much deeper than fashion.

I was making final adjustments to the seating assignments of the guests. Seating people at an event of this magnitude is like traversing a minefield, though potentially much more explosive. One had to have a working knowledge of not just everyone's life history—who they were presently and formerly married to, who they were dating or had dated, who their business partners and clients are and were, and who they were

All smiles. Sassy Jane Seymour would raise hell the following year at the Thierry Mugler show.

Sylvester Stallone, Jennifer Flavin, and director Joel Schumaker.

Johnny Depp became a regular at our events.

Composer/producer Quincy Jones was one of Gianni's best customers.

Jennifer Flavin with short hair in 1991 would stay on opposite sides of the ballroom far away from the ex-Mrs. Stallone, Sasha.

currently feuding with. One needed to know that the table purchased by Sylvester Stallone's former wife should not be near the table that Stallone would be sharing with his current squeeze, Jennifer Flavin. Put the wrong groups of people together and all hell could break loose. Insult major donors to the charity by putting their table too far back or not close enough to what many perceived as the VIP section (lining either side of the runway) and one could sabotage next year's donation. No matter how careful I was or how hard I tried to please everyone, there would always be someone who was not happy—who would make sure I and often everyone else knew it. This thankless job took sensitivity, knowledge, and guts. A little dumb luck was handy too. Still, year after year, it was one of the most important jobs for the success of these events.

After the afternoon's dress rehearsal—at which Gianni welcomed students invited from local design schools such as the Fashion Institute of Design and Merchandise and Otis Parsons to enjoy the show for free—I approached Gianni and Donatella, who stood at ground zero of our huge backstage preparatory ballroom. In her miniskirt, Donatella, looked more like a teenager than a mother of two. She was tanned, with long, bleached-

blonde hair framing her large Roman nose and full red hornet-stung lips from which an ever-present Marlboro dangled. One hand held a cell phone to her ear as Donatella talked into it in English and to Gianni in Italian. The other hand was extended out to her side, as a seamstress, periodically bombarded by falling cigarette ashes, vainly attempted to repair the arm of Donatella's beaded cashmere sweater. Donatella was a tough, no-nonsense woman and was not one to bite her tongue in deference to her famous brother, as I was about to see.

I held up the map of the ballroom for Gianni, explaining to him where each person was to be seated. He was particularly interested in where the press would be seated and, of course, the location of his close friends and clients. Suddenly, Gianni saw the name Mirabella on a yellow Post-it stuck to a table with a ringside location. He started to swear in Italian (I'm sure he was swearing, even though I don't speak Italian), spit twice on the floor in disgust, and pulled the Post-it off the map. The one word I did understand was "No!", over and over again as his hands chopped through the air. So much for old-world reserve. Abruptly, he stuck the Mirabella Post-it on the outskirts of the chart. "That's in the kitchen," I explained gingerly.

Actress JoBeth Williams was an early supporter of our AIDS fund-raisers.

Broadway star Patti Lupone wanted to sing, but the Versaces said no, thank you.

Actor Dennis Hopper with an unidentified guest.

Donatella quickly dismissed her phone caller with "Ciao," and sprang to her brother's side, ready for combat.

The Mirabella sticker on the chart, which now resided in the kitchen, referred to the publisher of *Mirabella* magazine and former editor in chief of *Vogue*, Grace Mirabella. Because there are few more important individuals in the world of fashion, she was someone we had to seat properly or have hell to pay later. As Gianni agitatedly paced the room, Donatella sheepdogged him, step for step, talking Italian to him through her cigarette-clenching teeth as rapidly as he was pacing. The seamstresses, although they all obviously spoke Italian, seemed unimpressed by the drama, ignoring the whole scene, probably having witnessed it too many times before. I had no idea what Donatella was shouting but, something like a kid who did not understand why his parents are fighting, feared it might be my fault. Finally, one of Gianni's assistants came up to me and explained what was going on. Apparently, back in the early days of Gianni's career when he struggled desperately for any editorial coverage from *Vogue*, Grace Mirabella, then at the helm, shut him out. Gianni had never forgiven her. But now the worm had turned, and *Mirabella* magazine was in hot pursuit of

some of the multimillion-dollar Versace advertising budget. Ah, sweet revenge. As the scene played out, Donatella handed me back my seating chart and discretely instructed me to seat Grace somewhere better, but out of Gianni's sight. I found a halfway decent table toward the back of the room that would be bathed in darkness. Gianni would never see Grace unless he had a flashlight.

Later that evening, as the guests were enjoying champagne cocktails and Absolut martinis in the foyer to the ballroom, a handsome woman with oversized dark glasses cornered me. She was looking for Gianni Versace, and she had a large manila envelope she needed to give him. Her name? Grace Mirabella, of course. "He's busy backstage," I said, hoping she'd walk away. "Take me to him," she ordered. I guess some playful trickster inside of me took over, because suddenly I couldn't wait to see this drama play out. "Follow me," I found myself saying. She took my arm as I led her through the maze of journalists, celebrities, socialites, and other assorted VIPs, then through the partition and into the backstage prep area. Her eyes searched the wild scene that precedes a major fashion show. I swear, despite all the bedlam, Grace and Gianni saw each other at the same instant, and like rabbits caught in the headlights of an

Versace Men's Collection, Fall 1991.

onrushing semi, they both suddenly froze. Then, "JOHNEEEEE" was shrieked across the huge dressing area, met with "GRACE," bellowed in reply. The two hurried toward each other through crowds that, as in a bad movie, parted for them until they met midway with lavish air kisses (one doesn't kiss a woman who is made-up for the evening, no matter how histrionic the moment). It did not escape Gianni's notice that Grace was dressed in Versace (black, of course, as is de rigueur for New Yorkers with any pretense, but unmistakably Versace). "Look what I have for you," Grace purred as she opened the manila envelope and pulled out a mockup of the May 1991 cover of *Mirabella*. And what might the cover model be wearing? What else, but Versace. Gianni seemed touched, even overwhelmed. Suddenly Donatella grabbed my arm and pulled me aside. As she blew cigarette smoke into my face, she instructed me, "Put Grace back at her original table." "I've already taken care of it," I exaggerated as I ran out front to switch some table numbers before the guests entered the ballroom. Shortly, of course, guests sitting at table number 3 questioned why their table was next to table 53 and why table 54 was next to table 5. My absurd explanation that I was dyslexic put an end to the questions. So we all, except for table 3, ended on a happy note, followed by major editorial coverage of our gala in *Mirabella* magazine and a hefty contribution to the charity from the magazine's publisher.

Rock star Rod Stewart and then-wife Rachel Hunter attended almost every event. Rachel modeled in several.

Another of my zany memories of the Versace evening involved one of my favorite people, Nina Blanchard. Through her modeling agency and her personal contributions, Nina had been helping us since way before it was cool to do so. Nina was a celebrity in her own right and had been a frequent guest on the old *Merv Griffin Show*. Nina and her date for the evening, the late actor George Peppard (famous for being Audrey Hepburn's romantic interest in *Breakfast at Tiffany's* and for being the leader of TV's *A-Team*), were both avid smokers and were seated at my table. Nina stood up, leaned over the table, and grilled me in her distinctive throaty voice, "Who put these goddamn *No Smoking* signs on the tables?" I cringed. I had grown to love Nina over the years, but sometimes she could intimidate the hell out of me—and lots of other people in Hollywood too. This was certainly one of those moments. "It was the fire marshal," I offered apologetically. "The Versace tablecloths aren't fireproofed." "Who invited the fire marshal?" she laughed. With that, Nina picked up the small plastic no smoking sign and with the accuracy of a Dodgers pitcher, threw it hundreds of feet across the chandeliered ballroom, right through the swinging doors into the kitchen. She then put a cigarette to her lips, as did George, and Nina defiantly lit both of them. I held my breath, waiting for one of the ever-present fire marshals to ask them to extinguish their cigarettes or to tell me to shut down the event. But when a fire marshal finally made his way through the crowded ballroom, all he could do was stare at George Peppard and ask him for an autograph. George, the cigarette still hanging from his lips, graciously complied with the request, as I watched blue smoke circle the fire marshal's head. I could not suppress my laughter as Nina lit another cigarette off the one that had now burned down to the butt and settled herself in for the show. The famous are blessed with their own set of rules.

Just moments before the show was scheduled to start my cell phone rang. What now? It was Cher's manager, Billy Sammath, calling me from his home. Despite announcements to the press, the detailed script, and expectations of Gianni and the celebrity audience, Cher had decided she couldn't present Versace with his award that evening. According to Billy, "She thinks she's too fat." Sure, Cher's fat and the Pope's Mormon. Why couldn't she have been too fat yesterday? Billy made it clear that Cher was not going to change her mind. Why not, she changes it often enough—just always in the wrong direction.

The Versace Men's Collection,
Fall 1991.

Who could we find to sub for the suddenly plump Cher? Who wouldn't mind
jumping in with a few minutes preparation to
potentially embarrass themselves in front of
Hollywood's elite? Scanning the room, we
decided to ask Gianni's great friend Sylvester
Stallone. After graciously allowing himself to
be photographed until he was seeing white
spots before his eyes, Stallone and his bodyguard were now sitting comfortably at his
runway table, waiting for the show to begin.
In his Versace tux with a banded shirt collar
decorated by an onyx button, Stallone was
anticipating no greater activity that evening
than throwing kisses to his date and future
wife, model Jennifer Flavin, as she strutted
down the tarmac that evening. But when we
explained that his friend Gianni had been left
in the lurch by Cher, Stallone immediately
stood up and said, "Sure, what'd I gotta do?"
He also said a few words about Cher, but I
won't print those. Cher's speech was quickly
rewritten for him and Stallone went backstage
accompanied by his bodyguard to memorize

the speech amidst the commotion. Standing
next to Stallone were two star couples who
would also be participating in the show that
evening, multi-Oscar-nominated actor Jeff
Bridges with his wife and frowning action star
Steven Seagal and his then-wife, actress-
model Kelly LeBrock. Seagal and LeBrock
were bickering loudly because she had
chopped off her long hair that afternoon.
LeBrock's hair was now short and spiky, and
Seagal, although a self-professed reincarnated
Buddhist lama, was livid. Hair is apparently a
big issue with Seagal, as he had sent his press
agent earlier in the day to grill the Versace
lighting designer to make sure no light would
be bouncing off the bald spot on the back of
Seagal's head, which even his ponytail could
no longer disguise. Seagal and LeBrock later
carried their short tempers right out onto the
stage, where LeBrock screamed at the audience, "Shut up!"

With all the noise from marital dishar-
mony and last-minute preparations, it was
clear that Stallone was having trouble

The always present and
always welcome Sandra
Bernhard looked fab in her
Isaac Mizrahi gown.

One of our Versace table settings.

memorizing the speech. To make a change to the text of the speech, Stallone reached out for a pen hanging around the neck of one of our volunteers, then—CRASH! Stallone had lost his balance as he reached out and had fallen over, knocking down and breaking a video monitor that had been displaying the stage and runway. To this day, I'm not clear whether it was the commotion, Stallone's dark sunglasses, or the four-inch-high lifts in his shoes, or the combination of all three that had caused the mishap. But Stallone immediately jumped up, brushed himself off, and went out onstage. He ended up ignoring the prepared speech and spoke movingly from his heart. Stallone really loved his Italian brother Gianni and made no secret of it.

One interesting table that evening had been purchased for $25,000 by the Marciano family who own the Guess? clothing line. They had insisted earlier that I messenger over the seating map for them to inspect "for security reasons"—which of course I did not do. Their table had the dangerous chairman of Neiman-Marcus's table on one side and the table of the blood-thirsty artist David Hockney and the ruthless singer-actress Lainie Kazan on the other, so the Marcianos skipped the dinner and arrived just before the show with three armed bodyguards. They insisted that their bodyguards stand surround-

ing their table, so we had to position the three where they would not block anyone else's view. Immediately after the show ended, everyone at the Marciano table got up and left, escorted by their guards. I hope they got home safely.

There was another last-minute arrival that night. As the lights went black and just before the show began, my walkie-talkie chirped the message, "E.T. is in the house." Elizabeth Taylor had arrived through the kitchen to avoid all the press and paparazzi. She was looking fit and chic in the sequined gown and jacket that Versace had designed especially for her. On the front of her gown, looking like a sequined Andy Warhol lithograph, was the image of Marilyn Monroe. Miss Taylor sure didn't have to worry that any other woman that evening would be wearing the same dress. We escorted her and her small entourage to a VIP table. With all the excitement and anticipation amid the darkness, it was easy to miss the petite legend. As the last model disappeared from the stage and the lights came up again, I noticed Elizabeth Taylor and her guests were gone. Her table looked as if no one had ever been there. How she escaped my watchful eye is beyond me. Fortunately, her visit to see her friend Gianni the day before the show had been much longer. It was early evening and only the Versaces, their staff, and a handful of volunteers were still working in the ball-room when Elizabeth Taylor showed up to visit with Gianni and Donatella and select some clothes for herself. Designers typically bring tons of extra clothes, not for use in the show, but to give as gifts to celebrities who will be later seen and photographed in their clothes. When the visit and comple-mentary shopping spree were over, Elizabeth, with her assistant carrying the clothes that had caught her fancy, quietly slipped off into the night.

My most delightful surprise of the evening came when model Naomi Campbell

Gianni Versace looks like he wanted to hug everyone in the sold-out ballroom. The feeling was mutual.

whisked out her checkbook and insisted that she was going to buy her own ticket to the event. Although she had flown out from New York to donate her time (her fee was then $10,000 a show) and was our guest for dinner, she wouldn't accept my "No, thank you" for an answer. She finally tore off the $350 check and stuffed it into my front pants pocket—a straight boy's wet dream.

Another delight was when Cindy Crawford wowed the sophisticated L.A. audience by making one last run down the tarmac,

this time with her personal video camera. She panned the camera left and right, zooming in on her friends. When she zeroed in on her then–husband, charismatic leading man Richard Gere, she flashed him the peace sign and he flashed one back to her. I still wonder if this was their way of making peace after some earlier squabble.

The show itself was spectacular. Swarms of the world's loveliest women converging on the runway in Versace's bright yellows, greens, blues, and reds. Handsome men in patterned

Gianni and Elizabeth backstage.

pants and suits. Fashions that broke all the rules, and accessories that looked as if they had been borrowed from a museum in Florence or from the Vatican. Music and lighting that seemed to have grown from the very fabric of each Versace masterwork. With the fragrance of the freshly cut roses, the voice of Pavarotti, the Italian feast, and the backdrop from La Scala, it was easy to imagine that the maestro had transported us all to Milan. The evening was perfection.

The audience went wild for the whole event—to such a degree that we had to station security at each exit to prevent our illustrious, well-heeled guests from walking off with everything in the ballroom not bolted to the floor. A few limited edition Versace lampshades or tablecloths were certainly desirable, but the Versace people were expecting to transport them back to Milan for another AIDS fund-raiser. Particularly flagrant was the fashion editor of a major New York style magazine. Hard as it is to believe, she was stopped trying to spirit out four lampshades (with the lamps attached), several tablecloths and napkins, a set of silverware, two place settings of china, and some crystal goblets—all under her big faux fur coat! As the editor unloaded her booty at a nearby table, I happened to overhear her say that I had given her permission. As we had never met before, I walked over to her and introduced myself. She immediately started to shake uncontrollably, and then I was slightly horrified to see that she had just wet herself and the front of the expensive Versace gown she was wearing. I grabbed her, gave her a big hug, a tablecloth, a lampshade, and a centerpiece of roses. In gratitude, the editor later raved about our event in her magazine, printing several stunning pictures. In subsequent years, she became a major sponsor of our show.

Several weeks after the event, I received a personal note from Gianni. In it, he praised the many volunteers who had donated their time and invited me to visit him next time I was in Milan. He thanked us for picking him as 1991's honoree and said how happy he was that we'd raised so much money for people with HIV and wished us luck with future endeavors. Ever playful and still boyish at 45 years old, Gianni closed his note with a small sketch of a red heart and the postscript:

I am still wondering why you picked me and not Armani. Perhaps someday you'll tell me.

I never had the chance to tell him the reason, "Because of your grace and style, and your openness about your lifestyle." I can still see him on that warm windy evening in February as he walked down the runway with his arms stretched out, as though he wanted to hug us all in the same moment. Six years later, like John Lennon, Andy Warhol, and others who have felt the dark hand of fame, Gianni Versace was gunned down on the steps of his South Beach mansion in Miami, Florida. When I heard the news, my heart ached. I looked for Gianni's note to me, but could not find it.

In September 1997, Gianni's brother, Santo Versace, became the new CEO of Versace, and Donatella became the head of design. Donatella's 11-year-old daughter, Allegra, was the sole heiress of Gianni's estate, including his mansions in Italy, New York City, and Miami. Donatella's son, Daniel, inherited Gianni's collection of paintings. As the design force in the company, Donatella informed the world, "I'm a Versace girl. I grew up with Gianni, I started work with Gianni, so I'm not going to have another philosophy." And what is that Versace philosophy as articulated by Donatella?

Break the rules. Do not be afraid of your sexuality. Show the attitude and personality, which all women have. Say something. Play hard and soft. Discipline or revolt.

6

Thierry
Mugler
—Prêt-á-Party

"It's **all** about image.
Life is about **image**."

—Thierry Mugler

In looking for a designer for our 1992 fund-raiser, after the spectacular success and the international publicity of our Gianni Versace 1991 event, we found we were not just playing in a different league; we were playing a whole new game. Besides ubiquitous coverage in the fashion publications, the Versace show had cracked into the popular media. Clips from the Versace evening appeared on MTV, *Dateline NBC, 20/20, Hard Copy, Extra,* and *Fashion File* and were played on monitors in trendy gay video bars and straight nightclubs all over the world. Suddenly, we weren't seeking and pleading and facing rejection but were being courted by many of the biggest fashion houses in the world. They wanted the spectacular showcase that our gala had become. Amazingly, in five short years, our event had become the most glamorous, prestigious American fashion occasion except for New York's Costume Council Awards. Chanel and Karl Lagerfeld, Georgio Armani, Donna Karan, Dolce and Gabana, Christian La Croix, and other world-

class designers were having their PR representatives call me to ask how their clients could become our next honoree. It wasn't necessarily the award they were interested in; they wanted our venue, our platform to show their stuff on the world stage. Many of the courting designers also sent us videotapes of previous fashion shows they had done, basically "audition" tapes, so we could get a feel for what their event might be like. When I saw the tape sent by Thierry Mugler's people, I took it to our steering committee and everybody loved it. It was so different from the Versace event. Now that we had a choice, we decided to start this year with an elegant serious designer one year and then a more whimsical, of-the-moment hot designer the next—alternating to keep the events interesting for the audiences and the press. After the Mackie evening, we did the Hollywood Costumes evening. This was partially because of a last-minute cancellation by the designer who we thought had committed and partially because we were tired of big names with difficult egos. Working with Versace had been such a positive experience and had shown us that a

A happy Jane Seymour during cocktails. Backstage, she was grumpy.

Rod Stewart and Rachel Hunter arrive at the Mugler event in 1992.

Two-thirds of the 1980s trio Wilson Phillips, Carnie and Wendy, arrive at the Mugler event.

Thierry's fabulous stage and runway looked like the Moulin Rouge à go-go.

designer could have an international reputation and a healthy ego but still be a gentleman—reasonable and a delight to collaborate with. The Versace show had also been an elegant, posh, formal affair, and our plan was to follow Versace with a designer who was more outrageous and controversial. Mugler's tape and his reputation made it clear to us that he would provide a sharp contrast with the previous year's gala. Also, Mugler was French. France was the birthplace of haute couture, with Paris still the couture capital of the world. It was time for us to tackle a renowned French designer. We also wanted to attract younger Hollywood to our evenings. Mugler made sense. He was French, whimsical and avant garde, with the money to put on a show. He was hot stuff in the fashion press—maybe the hottest right then. There was major friendly competition at the time between Mugler and Jean-Paul Gautier. Our fashion fund-raisers were now spawning copycats. Gautier had earlier been involved in an L.A. fund-raiser for a national charity that funded AIDS research. The grand Gautier event had been held at the Shrine Auditorium, the

mammoth theater in downtown L.A. that often hosts the Oscar and Emmy shows. The Gautier show had made headlines around the world both when a topless Madonna wheeled a baby carriage down the runway and again later when its financial records were audited. Despite filling 6,000 seats, the show apparently made little or no money for its charity. Many people were outraged when a *Los Angeles Times* investigation disclosed how much money had been wasted on luxury expenditures such as a helicopter to shuttle the show's producer from his five-star Parisian hotel to the De Gaulle Airport. So the Gautier-Mugler competition also made the Mugler selection a natural. Did we also want to show the other big AIDS charity how to do one of these events the right way? Not consciously, but I guess we all are a bit competitive, even when doing good works. After five profitable and successful events in a row, I guess we were a bit cocky, thinking we actually knew what we were doing. It would take a few humbling experiences in subsequent years to remind us of the luck with which we had been blessed and the substantial help from the

Contortionists added to the eclectic mix of models.

angels. The truth was that guiding one of these big charity events was like holding the proverbial tiger by the tail—you can't let go or you'll be eaten by the tiger and if you hang on, the only direction you can go is wherever the tiger wants to drag you. Most of our illusions of control would turn out to be just that, illusions. So far, we'd been very fortunate and would be again with Mugler. Later on, we would develop greater empathy with those who put together the Gautier fund-raiser and been mauled by the tiger.

This was the first year in which we had the pleasure of picking among designers instead of waiting nervously for one to say yes to us. For our 1992 fashion gala, we said yes to Thierry Mugler. Mugler was born in 1948 in Strasbourg, a city on the Rhine River in the northeast of France. Strasbourg is the major city in Alsace, a region that has repeatedly passed back and forth between the Germans and French since the time of Charlemagne.

Of his years growing up in Strasbourg, Mugler has said, "All my childhood, I was very, very lonely. People thought I was retarded." At the age of 14, he entered the ballet of the Rhine Opera as a classically trained dancer. Mugler also studied design at Strasbourg's School of Fine Arts while continuing to design and make his own clothes. "I set off to the flea market, transforming things, dyeing things, cutting stuff." Wearing his own designs in Strasbourg, however, he was often confronted with derisive laughter and ridicule. That changed when he left for Paris. "When I moved to Paris, at the age of 20, people stopped me in the street—the first day I came off the train—asking, 'Where did you get that?' It was a completely logical reflex. I never shopped in the stores, I just didn't like it. So I did my own fantasy on me, and people liked it." He worked originally as an assistant designer for the Gudule boutique, then designed for André Peters in London, followed by a period freelancing for fashion houses in Paris and Milan. In 1973, Mugler created his first line, Café de Paris, followed the next year by the founding of his own label. From his days as a ballet dancer, he kept his taste for the theatrical in his presentation and for an architectural approach to design—

One year earlier, Tracy Ross (Diana's daughter) was asked to model in Thierry's Paris show. The next season mum Diana replaced her. What was that about? Diana was a show stopper in Paris.

Barry Krost and our favorite character actress, Carol Kane.

Dana Delaney

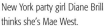

New York party girl Diane Brill
thinks she's Mae West.

Daryl Hannah in her freshly dry-
cleaned rhinestone romper looking very Marilyn Monroe.

"Dancing taught me a lot about the handling and structure of the clothes, and the importance of the shoulders, the head placement, and the play and rhythm of the legs." His exquisitely tailored designs are known for their precision and often for their classic, geometric structure. He can, however, also present softer, more fluid silhouettes seemingly designed for that icon of 1960s and 1970s fashion chi-chi chic, Babe Paley.

Beginning in 1977, Mugler started presenting his razor-sharp collections as theatrical events, with shows choreographed like grand ironic and iconoclastic postmodern operas. In 1984, he broke with tradition by presenting his winter collection not at the Louvre like every other designer but at a rock music stadium,

thereby injecting some much needed spectacle into the staid Parisian fashion world. Since that time, he hasn't let up in his desire to delight, surprise, and outrage. His twice–yearly futuristic fashion freakfests are perennially some of the hottest tickets in Paris.

His work and his shows, heavily influenced by movies and theater, are always rich in iconography, witty, erotic, and provocative. His designs can span from gaudy ornamentalism to rigorous minimalism. His postmodern playful irony has dressed his women as a seemingly inexhaustible variety of icons—futuristic, sexy Barbarella, flower child, opera, film, and rock divas, Ziggy Stardust-inspired space goddess, stalking glamazon, Tom of Finland leather dominatrix, angel and demon,

Rod Jackson and Bob Paris (former Mr. Universe) were actually husband and husband in 1992. Their two minutes on stage would shock some of our more conservative guests.

Like watching a Broadway play in Technicolor.

The Lady Miss Kier.

Gold lamé had a real presence in the Mugler show in 1992. It still does today in West Hollywood.

melodrama heroine, simple secretary, Marie Antoinette and Joan of Arc, and madonna and street tramp. This is how Los Angeles Times Syndicate fashion columnist Marylou Luther explained Mugler to me:

Thierry Mugler is the Steven Spielberg of international fashion, the creative visionary who has pushed the frontiers into both inner and outer space. His fashion expeditions have taken his Parisian audiences time-traveling from Stone Age to New Age. His extraterrestrial escapades have brought to the fashion stage the only living, breathing humanoid—or as Mugler preferred, the Imanoid, a red Plexiglas bodysuit named for and modeled by the supermodel Iman. The multitalented Frenchman has done more to celebrate the allure of Hollywood and its glamour goddesses than anyone since Adrian, Edith Head, and Bill Travilla—three of his heroes.

Mugler, a photographer since age 14, is also known for his photographic essay ad campaigns. He began photographing his own designs in the late 1970s. Helmut Newton, booked to shoot Mugler's advertising campaign, became so annoyed with the interfering and second-guessing designer that he stormed off, telling Mugler to do it himself. Since that

time, Mugler has created most of the advertising campaigns for his label and his fragrance, Angel, said to be so overpowering you either love or loathe it. He has also done featured pictorials for *Playboy* magazine and has published two books of his architecturally inspired photographs. Unlike other "renaissance" designers such as Karl Lagerfeld, whose attempts at photography and painting disappoint, Mugler's pictures are brash, exciting, and often capture the moment. Eschewing today's computer manipulation of images, Mugler, like Nazi documentarian Leni Riefenstahl, seems obsessed with the idea of the physical challenge of getting his shots. It's not easy being a Mugler photo model and it helps to be fearless. He has staged his shoots on icebergs, desert dunes, on cliffs, and apparently inaccessible ledges of skyscrapers—he even draped a model across one of the nickel gargoyles of Manhattan's Chrysler Building. Mugler himself recounted to me a story from one of his fashion shoots in Los Angeles. He had created a mock suicide, with the model apparently ready to jump off the Arco Towers in downtown Los Angeles. Frantic spectator calls to 911 quickly summoned the police and paramedics to the rescue. The crew of lighting, makeup, and wardrobe, as well as other assorted helpers cued the rescuers that this

Lypsinka strikes a pose.

The Rocky Horror Show.

Latin super diva Celia Cruz.

was not a real jumper. Thierry assured them that he had a permit and the model was attached to a safety line. To further his point, Mugler told the cop in charge, "Nobody commits suicide with this perfect makeup, this huge hairdo, and wearing such a magnificent Chinese dress." "This is L.A.," corrected the cop. "You wouldn't believe what we see." The dark humor of Thierry's story reminded me of the infamous Hollywood suicide of actress

Drag queen and entertainer Lypsinka doing her part in the fight against AIDS.

One of our models got into the spirit or the spirits got into her.

These girls got all tangled up on stage.

And we thought Sandra was tall.

Lupe Velez in 1944. Velez is probably best remembered for her starring role in the series of Mexican Spitfire films and for her failed marriage to "Tarzan" Johnny Weissmuller. Some claimed that Lupe Velez decided to take her own life because her career seemed over, while others blamed it on a pregnancy out of wedlock. She meticulously prepared the perfect setting in which to be found dead— soft candlelight, a bedroom full of flowers, a silver lamé nightgown, silk sheets and pillow-cases—then washed down her sleeping pills with liquor. Unfortunately, Lupe had also had a last meal of Mexican food. Before long, she became woozy and nauseated. As she stumbled into the bathroom to be sick into the toilet, she slipped on the floor tiles and smashed her head. Instead of being discovered dead in her perfect silk setting, Lupe Velez was found drowned with her head in the toilet.

Mugler's shows present his designs in dramatic narratives rich with visual and thematic references from Hollywood glamour and sexual fetishism to science fiction and politics. He was the first to use stars and media personalities from outside the fashion world in his shows and is known to court celebrities with the zeal of a fan and the per-sistence of a stalker. He has used transvestites to spice up and confuse his sexually charged extravaganzas. He has shown a dress in which the sheer front drape is held up by nipple-piercings on the bare-breasted model. Even the supermodel Iman, who retired in 1989 after sixteen years at the top, uses a Mugler moment to explain why she won't return to the runway: "People still come up to me and say things like, 'I will never forget seeing you on the catwalk for Thierry Mugler with a monkey on your shoulder and holding onto a leopard.' I think to myself, how would I ever top that if I came back to modeling?" In a documentary film presentation of his 1985 designs, Mugler portrayed actress Juliette Binoche as France's patron saint, Joan of Arc, first in white, pure and innocent, later in black, facing death on the hills of Orleans. Carrying his theatrical irreverence (some might say blasphemy) even further, he sent avant garde model Pat Cleveland to fashion heaven as the Virgin Mary one season, then banished her to hell as the bride of Lucifer the next. Growing up in the shadows of the eleventh century Notre Dame of Strasbourg Cathedral might help explain Mugler's recur-ring use of religious iconography, but what

Another beautiful model donates her time to raise money for AIDS services.

Super star Sharon Stone looking like a vixen—and ready to whip up the crowd.

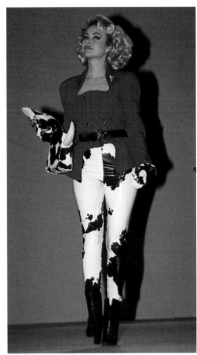

Actress Michelle Phillips threw condoms into the audience, where they were used as balloons.

type of childhood experience might have inspired his tulle tutus or the chrome bustier in his biker collection?

No wonder we were all so eagerly anticipating the arrival of Thierry Mugler and his team. What kind of wild show would this alchemist of the imagination create for us? As was the case with our other European designers, Mugler agreed to hold his show at the Century Plaza Hotel Ballroom. We knew it wasn't his typical bold backdrop and were grateful that he gave such importance to our needs to control costs. In sharp contrast to other designers who tended to arrive in Los Angeles just a day or two before their shows, Thierry arrived from Paris a full month before our sixth annual gala. He moved himself and his entourage into the Chateau Marmont Hotel on the Sunset Strip in West Hollywood. This 63-room landmark was built in 1927, based on an actual French chateau. Movie stars, writers, musicians, painters, photographers, and other A-list arty types have been ripping this place up since the Great Depression. F. Scott Fitzgerald and wife, Zelda, stayed there, as did Greta Garbo, Jean

Harlow, and Errol Flynn. Howard Hughes took over the penthouse for months, ogling the poolside beauties through a telescope seven stories up. In 1939, Columbia Pictures founder Harry Cohn rented the penthouse for his young male stars William Holden and Glenn Ford to get into trouble discreetly. Later, Robert De Niro lived in the same penthouse for two years. This is where Jim Morrison lived for a while. His drunken night on the Marmont roof was depicted in the Oliver Stone movie *The Doors*. The bungalows away from the main building are favored for privacy, and in 1982, John Belushi died in poolside bungalow number 3. Even after a $100-million, four-year makeover, the walls of the Chateau still drip with Hollywood history and lore.

Thierry's purpose in arriving in town a month early was to cast his show. In residence at the Marmont was a small army of Thierry's staff, including a producer, a publicist, and his personal weight-lifting trainer, who strangely enough always wore black-and-white harlequin-print Versace jeans. It was a handsome group, spirited and gossipy, energetic, and fun-loving.

Matching faux snakeskins.

Lesley Ann Warren looking like Cinderella.

Judy Jetson.

Lady Miss Kier.

A buff Linda Hamilton modeled while her then-husband, director James Cameron, yelled "Baby" from the audience.

Thierry himself is a French hunk with movie-star good looks who stands out in a crowd. His short-cropped blond hair, chiseled cheek-bones, and sexy French accent cast a spell on many an Angeleno, male and female alike. It's no wonder that most of Hollywood found it hard to say no to him when he asked them to model, present, or attend his show. Any night of the week would find Thierry and his entourage at the trendiest dance clubs or hottest parties in town—sans shirts, they would dance and drink until the morning hours, with Thierry always alert for potential models for his show. Thierry would literally approach strangers, men and women, in the clubs or on the street and cast them in his show. Such an approach might seem to be fraught with potential peril, but Mugler's good looks and charm seduced even those who were not familiar with his name.

Thierry played by his own rules and he played hard, but like all the European designers we worked with (and a couple of the Americans), he also played fair, keeping in mind that this was also an event for charity and not for showing his latest collection. Like Versace, he picked up all expenses for himself

and his staff, and he paid for all the extra glam that accompanies a major fashion show. He could be indecisive and perfectionistic, but the expense added by his actions, quirks, and precise desires all came from his pocket and did not reduce the amount we could turn over to the charity to support people living with HIV. For instance, he didn't decide on using neon for the set until just a couple days before the show. This indecision and last-minute rush job added tremendously to the expense of the set, but the extra expense was borne by Thierry's company.

The end result of Thierry's artistic pro-crastination was an impressive stage, backlit with neon, looking modern and retro, colorful and loud, very 1960s Hollywood à go-go and très Moulin Rouge. The ballroom itself was mostly white on white, simple and elegant, to avoid distraction from the bright neon of the set design or the clothes. There were white linen tablecloths and napkins, white linen chair covers, white china with French crystal goblets, white votive candles and bunches of white French tulips, and each table was pin-spotted with white light. The runway was white and lit white. Even the waiters and volunteers would be dressed in white with black tuxedo pants.

In a striking departure from the glamour of Bob Mackie and Gianni Versace, the Thierry Mugler show was outrageous, flamboyant, and extravagant. When asked today which was my favorite show, I say it had to be the Mugler gala. Never have I seen such a wild, eclectic collection of models: amateurs from the streets; supermodels, movie stars, and performance artists; rock legends; supreme divas Sharon Stone and Salsa Queen Celia Cruz; video porn legends Traci Lords and Jeff Stryker; New York party girl Diane Brill and transvestite entertainer Lypsinka; rave DJ and Dee-Lite vocalist, famous for her drag queen wigs and iridescent gowns, the Lady Miss Kier; a former Mr. Universe and his buff male spouse; and a woman famous for being the jilted ex-wife of a billionaire, Ivana Trump. It sounds like an old *Ed Sullivan Show* as booked by John Waters, whose preferred title is "The Pope of Trash." Maybe Waters and Mugler do have similar casting instincts as they had each previously employed Patty Hearst ("the Lindbergh baby who lived," according to Waters), and not many impresarios can say that.

Mugler Men's Collection, 1992.

The day of the show, dress rehearsals began at 4 P.M. Thierry was meticulous and demanding, though polite, as his voice boomed directions through a microphone. Thierry did not get up on stage with the models but directed from the shadows of the darkened ballroom. He took such a long time with each sequence that the cast members

Backstage with our Mugler men. One model got so excited it showed.

A few days earlier, Thierry had asked me to zoom over to a West Hollywood condo, in French-country style much like the Chateau Marmont, to pick up a costume from a legendary supermodel and her rock star husband. After a call upstairs by the doorman, I was let into the building. The supermodel opened the door, invited me in, then excused herself as she headed off through the spacious digs, filled with African art, to fetch the costume. As I stood in the foyer, I could see her husband stretched out on the oversized divan reading his *New York Times*. When he suddenly peered out at me from over his paper, I was startled by his vivid eyes, which were two differ-

Thierry takes his place on the run-way during the finale.

ent colors. It was freaky, like one eye was glass. "Are you French?" he inquired. Still a bit shaken, and, I guess, because this talented and ultra-cool man had been a prime idol of my formative years, I absurd-ly replied, "No, sir." "Sir?" he laughed back at me. Right then, his wife returned carrying a large black garbage bag. At that moment, I thought of Cecil Beaton's *My Fair Lady* ball gown for Audrey Hepburn, which had been thrown away because it was stored in a garbage bag. I would soon discover, however, the wisdom of storing this valuable costume in an airtight bag. I was surprised at the weight of the bag, 35 or 40 pounds, as she handed it to me. "Do you work for Thierry?" she asked. I was taken by her gazellelike neck and statuesque, sleek beauty. She was wearing a white, rib–knit T-shirt and beautiful silk pedal pushers in a soft plaid of gold and earth tones. When I answered, "No, actually, I'm the chair-man of the event," the wary supermodel eyed me dubiously. Sure, the chairman was out schlepping around dresses. I must have sounded like some delusional delivery man. "Okay," she responded, still staring down at me with those beautiful eyes, but stumped for what to say next. "Thanks," I said and headed for the door as I slung the heavy bag over my shoulder. It felt like there was something dead inside—limp and dead. I tossed the bag in the back of my car and started driving back to my home office. Along the way, I was bothered by a nasty odor that seemed to be wafting into my car.

I rolled up the windows and put on the air conditioning, but the smell just got worse. Not until I parked and retrieved the bag did I realize that the stench was coming from inside the black garbage bag.

When I walked into my office with the bag, my assistant Dee Dee was eager to see the Mugler costume. (Dee Dee had her own peri-od of fame in the early 1960s with the pop, blue-eyed soul duo from Los Angeles, Dick & Dee Dee. They hit number 2 on the charts in 1961 with the moody midtempo ballad "The Mountain's High" and also had hits with "Thou Shalt Not Steal," "Turn Around," and "Young and In Love.") When Dee Dee and I opened the bag and looked inside, we jumped back and grabbed our noses because of the noxious fumes. It smelled of rancid perspiration, cigarette smoke, stale beer, old perfume, and sourness. When I pulled out the costume, Dee Dee and I laughed hysterically as we played hot potato with it, tossing it back and forth, neither wanting to hold it. I finally put the garment out on the patio to air out. It was a pretty black velvet romper with a rhinestone breastplate, but boy, did it stink. Not having any one-of-a-kind, rhinestone-studded garments myself, I had to decide where to have it cleaned. As I looked through the Yellow Pages, Dee Dee and I watched through the sliding glass door as my three Dalmatians approached the bag and garment. They sniffed cautiously, then backed away. Betty barked at it threatening-ly, but it was Big Boy, the only male, who settled the issue. He mustered his courage, then ran over to the garment, lifted his rear leg, and peed on it.

Dee Dee and I finally located a Beverly Hills dry cleaner that specialized in expensive clothing and theatrical costumes. When the romper returned, most of the stench was gone, but not quite all of it. This is where Daryl Hannah's head cold, bless her fevered head, came to the rescue, as she was scheduled to wear this costume in the show. She was so congested from her illness that she couldn't smell anything. And after all, the outfit was clean. Daryl looked amazing in the rhinestoned romper. In her high heels, she looked all legs, and in her platinum wig, she vamped like Marilyn Monroe. Later in her tulle tutu, Daryl looked like a fairy princess floating on the stage. At that moment, I loved her for being so beautiful, for her tremendous professionalism and stamina, and for her unwavering commitment to people with HIV.

Talissa Soto

Diane Brill was one of Thierry's
favorite models.

Sharon Stone as an archangel.

waiting backstage, with ample champagne and little food, were definitely relaxed but slightly goofy.

The first celebrity model to arrive on the day of the show was Sandra Bernhard. Sandra's ferociously critical comedy and public persona have gained her entrée into different media worlds, none of which has ever quite understood what to do with her. She's been a comedic film actress, author of provocative books and magazine articles, stand-up comedienne and one-woman show, chanteuse, and B-movie hostess on USA Network. Her acidic commentary has a bitter, angry edge that suggests you'd better laugh or she'll leap from the stage and scratch your eyes out. Sandra is best known to most Americans as former Madonna gal-pal and for her recurring role as a lipstick lesbian on the *Roseanne* sitcom. Slowly and surely, Bernhard's star has risen since she began her stand-up comedy career at age 19—though it is impossible to predict just where it might be going. Sandra is a tireless worker who can also be a real pain in the patootie.

Sandra became a regular attendee of our later events, but this was the only one in

which she would be a model in the show. She arrived with an unusually large entourage of hangers-on and Hollywood hopefuls—the kind of people who always attach themselves to stars on the way up. Whether they're just living vicariously through the celebrity, are hoping to be discovered themselves, or actually serving some supposed purpose such as publicist, stylist, or bodyguard, they stick to the celebrity like leeches. From the point of view of someone trying to pull a show together, these celebrity corteges mostly get in the way. And it's a Hollywood rule of thumb that the more minor or nouveau the celebrity, the bigger their retinue. Whatever the purpose of arriving with a large collection of sycophants, helpers, and friends, the unintended result is to announce to all that the celebrity is very insecure about his or her position in the Hollywood constellation. With few exceptions, the truly big stars, the legends such as Myrna Loy, Claudette Colbert, Carol Burnett, Carol Channing, and Audrey Hepburn, arrive either alone or with a spouse or a friend. In these times when the dark cost of celebrity has been made too apparent by news stories of deranged star stalkers, it would be hard to

Bustiers at the silent auction.

Sandra Bernhard and the ex-Mrs. Stallone, Brigitte Nielsen.

After breaking an ankle, Brigitte Nielsen was bound and determined to be in this show.

disagree with any celebrity who felt it necessary to have a bodyguard, but do they really need to show up at a charity event with publicists, managers, agents, hairdressers, makeup artists, dieticians, trainers, and spiritual advisers? One exception to the above rule of thumb was the undeniable diva Diana Ross, who did travel with an assemblage. It amused me that Sandra issued orders that no one was to speak to her unless spoken to first, and Diana had a similar rule. Was Ross the role model Bernhard was emulating? Actually, Ross's rule went even further. Miss Ross also refused to touch anything; instead she pointed and instructed that whatever she wanted be handed to her. It all seemed a bit incongruous and vaguely unhealthy, like late-stage Howard Hughes.

When Sandra Bernhard arrived, Thierry quickly picked out the clothes she would be modeling, then whisked her off to makeup, where she would spend the rest of the afternoon surrounded by her pals who kept volunteers and staff at bay. During the course of the afternoon, the makeup artists, stylists, and fit-

ters would transform the eccentric-looking Sandra into a Mugler vixen. The dress she modeled later that evening caused quite a sensation. Mugler had made the dress out of tiny mirrors held together with transparent thread. As Sandra strutted down the catwalk, the ballroom and stage lights reflected in the dress mirrors. Even more spectacular for many was the sight of Sandra's bare derriere and of her very, *very* privates. Without panties, Sandra's sub-micromini dress didn't hide much, particularly when she was four feet above our heads on the runway. Speculation and bad puns rippled through the room as audience members wondered if she'd been bushwhacked and had her undies snatched. Clearly, this was exactly the stunned delight and outrage that she and Mugler had intended. Sandra loved the uproar, and she growled and snarled her way down the tarmac for a second trip. I imagine that most of the Sandra pictures that the paparazzi took that evening weren't publishable until the photos were cropped.

Throughout the rehearsals and as show time neared, the place to be was backstage.

Our fairy princess, Daryl Hannah.

Lunching With Debi Mazar, April 1999

• **How did you get involved with our Thierry Mugler show?** I don't remember who asked me exactly… I think it was a request from Thierry through Deniello [the New York hair stylist]. I had worked for Thierry once before and I loved his designs. I loved the lines of his clothes—like he was designing clothes for the space age. It was also a time when I was losing lots of friends [to AIDS], and I just wanted to get involved, to do something to help. • **How did you first meet Thierry?** My friend Deniello was going to Paris to do a show. I needed a vacation and went with him to just hang out. I'd been to Paris before but I'd never been to a real French couture house. It blew me away—see-

Our sweetheart
Debi Mazar

ing all these seamstresses sewing wings on butterflies and making insects. It was couture come alive. While Deniello was styling wigs for the show, I was skipping around checking things out. Thierry saw me and recognized me from *Goodfellas* and a couple other movies I'd done. I had my own look going and he asked me to do his show. He threw me in a dressing room, stripped me naked in front of everyone, and started taking very detailed measurements of me from wrist to wrist. He created a cos-tume for me and put me in the show. Being an actress, I loved it—although I was the shortest model in the show. I'm only 5'4". • **Do you remember who else was in that show?** Carla Bruni, Tracy Ross [Diana Ross's daughter]. It was so funny because years before I had done Diana's makeup and she was really rude to me. [And now] her daughter was dressing next to me. When I came back to change cos-tumes, Diana was sitting in my chair. I had to put my stockings on so I said, "Excuse me, Miss Ross," and she was like, "Well, well." It was a fun moment for me. Let's see, who else was in that show? Traci Lords, Cindy Crawford… I can't remember. Then Thierry and I became friends after that show. I love leather and Thierry uses lots of leather, so we started hanging out together. We have lots of mutual friends. • **What stands out in your mind about the Thierry Mugler show in L.A.?** There was a little earthquake that day—and me being a New Yorker—and I was in a huge hotel in the basement with these enormous chandeliers swinging back and forth, as some makeup artist was beating my face. But then all these great friends of mine who were working on the show began arriving. I saw Sharon Stone and Julie Newmar, whom I'd never met before. Remember Julie crawling down the

Debi Mazar wanted purple poodles but had to settle for this
adorable bulldog puppy.

The behind-the-scenes landscape was domi-nated by cases of Cristal champagne and was cluttered with makeup tables, mirrors, acces-sories, cell phones, tutus, Chanel travel bags, friends, publicists, groupies, and even ageless rock cutie Jackson Browne, who was watching over his then-girlfriend, actress Daryl Hannah, who was running on empty. Daryl was battling a bad cold but, ever the trouper, she insisted on ignoring her fever to keep her commitment to Thierry and us. For some bizarre reason, Daryl's head congestion from her cold actually turned out to be a blessing in disguise.

A hush fell over the entire backstage sud-denly when, unannounced, Elizabeth Taylor popped in with her assistant. As I mentioned earlier, big stars don't need or want an endless

entourage to make an impression. Thierry stopped the rehearsal to visit with Taylor and escorted her through his collection so she could make a few personal selections. She soon left as unobtrusively as she had arrived, and bedlam was once again restored backstage.

One celebrity model demanded and received a special dressing room, complete with a security guard stationed outside the door. Her own hairdresser had to be flown in from New York at our expense. This celebrity was celebrated merely for her famous ex-husband and her early years as an internation-al party girl. Once again, the smaller the celebrity, the bigger the demands. A security guard? She'd be lucky if anyone even wanted her autograph. But fearing one of her famous tantrums, we met this woman's every whim.

runway in that cat suit? And then I had dinner with her the next night and she ordered CATFISH! I was hanging out with Miss Kier the night of the show and everyone in town was there. It was so playful and fun. Diane Brill, a girlfriend of mine, was in the show. And everyone was having to hoist up their tits—all us girls having to cram our tits and asses into things that we could barely zip up. And people sticking things in our faces and pushing up our cleavage. Then I begged Thierry to hire me a dog as prop so I wouldn't skip down the runway. I thought it would look cool. I wanted French poodles, tinted to match my outfit, but all they could find at the last minute was that bulldog—but he was great. I had a real nice time and that dog saved my life; he kept me from skipping. • **How has AIDS affected you personally?** First of all, it [affected] my sex life as it did everyone's. At the age of 21, I started watching my friends get sick. I didn't understand it. I couldn't believe how much death I was seeing as a young adult. It gave me a whole new outlook on life—it changed me. I stopped thinking about myself and got involved trying to help my friends who were sick. I'd go to the hospital and massage them. And lots of other people said, "Ew! How can you touch them?" I would take some of the flowers in their rooms and perform "flower theater" for them, to entertain them. • **Is AIDS still an important issue in your life?** Oh sure, I still have the fear of detecting it in myself. I have younger brothers and sisters I worry about. My connection to the disease has nothing to do with being a celebrity. I do what I can to promote awareness with younger people. I do the dance-athons and whatever else will make people aware. It's been the cause I fight hardest for because there is no cure. • **What would surprise people about you who only know you from your work?** Most people who don't know me think I'm this loud, obnoxious girl from Brooklyn. They'd be most surprised at how simple I am at the end of the day—I don't like clutter in my mind or my life. • **Do you have a favorite color?** Red. It's beautiful, rich, it makes me happy. It's a sexy color and you can play it up or down—and I look good in it. • **Is any film director a favorite of yours?** I have a couple. Busby Berkeley really inspires me. You don't see that vision any longer. And Martin Scorcese, with whom I've worked a few times. • **Is there any period in history that attracts you?** I love the 1930s—the streamlined architecture, the films, the greased-back hair, the decadence. It wasn't so much about big tits then. The clothes were glamorous; they draped the body. I love the way they processed film, the silver gelatin—it all looked so bright. The graphic designs, the ads, I love it all. • **If it could be anyone, living or dead, with whom would you like to have lunch tomorrow—since your luncheon today is already spoken for.** Cleopatra. • **What do you find sexy in a man?** Humor and brains. His hands. Style. • **What about in a woman?** Humor. Cleanliness. • **What is the most common mistake made by people when they get dressed?** Their shoes.

And did this ultrarich woman donate a cent for the charity or for her A-table and wonderful French cuisine? I imagine you've guessed by now.

Another early arrival that afternoon was the dark-haired, blue-eyed character actress Debi Mazar. Before becoming an actress, Debi had been a successful makeup artist. In her feature film debut, she really caught Hollywood's eye as Ray Liotta's junkie mistress in Martin Scorcese's *Goodfellas* and has since worked steadily in theatrical and TV movies and in television series. Debi's portrayal of the cynical legal secretary Denise Iannello in the ABC drama *Civil Wars* was so memorable that, when *Civil Wars* folded, NBC, in a rare move for TV, brought Debi over to reprise the same character during the

final season of *LA Law*. She's one of the few actresses in Hollywood who's working constantly, appearing in an average of four movies a year. Debi and I recently sat down for lunch in her favorite vegetarian restaurant on La Cienega Boulevard in West Hollywood. The restaurant is clearly a star hangout—also lunching at the same time were actress Rae Dawn Chong and MTV's hottest VJ, "Downtown" Julie Brown—but Debi's entrance still turned heads. She was on her way to the Van Gogh exhibit at the L.A. County Museum and was looking very Katharine Hepburn-ish in gray flannel slacks and a bone-colored long-sleeved T-shirt with hair pulled back and oversize sunglasses. I just had hot Earl Grey tea with soy milk while Debi enjoyed a four-course lunch, as we

Spiderwoman.

talked about Thierry Mugler, the AIDS epidemic, and shoes.

As the afternoon and the rehearsal wore on, the backstage began filling up with stars and celebrities of every ilk. There was Sharon Stone, hot off the notoriety of her bisexual ice queen role in *Basic Instinct*. Actress Linda Hamilton showed up looking buff as did former Mr. America and Mr. Universe body-builder Bob Paris and his gay spouse, Rod Jackson. One diva even showed up with her resident clairvoyant and fortuneteller in tow to clean up the energy and to warn the star whom to stay away from. While the star was being made-up, her psychic was getting lit up from all the freely flowing champagne. Recognizing a business opportunity, however, in her own future, this chunky Iranian spiritualist with bobbed black hair, bushy black eyebrows, a light moustache, and no neck, spread out her Tarot cards and started telling fortunes for $10 a pop. Ironically, the seer was confused about present events, but even more confused about future events for her customers. She repeatedly told them, "You are here to help the people who have the cancer in their breasts. This is very good for your career in show business." She told the *very* gay bodybuilder Bob Paris, "You will marry a

Gay porn icon Jeff Stryker.

beautiful woman and have many children together."

When Celia Cruz, the salsa diva, arrived, she looked so small and plain that I might have guessed she was an elderly seamstress. Shortly, though, she would be glammed up by the Mugler crew and would emerge as the Latin Queen loved by millions. Mugler had designed Cruz a special outfit for the evening—a precisely tailored plum-colored suit with a floor-length skirt and matching six-inch-high platform sandals accented by brightly colored clunky ornamental jewelry. It was funny watching Cruz as she spotted the fortune-teller reading cards. Cruz eyed her suspiciously, then made a wide berth around her. I figured that Cruz didn't want to contaminate her Puerto Rican gris-gris with any of this Iranian mojo. With everyone having downtime to kill backstage, though, our resident soothsayer raked in the money.

Another highlight was when she told Jeff Stryker, possibly the biggest star in the history of gay male porn videos, "You will someday be as big as Clark Gable." For those who had seen Stryker's films, this was giving Clark Gable the benefit of the doubt in terms of size. Stryker even had a nationally publicized L.A. lawsuit in which he sued a company for

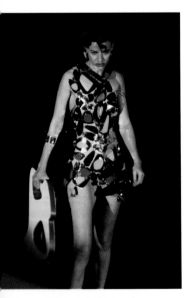

Sandra Bernhard in her micro-mirror-mini dress left nothing to the imaginations of the people sitting closest to the runway.

A playful moment onstage at the Mugler show.

Mugler swimwear.

"appropriating his likeness" in their production and sale of a Jeff Stryker dildo.

Stryker had been peerless in gay male porn, a big business, for more than a decade. This is a porn accomplishment comparable to Katharine Hepburn's duration as a leading lady. Considering he took off his clothes and had sex for a job, Jeff Styker strangely insisted on having a private dressing room. When he too became pretty relaxed from the champagne, my assistant and I had to walk him outside in the fresh air to help perk him up before he went on stage. Hey, someone had to do it. Jeff pulled himself together and performed like a pro. He went onstage wearing black leather chaps, vest, and boots, then stripped down to black leather briefs, which read in sequins on the rear—"Lucky Me." Because the show performance was before the dinner this year, the audience loosened up from all the liquid refreshment and went wild for Jeff. Several groups of gay men and some women cleared their place settings and began dancing on top of their tables. Whoa, this was going to be a lively night.

Actress and model Iman and her rock star husband, David Bowie, opened the show with a bit of verbal shtick that played like bad Sonny and Cher repartee. Iman played the smart one with Bowie playing the fool. It didn't work. I didn't get it, nor did the audience or the other celebrities watching on monitors backstage.

The first celebrity model on stage that night was Ivana Trump. She wore a Jetson-looking suit, with a red jacket and black skirt. Covering the lower half of her face, a black scarf served as a bandit's mask. When Ivana pulled off her mask and threw it into the audience, everyone loved the camp touch of casting Ivana. Julie Newmar is best remembered for her roles as Stupefyin' Jones in *L'il Abner* and as the original Catwoman in the old *Batman* TV series. Julie revived her Catwoman persona for her slink down our catwalk, purring at the audience and looking fabulously sexy. Debi Mazar herself had cat-eye, Egyptian-looking makeup as she walked her bulldog down the runway. Debi wore a form-fitting suit with a gray jacket and black skirt and her bulldog wore a matching outfit.

Our fortune teller backstage needn't have worried her diva boss about bad energy: the energy that evening was barely believable. The noisy enthusiasm kept building and building, with catcalls, wolf whistles, screams, and thunderous applause, as celebrated model after celebrated model paraded down the tarmac. The models backstage couldn't see what was causing all the noise and excitement so they cut peepholes in the ballroom's red theater curtain. The hotel management was naturally upset, and we had to assure them that our insurance would cover any damage. By the end of the show, those curtains were in shreds!

During the men's swimwear sequence, a young and novice male model who had spent the afternoon drinking champagne suddenly became aroused when it was his turn to parade down the runway. With five other handsome young men in yellow and black Spandex swim trunks, their arms around each other's necks, our excitable young man grew bigger and bigger the farther down the 36-foot runway he got. The bright yellow surprise delighted the audience, and giggles could be heard two floors up to the lobby of the Century Plaza. Now, curious hotel guests were wandering down to the ballroom to see what all the excitement was about.

Next on stage were Bob Paris and his spouse, Rod Jackson, both in their well-oiled Adonis-muscled bodies and not much else. Bob had made headlines when he announced to the professional bodybuilding world that he was gay and he was going to marry Rod. Having won the Mr. America and Mr. Universe titles, Bob was then one of the most famous bodybuilders in the world. Despite the rumors, innuendo, and jokes about pro bodybuilders, no one had ever announced that he was gay and the shock waves were tremendous. Bob and Rod then produced a joint biography, exercise videos, and a picture book photographed by Herb Ritts, and took to the lecture circuit as gay role models. Their message?—"You too can be a happily married gay couple if you are fabulously beautiful, unbelievably muscled, and filthy rich." A few years after our show, they divorced, but we take no responsibility. Well, much to the surprise of everyone in the house, including me, Rod and

My friend model Lynne Koester was faboo in this futuristic Thierry Mugler.

It was not until the following year that I found out just how much Bob and Rod had upset some of our audience. In reviewing ticket sales for "The World of Calvin Klein" show, I took notice that the owner of the California Mart (Los Angeles's equivalent of Seventh Avenue) had not purchased his usual tickets. I called him up to inform him that we were close to selling out but still had tickets reserved for him. Faster than you could say "Mugler," he started spewing

Bob Paris, fooling around in the background. We lost a couple of our key supporters because of this scene.

obscenities. No, he was not coming to the Calvin Klein evening or any other AIDS event ever, "because of those two disgusting homosexuals last year." Questioning him, it was clear that Sandra Bernhard baring her privates and Sharon Stone dressed as a dominatrix had been fine. I found his fury at homosexuals surprising, considering he worked in an industry where gay men were prevalent. What I found disgusting, however, was his willingness to use antigay epithets, such as "perverts" and "queers." This was a man who was active in the Democratic Party and in liberal causes and support for Israel. Would he think it okay if I started using ugly anti-Semitic slurs in conversation with him? I ended the conversation with the suggestion that he say ten Our Fathers and ten Hail Marys. We never did see him again at any of our fashion events or at any other AIDS fund-raiser. Although I later heard on the q.t., that he had also forbidden his wife from attending our fashion galas, she continued not only to attend but to buy a table each year. She wrote us big checks, but always on her personal account, not on the Cal Mart account as before. Apparently, two sexy men rubbing against each other hadn't disgusted her.

Bob, who came out onto the stage merely hand-in-hand, suddenly started simulating sex (or maybe they were just doing that 1970s dance "The Bump"). Boy, Thierry sure could figure out new ways to delight and scandalize an audience.

Backstage again at the Mugler event, I was preparing to go out on stage with TV and movie actress Dana Delany as copresenters. Dana and I had become friendly when we were neighbors in Santa Monica, and she quickly said yes when I asked her to be in the show. Dana, perhaps best known for her nurse role on the Vietnam War TV drama *China Beach*, had been dressed by Thierry in a short black cocktail dress with black mesh netting at her firm midriff. We were watching the monitors, waiting to hear our introduction. Suddenly, we were distracted by the bellyaching of actress Jane Seymour, star of CBS's *Dr. Quinn, Medicine Woman*. Seymour was

complaining about the show's lineup. She felt she outranked other presenters in the stardom hierarchy and should go out first. Seymour had also been griping earlier in the evening about the tablemates she had been assigned. She wanted to be moved to what she regarded as the A table, where Sharon Stone, Daryl Hannah, Jackson Browne, Rod Stewart, and Rachel Hunter were seated. We had moved Seymour to that table, but it was impossible to change the show's lineup at the last minute without serious miscues of music and lighting. There was nothing I could do but tell her no. Seymour obviously wasn't used to that word and started a shouting match with me. Now our star divas were sticking their heads out of their private dressing rooms to see what all the excitement was about. Next thing I knew, my TV nurse got up right in the face of this loud TV doctor and told her to "Go home, or shut up and follow the script!" Then the two

The Thierry Mugler show was my favorite.

Ivana Trump thought she had us all fooled in her red and black Thierry Mugler suit.

of them brought out the artillery. It wasn't pretty. Finally, the frontier doc backed down as Sharon Stone, Linda Hamilton, Daryl Hannah, and Jackie Collins, who was busy scribbling notes for her next novel in a notebook she had pulled out of her Judith Leiber handbag, gathered around and threw their support to sticking with the script. So our medicine woman took her assigned place in the lineup and did a wonderful job on stage.

The other big battle that night was among our various divas dueling for the limelight at the finale of our one-and-a-half-hour spectacle. Sharon Stone, Sandra Bernhard, Celia Cruz, and other supreme divas were obvious contenders for the crown, but there was a last-minute entry in the contest for chief diva. The females were suddenly upstaged by a male media mogul who had run a studio and a network, and was now plunging into cyberspace. In the middle of Sharon Stone's archangel scene, just before Thierry was to make his entrance, this master of the theatrical (supposedly, an important supporter of the charity) stood up with his entire table as bit players and stormed out of the ballroom as he bellowed, "This show is longer than a miniseries!" Later, Sharon Stone remarked about the drama queen mogul, "Why were his panties in such a wad?"

The battle continued at full swing after Thierry had made his bows and all the models came back onstage to applaud him. It was the gunfight at the I'm-OK, You're-not-OK corral, as our dueling divas pulled out every trick in the book to capture the attention of the 200 cameras snapping pictures. If victory was determined by whose picture appeared in print the most, then the undisputed Champion of the Flashbulb was Sharon Stone, who continued posing on stage long after Celia Cruz had cha-cha-ed off and Thierry had thrown his last kiss to the audi-

ence. As one superdiva quickly headed to her waiting white Rolls-Royce, she exclaimed, "Someone quick, get an exterminator!" Sharon finally left the stage when the lights were turned off on her.

The other models, still in costume, finished off the magnums of Cristal champagne, then headed out front for the dinner party following the show. As Thierry made his way through the 1,400 well-wishers, a fast and agile Suzanne Bartsch (well known for creating the Love Ball AIDS fund-raiser, first in Paris and later in New York) made a broken-field run across the ballroom and pinned Mugler against the runway. Suzanne wore a black feather headress, a black see-through negligee over her pasties-tipped breasts, and a black horsehair tail that trailed behind her like a centaur's flounce. She forced her tongue into Thierry's mouth and bear hugged him as he fought to get loose. Despite his weight training and taut muscles, it was quite a struggle. Once free, Thierry straightened his linen jacket and remarked to the enthralled onlookers, "That bitch is strong!"

The Mugler evening was a phenomenal success in every way possible. The show netted $700,000 to assist people living with HIV and garnered worldwide publicity and goodwill for Thierry, his company, and everyone involved. If our audience's reaction was any kind of a barometer, we had the most fun-filled, wild, and memorable evening Hollywood had seen in years. Hollywood, too, was finally over the fear of joining the battle against the AIDS epidemic and was now actively engaged in spreading awareness.

The Mugler event also irrevocably changed the nature of our future events. It reminds me of a scene in the Blake Edwards' satire about Hollywood, S.O.B. Robert Preston is an unscrupulous celebrity, Dr. Feelgood, preparing to inject a girl he picked up on the Coast Highway on his way out to Malibu. He says to the druggie girl, "I hope I won't jeopardize your amateur standing by using a clean needle." Well, the Mugler event did cost us our amateur standing as fund-raisers. We were no longer virgins; now if we could just avoid being raped in the future.

We were quickly approached by the Yves St. Laurent fashion house asking to be our 1993 honoree. Yves St. Laurent is not just a notable fashion designer; he is one of the most famous designers of this century and an acknowledged genius. He is one of the few living designers whose fame will clearly survive him. Of course we said yes! St. Laurent promised to create a retrospective of his legendary career and to make a personal appearance. Our announcement was met with amazing fanfare, and then whispers of, "Make sure you have a plan B. He's too unpredictable," from magazine editors who knew him as well as his reputation. Sure enough, in late fall of 1992, long after the announcement of YSL as our 1993 honoree, we were informed by fax that the YSL company had been sold and the new owners were canceling the show. We later learned the real reason, which is certainly more colorful. Pierre Biergé, the lifelong business and personal partner of Yves, was courting a young designer. To add to the insult, Biergé had let his blissfully untalented paramour present a collection of his own designs under the label YSL. This double betrayal created such turmoil in the YSL household and business that Biergé felt it necessary to pull the plug on our event.

So we were high and dry with only six months to find a suitable honoree and produce a show. With the help of Keeble, Cavaco, and Duka, the PR firm who produced the Calvin Klein press shows in New York, and with further assistance from Klein's friend, music and film mogul David Geffen, Klein jumped at our invitation. Geffen's push for Calvin to do the show apparently carried more weight than just friendly advice, as Geffen at the time owned the majority share of CK Inc. and called many of the shots for the company. Luckily for us, Calvin loved Hollywood and the limelight that an event of this magnitude would bring him and his ailing company. He also wanted to please his friend Geffen to whom he was beholden to the tune of $65 million. By Christmas Eve 1992, we had our 1993 honoree, and visions of sugarplums in CK briefs danced through the heads of many in Hollywood.

Jeff Stryker in a pair of leather briefs. Just what every guy needs in his wardrobe.

7

Calvin Klein
—Beige, Booze, Babes,
and Boys in the Bowl

"It's important that we use only arugula lettuce in the salad and no tomatoes! The salad has to match the chicken, the pasta, and the **table linens!**"

— Calvin Klein

Compassion, commitment, and modest means were the operative words when we started the AIDS benefit fashion shows in 1987. But in 1993, the operative words changed to passion and obsession, words indelibly linked with our honoree—Calvin Klein. Some (such as Jeff Yarbrough, then editor in chief of the national gay news magazine *The Advocate*) criticized the choice of Klein as an honoree by an AIDS organization because, to that point, his efforts in supporting AIDS or gay issues were minimal at best. Still, more gay men and women than ever before were wearing his CK clothing, particularly his underwear. In the end, the excitement Klein's name generated helped us raise 1.2 million dollars.

While the saying "Less is more" may describe many of Calvin Klein's designs (less clothing, more skin), when it comes to putting on a show, his philosophy changes to "More is more." As a showman, Klein was more like Marie Antoinette. Just like the people who built Hollywood from the ground up, the Kleins (Calvin and his then-wife Kelly worked as a kind of tag-team) understood with intuitive precision the three rules that are the bedrock of Hollywood success: Image! Image! Image!

The stage was now set for what would turn out to be an epic story embellished by glamour, sex appeal, and high drama, and, like many affairs of operatic proportions, populated by a large cast of strange bedfellows. As

Calvin and Kelly Klein in happier days.

1993's guest artist, the divine and dynamic Tina Turner sang her powerful and prophetic lament *You're Simply the Best … Better Than All The Rest*, entering from center stage our star-crossed leads: Calvin and Kelly Klein.

Tanned, scrubbed, looking every bit Californian, especially for a couple revered as the prototypical jet-set New Yorkers, Calvin and Kelly blazed into Los Angeles as if riding on the golden rays that kiss our sun-drenched city. Their arrival heralded the beginning of painstakingly detailed preparations in a signature style that is the hallmark of a Calvin Klein fashion extravaganza. While Calvin's eye for detail is a legend in the fashion biz, we were amazed that nothing (and I do mean nothing) associated with this benefit escaped his obsession for beauty. From the linen and roughage, to the lighting and 126-foot runway, to each of the 350 models, Calvin had his hands on everything.

Preparations began with searching for the perfect location. Location, as anyone living in L.A. knows, is *everything*. Crafting an event befitting Hollywood royalty, barons of industry, and the fashion elite, not to mention

Tina Turner sang her heart and soul out to help us raise more than $1.2 million.

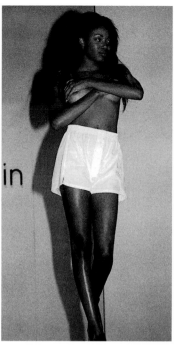

Grease producer Allan Carr with Studio 54 party gal Nicki Haskall. Carr would later die of cancer in 1999.

Eye candy for the more than 3,700 people who attended the CK show in 1993.

Mark Wahlberg, before he dropped his pants and received a standing ovation.

befitting a collection of beautifully tailored beige, black, and ecru designs that are staples of Klein's Classic American Look, required that the choice of venue be as imperious as the event would be imposing. Klein determined that L.A.'s Hollywood Bowl, one of the world's largest natural amphitheaters nestled in the hills above Los Angeles, would provide the appropriately audacious backdrop no mere hotel ballroom could ever command. The Bowl's grandeur and classic architectural purity, with its world fame as the venue of legendary performances by everyone from Pavarotti and Bernstein to Yma Sumac and the Beatles, perfectly suited the CK standard—and it didn't hurt that it had 18,000 seats!

No simple catered affair, the Calvin Klein event would be history in the making. No one had ever before attempted to do a live fashion show at the Bowl. Propelled by the Calvin Klein machine, a fine-tuned engine of advertising, public relations, and event specialists-in-waiting infused their own brand of expertise into the overall execution of the designer's precise artistic inspirations.

Not only did the food itself have to be approved by the Kleins, but the *color* of the food was critical—the complementary shades of arugula and skinless roasted chicken, the pale yellow of a poached Bartlett pear. Our first meeting took place on a beautiful spring day on the enormous Hollywood Bowl stage, which looks out at the lush tree-covered hills, ivy-covered walls, and those anxiety-inducing empty seats. Arriving from entertainment impresario David Geffen's home, where they were guests, Calvin was in khakis and white polo shirt and Kelly looked pretty in a simple white sundress. The discussions of the set design got underway but were shortly brought to a halt for the Kleins' unexpected, late-morning coffee klatsch, served on silver and china, for two, by their impeccable chauffeur and man Friday.

When the meeting resumed, the Kleins made their way to the lavish tables of food lovingly laid out by the caterer seeking the coveted contract to cater one of the biggest parties in Hollywood history. Kelly, starting with the salads, picked up large handfuls and tossed them into the air, then watched intent-

Producer Barry Krost arrives with his star Angela Bassett. *What's Love Got To Do with It?* opened to rave reviews the following week.

Ali MacGraw looking gorgeous
as usual in her gray Calvin Klein
suit.

Actress Annette Bening, husband Warren
Beatty, and fan David Geffen. Geffen
owned controlling stock in CK in 1993.

Dallas star Linda Gray at CK
in 1993

ly as some of it made it back into the salad bowl and some of it didn't. "Is there a lettuce leaf that is a lighter shade of green than this? Maybe arugula? And no avocado; we don't like that color of green." Next, Kelly tasted each bowl of pasta and rice salads, checking for texture and consistency. Suddenly, she picked out pieces of tomato and pimento and exclaimed, "No red!" The intensity of Kelly's orders and the precise arbitrariness of her opinions couldn't help but recall Faye Dunaway as Joan Crawford in *Mommie Dearest* when she terrorizes her daughter, Christina, with, "No more wire hangers!" Amused and intrigued as we were, we had little time to contemplate the possible origins of Kelly's suggestive obsession against the color red before we had to shift our attentions to the fastidious Calvin.

Setting his sights on the roasted chicken, Calvin began to rip the skin off and then held the poor old naked bird next to the near-colorless china and table linen. "It's got to be skinless," he told the caterer. "Looks better with the napkins." Between the two of them, the Kleins managed to dissect, push, toss, or taste nearly every plate of food the caterer had

prepared, finishing just in time for their chauffeur to whisk them off to lunch at Morton's. Morton's is Hollywood's premier restaurant in which to see and be seen, make a contact, or close a deal. Interestingly, it was the owner of Morton's and the Hard Rock Cafés, the generous Peter Morton, who donated the main course, chicken, to feed the 3,800 guests assembled for *The World of Calvin Klein.*

That was just the beginning of the Kleins' concentration on detail. When we gathered next, it was time to cast the show. In order that all of his well-tailored black, beige, brown, and ecru not be overwhelmed by the majestic location, Klein needed 350 models to fill the immense stage and its 126-foot runway. From the bike paths of Venice Beach to Gold's Gym to the trendiest gay bars and dance clubs in the entire metropolitan area, flyers spread the intoxicating siren call: *Calvin Klein is casting a fashion extravaganza in L.A.!* In a departure from the previous shows, this time the focus seemed to be on the near-naked physique rather than on the clothes themselves. Clearly, the models were more attractive and younger than ever before.

Jacqueline Bissett and her brother arrive at the CK event in 1993. Her brother donated two 1994 BMWs that were auctioned off.

Connie Stevens arrives with daughter, Joely Fisher.

Julie "Catwoman" Newmar had knocked everyone out the previous year when she modeled in the Mugler show.

(When we started to cast male models for the show, we couldn't help but think back on that moment of the "naked chicken." With the parade of young wannabe Calvin Klein poster boys all stripped down to their skivvies—if indeed they had any on—it was naked chicken, okay, but this time we were taking pictures of it.)

The usual celebrity models were eschewed for even more godlike boys, men, and women (well, mostly boys) who we referred to as the "beautiful nobodies" (who all had quite the "some-bodies!"). The quest for these fab nobodies was entertaining in itself. The casting took place at both the Hollywood Bowl and at Herb Ritts's photography studio on Santa Monica Boulevard. The criterion was simple—no experience required—only beautiful people need apply. You had to be tall, drop-dead gorgeous, muscular (for guys) or paper-thin (for girls), and younger than springtime. Kelly interviewed the girls and left the boys to Calvin. First, each boy removed his shirt. They were then asked to drop their pants for further inspection. For all those boys who didn't measure up, it was

adios! The models who met these demanding criteria were photographed and would be contacted later. Incredible as it may sound, the waiters later also had to pass the same kind of inspection and be photographed. After all, they would be serving the elite of Hollywood and New York society and had to look impressive in their tight black T-shirts and even tighter black Calvin Klein jeans. One might think that the number of models in the show would have made for a hair and makeup nightmare. Wrong! Remember, in 1993, the grunge look was the rage. So, even though the best stylists in Los Angeles and New York offered to donate their services for the evening, the Kleins insisted on using only two stylists—a "his" and a "hers."

There actually were three celebrity models who took part in the show. There was the waifish Kate Moss, a recent Calvin Klein discovery. There was the attractive 15-year-old actor Edward Furlong, then known for his film debut in *Terminator 2* but not yet the matinee idol of today. He arrived backstage chaperoned by a woman I thought was his mother, but who turned out to be his manager

Supermodel Beverly Johnson.

Manager Sandy Gallin and
author Jackie Collins arrive at the
CK event.

We were all wondering where Barry Diller's longtime
gal pal, Diane Von Furstenberg, was. Here he is with
Revlon's Ron Perelman.

Ronnie and Vidal Sassoon.

and girlfriend. Furlong changed into his black CK pants, oversized white tuxedo shirt and black vest, and had no modesty undressing with the other 350 models. The third celebrity model was the remarkable Mark Wahlberg, who was then the CK-underwear model in magazines and on billboards. Few people suspected—if any—that the younger brother of New Kids on the Block vocalist Donnie Wahlberg would have much of a career when he came onto the music scene in 1991 as pop-rap singer Marky Mark. But with his group The Funky Bunch, Mark quickly scored a number-one-hit single and a platinum album. After tremendous exposure as the Calvin Klein underwear model, and a name change back to Mark Wahlberg, he turned to acting with equally surprising skill and success in movie roles as varied as a young addict thug in *The Basketball Diaries* and a naïve but well-endowed porn star in *Boogie Nights*.

It was backstage on the night of the gala that I first met the personable young Mark Wahlberg. I spent some time in Mark's dressing room with Mark, Kate Moss, and a few production team members as we shared champagne to calm our before-the-show jitters. It

wasn't really a dressing room, more a tent, as there aren't many dressing rooms backstage at the Hollywood Bowl. Mark didn't need much time to prepare himself for the show. He didn't need makeup and he had arrived in the clothes he would be wearing onstage that evening, CK jeans. On a hanger in the tent, with Mark's name attached, was the outfit he would be modeling—a pair of white Calvin Klein boxer briefs. As we hung out, Mark graciously allowed me to ask him a few questions.

I liked Mark. Everyone seemed to. He had a street-smart but sweet sensibility about himself. He was modest, and even a bit shy, but also a real professional. When show time came, Mark was ready to attack the hungry, drunk, and very live audience eagerly anticipating his appearance. After a taste of champagne, all the models took their places, with Mark bringing up the rear—a position for which he was imminently qualified. Wahlberg then delighted the crowd by dancing shirtless down the runway and at the end of his routine, dropped his jeans and grabbed his—paycheck! The audience went wild. It was

Talking With Mark Wahlberg, June 1993

• **Why did you pick this event?** Calvin Klein asked me and Kate. It's in my contract that I have to do so many personal appearances. • **What do you think of all this?** I love it. • **Have you met Tina Turner?** Yes. • **Do you like her music?** It's rock and roll; it has its place in history. • **How about you and Kate Moss, do you see each other socially?** No, never. • **Why do you suppose Calvin Klein picked you to represent his underwear line?** My personality. • **How does it feel to be a gay icon?** I don't think I am … um … and I'm not gay! • **I've heard that before you were chosen as the Calvin Klein poster guy, Calvin had his friends give you their final nod.** Very true. • **Do you wear Calvin Klein underwear?** Sure—when I wear underwear. •

Mark Wahlberg and CK share a moment backstage.

What's next for you? Are you going to do anything in music? Maybe. But I've had some offers to do movies. • **Did you hear that the Calvin Klein advertising department flew a four-story-high banner of you in your underwear up and down the beaches over Memorial Day weekend, with my home telephone number on it by mistake?** No, that's funny, though. Did you get any calls? • **Yes. More than four hundred.** Wow. • **Are you ready to go out and entertain the audience?** Yeah, but I'm a little nervous. • **Why?** Because I'm not used to doing this kind of thing. I'm used to working in a studio with just a few people around. • **You'll be great.** Thanks. • **How does it feel to see yourself on billboards in Times Square, in magazines, on TV, all in your skivvies? Do you ever think of it as demeaning?** Sure, but it pays good. Now I can appreciate what girls must go through when they are exploited and not compensated in the same way I am. • **Thanks, Mark. Good luck.** See you at the Roxbury [the after-gala party at a nightclub on Sunset Boulevard].

Wahlberg's undress rehearsal for his final scene in *Boogie Nights*.

We were not without the usual traumas that had become a hallmark of these events. A major movie star I'll call "Monica" went to elaborate lengths to be part of the show. In my naivete, I thought she wanted the thrill of working with Calvin. Several days before the event, she had her people call to ask if she might be the finale of the show. It was explained to Monica's people that the show had already been cast, but her offer would definitely be passed on to Calvin. "By the way," I inquired, "what dress size is she?" "A *small* 14," came the response. Yikes! was my only possible thought considering the rigid criteria for being a CK model—size 1 or 2. Nonetheless, I passed the information on to the Klein camp and didn't think about it again until the day of the event when Monica herself called. "So, what's *his* decision?" she asked authoritatively. "I passed your generous offer on to the Calvin Klein people," I said. "They haven't contacted you?" "No!" she snapped back. "Well, do you need anyone to make an introduction ... perhaps I could introduce Calvin?" she suggested in the coquettish voice I remembered hearing in almost all of her movie and TV roles. "No introductions," I told her. "Can you tell me where I will be

CK Fall Men's Collection, 1993.

Annie Hall lives again. Menswear on women was big in 1993.

I heard from the CK staff that Calvin never wore the same pair of underwear twice—"wears them once and throws them away."

Silver lamé dominated the CK
Swimwear Collection for women
in 1993.

Although there are no jockstraps
in the CK underwear collection,
our model had to have something to wear with his CK T-shirt.

CK lingerie. More like C-*through*
lingerie.

sitting?" came her next question. I knew she had not purchased a ticket and all of the good seats had long ago been sold. "Are you coming as someone's guest?" I asked wistfully. "No, I will be coming with my publicist and a friend," she told me. Abruptly, the phone went dead. I scurried to my wall-sized seating chart to try to find a place for her and her guests.

The best I could do were seats several rows back and quite far off to the side. I added her name to our VIP list at the gate and left her tickets at Will Call.

That evening, as I sat in my box with my friends enjoying the last part of the fashion show, I noticed Monica had moved herself into a box directly next to the runway. The

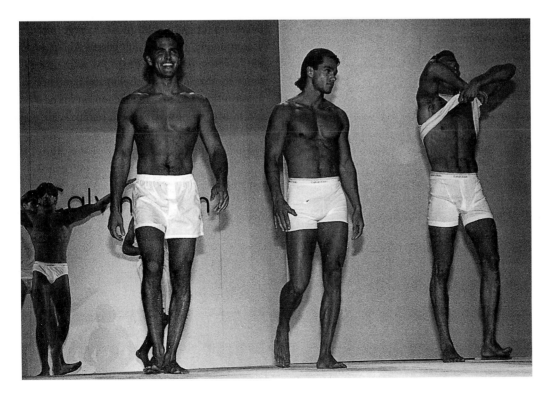

This is what our audience was
wishing and hoping would happen: bare-chested underwear-
clad boys and girls.

Yum!

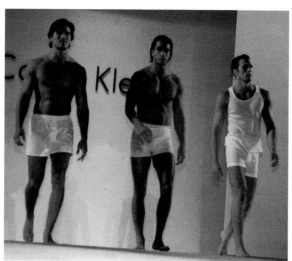

Boys will be boys. Most had
instructions to keep their T-shirts
on—but with 3,700 people yelling
for you to take it off, what's a guy
to do?

It takes a special girl to wear Calvin's sexy lingerie.

people into whose box she had ensconced herself seemed overwhelmed by her presence but
were obviously impressed that such a big star
had joined their party. As I watched, I saw
Monica drinking straight out of one of the
wine bottles. Oh well, she seemed happy and

Grunge was the look in 1993
and Calvin embraced it in his
younger collections for men
and women.

content at this point. Who was I to question
all that fun she was having?

As the last model left the runway, Tina
Turner took center stage to wild applause.
Tina (God bless her) was the brightest star of
the evening. She had unselfishly chosen our
benefit to preview her "What's Love Got to
Do with It" world tour (to promote the new

movie about her life and its soundtrack
album) and had canceled her later scheduled
Hollywood Bowl appearance to do it. She lost
a lot of money canceling that paid appearance
to help us for free and probably didn't endear
herself with the Bowl management either. But
Tina's name and the prerelease excitement
about the film based on her life (produced by
the same Barry Krost and Doug Chapin who
had helped us make the Adrian event a star-
studded evening) certainly helped us fill the
seats in the Bowl—even though we had twice
as many tickets to sell this time. It was a
delight to see Angela Bassett and Tina Turner
chatting each other up with girl talk backstage
before the show. Angela Bassett was already
getting tremendous buzz around Hollywood
for her portrayal of Tina Turner in *What's
Love Got to Do with It?* which would open in
theaters just one week later. The best cinemat-
ic portrayal of a singer since Sissy Spacek won
an Oscar for playing Loretta Lynn, Angela
Bassett's performance would later win a
Golden Globe and receive a Best Actress
Oscar nomination. When Miss Bassett arrived
that evening on the arm of Barry Krost, the
paparazzi went bananas. Only Warren Beatty's
arrival with his wife, Annette Bening, came
close to generating that level of excitement
from the crowds outside the Bowl.

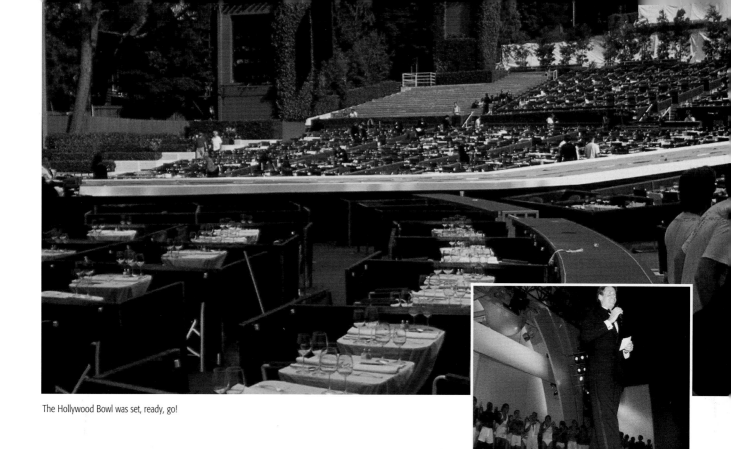

The Hollywood Bowl was set, ready, go!

Calvin outspent all the other designers producing this event.

The audience in the Bowl was standing, whistling, screaming, and dancing in the aisles as Tina Turner ripped into her second set, *We Don't Need Another Hero*. Suddenly, my walkie-talkie went off! Security asked me to look to my immediate right and wanted to know what, if anything, they should do. I looked over to see Monica drunkenly trying to raise herself up onto the five-foot-high runway. A second later, Monica was pushed up onto the runway by one of her adoring fans. To Tina's surprise, and the audience's delight, Monica began to dance the "Monkey," the "Pony," and a dance I didn't recognize from any known animal kingdom.

As Tina moved away from our movie star and back toward

The flip side of Tina Turner.

the security of her band, Monica wrapped up her routine with a burlesque version of the "Dance of the Seven Veils." She then curtsied, bowed, and flung herself off the stage as if she were Iggy Pop. The audience members not only caught *her*, but a good deal of her undigested dinner and wine as well! To this day, I'm sure that somewhere on Monica's resume is her "Live Appearance at the Hollywood Bowl."

As at all of these events, there was the usual demand for backstage VIP passes. Most of these requests came from the stars and their entourages who didn't want to use the public restrooms, not realizing that the toilets too had undergone their own CK metamorphosis. As each publicist called me for that prized yellow pass, I would explain the elaborate preparations the CK folks had taken to assure

Tina Turner lights up the Hollywood sky.

Calvin's clothes were as simple as black and white compared to some of the other designers we honored.

There were an amazing 350 models in the CK show.

the proper restroom *image*. The public toilets at the Bowl had each been steam cleaned, scoured with disinfectant, painted white, and decorated with large bouquets of white Casablanca lilies, fresh linen towels, and pre-

screened atomizer-holding attendants to give the restrooms a healthy whiff of Calvin Klein's own Obsession cologne after each and every use. This inside information happily satisfied most of them—but not all.

On the day before the event, I received a barrage of anxious calls from the wife of a big Hollywood producer. Her guests for the following evening were a famous oil and film tycoon and his socialite wife. She wondered if the tycoon and his wife could purchase an adjoining box so that the tycoon might be more comfortable—a euphemistic reference to said tycoon's incredible girth. We were able to accommodate this pressing need, though we never did receive the promised $5,000 (billionaires can be so cheap). But the later frantic requests for a backstage pass to allow the socialite wife of the tycoon to use the back-

Fifteen-year-old Eddie Furlong models in his first fashion show. We thought the woman accompanying him was his mom—but in fact it was his girlfriend.

CK promwear.

CK Men's Collection, Fall 1993.

CK Briefs. I wondered what happened to them after the models returned them at the end of the show.

stage bathroom had to be repeatedly, though gently, declined. Yet, on the evening of the event, there was the oil tycoon's wife bursting forth from Tina Turner's private backstage bathroom with the all-access backstage pass around her bejeweled neck. Though the bright yellow plastic clashed badly with her burgundy Adolfo, she wore that pass as proudly as if it were an Olympic gold medal. Considering all of the pleading phone calls and anxious arm-twisting that it must have taken to finagle that pass from who knows who, I guess, if not a gold-medal performance, it may have been a personal best.

Then there was the famous couture designer for a former First Lady. The Designer was seated in a box next to that of his biggest customers—the equally famous president and chairman of a major California retailing giant. Given the plentitude of champagne and wine, our Designer got, well … hammered. Naturally, at a certain point in the evening, he had to relieve himself. But in the dark and in his drunken state, he stood up, spun around a few times desperately trying to get his bearings, then unzipped his pants and did his business into the next box, all over its occupants—his best customers! Not waiting for an encore, we immediately removed our distinguished Designer and his party from the

Mark Wahlberg applauds
Calvin Klein.

Bowl. The following day we heard that he spent more than $10,000 on roses, champagne, and gifts from Tiffany's for everyone in that neighboring box. But then, $10,000 is a wee amount by Hollywood standards.

Of course, the dilemma of too much drink with too little food—meager portions of beige food were complemented by a full bottle of wine for each guest—led to other precarious situations that evening. A favorite incident involved a famous producer who was dressed in his usual whimsical fashion. Although his entrance bore his traditional floating grace, he had some trouble maneuvering his exit. As he fell and rolled down a very

steep hill, his floor-length gown spun like kite string up around his pudgy little neck. When he managed to get to his feet, he swore he would sue us and the Bowl. But as time passed, we heard nothing more from him. Perhaps he forgot about it (or couldn't remember it) but for those of us who witnessed this scene, we never will!

The evening's piece de resistance for sober chutzpah involved that notorious girl-friend columnist for a Condé Nast publication. Although we were always happy to provide tickets for members of the press, this was usually limited to two. This member of the press somehow managed to get his hands on

The average age of our CK models was just 17 years old. Very few were professional models.

MacGraw. Ali bought four full-price tickets for herself, her date, her son, Josh Evans, and his date Natasha Wagner, the daughter of Robert Wagner and Natalie Wood. Even more generous, on the corporate level, were *Bazaar* magazine's Liz Tilberis and Veronica Hearst, who helped underwrite the evening with a $250,000 donation. Another fond memory was finding an excellent seat for a delightful 75-year-old retiree who for many years had tirelessly volunteered her time to help people with HIV and AIDS. She deserved a good seat and we found one for her—an unused empty seat in the box purchased by a New York billionaire whose personal care products company would later become infamous as the employer of last resort for Monica Lewinsky. This rich businessman, though a bit nonplussed by his surprise guest, was also a good liberal Democrat who certainly wasn't going to make a scene about an elderly African American woman unexpectedly joining his party.

And then there was the show! One of my favorites, really. More like a corporate presentation than a fashion show—350 models converged on stage, one by one, hunk by hunk, babe by babe, one more beautiful than the last. We saw Calvin Klein denim and sunglasses, swimwear and sportswear, overcoats, shoes, socks, and finally that part of the evening that everyone had prayed for—underwear-clad boys and topless girls. To prove once and for all the CK dictum that less really is more, bottomless boys in torn T-shirts that were ripped off so fast you would have thought the runway had become one giant Hollywood casting couch! As all the models in their CK gear made their way back onstage for one final appearance, Martin Luther King Jr. could never have dreamed that his famous *I Have A Dream* speech (the disco version) would be blaring out over the loudspeakers as

One of our volunteer models being fitted backstage at the Hollywood Bowl.

six complimentary tickets. Just moments before the evening was to begin, I was informed that Girlfriend was out front *scalping his tickets!* Ever vigilant, I confronted him on the subject of his nefarious activities. Girlfriend was surprised and outraged. He vehemently denied any wrongdoing and threatened to have his "New York boyfriend take care of you if you don't leave me alone!" Girlfriend then let out a shriek in the direction of Kelly Klein, turned away from me in his trademark black Gucci mules and, holding on to Kelly for dear life, escaped into the safety of the crowd.

In sharp contrast to so many celebrities and powerful people who think they deserve free tickets just for gracing our event with their radiance, even though it's a charity event, there was actress and humanitarian Ali

"You don't want to know," she giggled. "I'll leave it to your imagination!" Carolyn was the kind of person who made me want to do events. In a quiet moment, amid the hubbub backstage after the show, Carolyn and I had a brief debriefing about the show and life at Calvin Klein.

All quips about the process aside, the results of the event spoke louder than any laughs or laments. We raised more money for people living with HIV and AIDS than ever before, and the evening has entered the Pantheon of Hollywood legend and lore. It had been a perfect night for the show, warm and balmy with the diamond-studded Hollywood Hills shimmering brilliantly against an indigo sky. On that June 1993 evening, we were once again kissed by the angels, perhaps the very souls we were too late in helping and comforting.

accompaniment to a final group hug in salute to our man of the hour.

Later, as photographers snapped pictures backstage of Hollywood's beautiful people, I thought to myself that the photographers were missing the shot that should have been recorded for posterity—the sight of more than 150 models returning their borrowed, just-worn underwear. As all those body-tempered briefs were obediently deposited into waiting laundry bins, I had to wonder about their destination. Were they to have been given to some unspecified charity or returned to Calvin? Would they be laundered or left *au naturel*? Whatever!

Several months later, I would ask Carolyn Bessette, a publicist with the CK Dream Team (later Mrs. John F. Kennedy Jr.), "Whatever happened to all those undies?"

Kate Moss without makeup.

Underwear ruled—people still talk about it today.

Talking With Carolyn Bessette, June 1993

• **Did you enjoy the show?** I'm glad Calvin did it. He should have done it a long time ago. I hope he does more events like this. • **Carolyn, you have a fabulous job…am I correct in assuming so?** Yes, it's great, though I never want to work for another mogul again. • **Was this a hard decision for Calvin to make, coming to Los Angeles and doing an AIDS benefit?** Yes. • **Why?** I can't really comment on that. • **Who is your favorite designer?** (She just laughs.) • **What was your favorite part of the show tonight?** It was getting ready for the show. It was arriving last Sunday and working on it with a bunch of dedicated volunteers like you that made this week so special and memorable. This is one show I don't think I'll ever forget. It's been an incredible experience. • **So what's next on tap at Calvin Klein?** We're leaving tomorrow to go back to New York to do a fund-raiser for gays in the military for David Geffen. [David Geffen, founder of Asylum Records, Geffen Records, and cofounder of DreamWorks Studio, hosted the event, which was held at Calvin and Kelly's house in The Hamptons on Long Island, New York.] • **Why has Calvin become so proactive in issues of concern to the gay community?** Calvin has always been pro gay. But this is more for his friend David Geffen. • **Will you be doing a fashion show?** Yes. • **Do you think that Calvin Klein ever crosses the line as far as the sexual connotations of his advertising?** No, I never really think about it. There's nothing wrong with the human body, and our marketing has always been, for the most part, directed to people who are very health conscious. I love the human form and so does Calvin.

Isaac Mizrahi

—Le Miz at the Chinese Theater

"Fashion is about women not wanting to look like cows— although COWS are kind of charming, aren't they?

It's almost impossible to have style nowadays without the right dogs.

Everything is frustrating except designing clothes—that's beautiful and liberating."

—Isaac Mizrahi

It was four-thirty in the morning on January 17,1994, and I awoke unexpectedly. No, it wasn't another dream about a Bob Mackie gown. I didn't know why I awoke with a start but I was about to find out. Apparently, I was the only simple beast in the room who could sense impending natural disasters. My three Dalmatians were snoring comfortably. Then, BOOM! Had a 747 crashed into the building? Maybe an explosion. The TV flew off the nightstand and smashed into pieces, sending glass and parts everywhere. My antique armoire tipped, rocked, then crashed down. My dogs were terrified and jumped into the bed. The whole room was shaking and rolling, then I knew. Was this "THE BIG ONE"? That was the question every Angeleno who'd lived in this city for more than a few years was asking as they watched for more falling and flying objects and wondered, how much longer can this go on? No, I later found out, it wasn't *the* big one, only *a* big one, 6.7 on the Richter scale and centered on the other side of the Santa Monica Mountains in Northridge, a

Los Angeles suburb in the San Fernando Valley. I was in Santa Monica, 20 miles away. No, it wasn't the big one but it would kill 51, injure 9,000, leave 22,000 homeless, and amount to the costliest disaster in U.S. history. Right now, all I knew was there was no electricity, all was pitch black inside and out, and I couldn't light a candle because I was smelling gas! I had to get myself and my dogs from my bedroom and out of this building fast. But the armoire had fallen in front of the only door out of the bedroom. I guess I was like one of those mothers you read about in the papers who lifts a car off her injured child; somewhere, I found the strength to right the armoire and get outside my bedroom and condo, my three dogs clinging to my side.

Finally, I could take a second to catch my breath. I'd never seen L.A. like this—pitch black. My God, there were stars! I heard my neighbors from the other three condos in my building and hurried to them. None of us was seriously hurt, but all were badly shaken. Then I realized I was in nothing but my boxer shorts and I was freezing. I asked my neighbors to hold my dogs, who weren't going to let me leave their side, and I ran back into the

Our 35,000-square-foot dining tent was pitched in a parking lot behind the Chinese Theater.

Linda Evangelista in taffeta and down.
This was Isaac's Eskimo period.

of this location would only become obvious the next day when we saw TV pictures of a formerly three-story apartment building that was now two stories, the bottom floor having been leveled, killing two dozen people. When daylight came, my bravest neighbor, a female set designer for one of the film studios, went around with a wrench and turned off everyone's gas. We aired out the building and eventually went back into our homes to try to clean up some of the havoc.

We still had no electricity or phones. Then, around 10 A.M. all six phone lines into my home office started ringing at the same moment. I figured it must be my family wanting to know if I was alive. I quickly grabbed a phone, but it wasn't my sister, not my father, and not even a dear friend from out of state. No, it was Isaac Mizrahi. Yes, it was our scheduled honoree for 1994 and it was so wonderful that he was worried about *me*. Right. Isaac, in a panic, screamed into the phone, "Is the Chinese Theater still standing?" "I don't know, Isaac," I answered dryly. "I'm still standing; aren't you happy to hear that?" "Sure, honey. Can you drive over to the Chinese and call me from a pay phone?" "Isaac, the city's in

building and grabbed some clothes. Shortly, we would all huddle together in one of the cars in the parking garage located under our building and listen to the radio. The stupidity

The Mizrahi troops occupied the Chinese Theater for three days prior to the event in 1994.

Christina Applegate with pink hair arrives at the Chinese Theater.

rubble. They're warning everyone to stay off the streets and leave them clear for emergency vehicles." Isaac, undeterred and with a sense of proportion only a fashion designer could truly understand, said, "This *is* an emergency." I explained, "If I go peeking around the Chinese Theater, they may shoot me as a looter, and they say to expect aftershocks almost as big as the first quake." "You'll find a way, honey," Isaac reassured me and then hung up. Well, there you have it, the designer to be honored at our eighth annual fashion gala and our venue— Le Miz at the Chinese Theater!

The really absurd thing about this story is that I actually did get into my car to go check the Chinese Theater for damage. Maybe it was shell shock or maybe it was the weird, delirious energy that Isaac could spread in his wake, but there I was on the Santa Monica Freeway heading right toward the two big sections of the freeway that had crashed to the ground. Fortunately, the police were directing all the cars onto surface streets. No stoplights working, walls and chimneys in rubble, a strange yellow pallor hung over the city as I crept my way toward Hollywood Boulevard. The boulevard was deserted as I parked directly in front of the Chinese Theater, a spot typically filled with tour buses. As I walked across the hallowed star concrete footprints, I didn't see any obvious new cracks but I did notice how much bigger my feet were than Fred Astaire's. I banged on the large glass double-doors, but no one answered. I walked around the perimeter of the building and everything looked okay. It was about this time that I felt just how absolutely stupid I was to have gone out into a city in turmoil just to comfort Isaac. I tried to hurry back to my dogs before the next aftershock. Almost four hours after I left home, I made it back safely. I called Isaac in New York and got his answering machine. I left a message, "The Chinese is all rubble, Isaac. It looks like we'll be holding your show at the Holiday Inn after all." I hoped that would straighten his curls.

Isaac had been to L.A. about six months earlier, but he really considered only one location for his show, the Chinese Theater in Hollywood. Isaac later told the *Los Angeles Times*, "I wouldn't have done this [show] if it

wasn't at the Chinese. It's like the Louvre of California, one of the natural wonders of the world." One of the unnatural wonders, I imagine he meant to say. He had a particular fondness for the hand and footprints of Tyrone Power and Rita Hayworth. So, assuming we could get it, a big assumption, Isaac was all set on the Chinese Theater. He did have one problem with the setting, though, the very unattractive and very tall Holiday Inn visible several blocks behind the theater, on Highland Boulevard, about halfway up to the Hollywood Bowl, where we'd just raised $1.4 million in a single evening. With the grandiose vision of a megalomaniacal Hollywood director, and a fair amount of playful camp, Isaac, dressed in New York black with his wild curls squirting out above his trademark blue bandana headband, waved his hand and cigarette in front of the eyesore Holiday Inn and proclaimed, "Let's just tear the fucking thing down for the evening."

Isaac and actress Kelly Lynch exchange phone numbers.

Anjelica Huston and her artist husband enjoy watching the stars land.

Our favorite groupie, Sandra Bernhard, waits for the show to begin.

turer, with teaching him everything he knows about cutting and sewing—"My father personally custom fit my powder blue bar mitzvah suit." Isaac credits his mother, Sarah, with whom he has an almost stereotypically close and maddening Jewish mother-son relationship, with forming his taste, which British *Vogue* called "the classiest in America." Isaac now admits to his mother that, as a child, he used to steal money from her purse to buy fabric. Isaac's New York City design studio is on Wooster Street in Soho, though he claims to get his most dazzling ideas while in bed. He also is inspired from the television shows of his childhood, particularly from the *Mary Tyler Moore Show* and the *Dick Van Dyke Show*. He asserts with his characteristic understatement that, "Between Mary Tyler Moore and Jackie Kennedy, they shaped this country. Why do I like Mary Tyler Moore? Because I'm an American. And because I'm not a stone." Isaac is also heavily influenced by "the early twentieth century in Hollywood, from the 1930s to the 1960s and especially the 1950s. They were glamorous, apolitical, the absolute peak of Technicolor, optimistic, and the last time we had real shape in fashion." The "Eskimo chic" collection that Isaac would show at our gala, which is also featured in the documentary *Unzipped*, was inspired by

It had been a few months before that, in spring 1993, when Isaac Mizrahi and his PR rep Nina Santini had contacted us through *Elle* magazine, whose parent company was financing a movie about Isaac that would eventually be entitled *Unzipped*. Isaac's proposal came to us fully prepared with financing already in place. We liked Isaac's long history of involvement in AIDS fund-raisers across the country and overseas, and Isaac's openness and ease with being gay was refreshing. In fact, Isaac was so flamboyant, sort of a rococo Nathan Lane, that he couldn't have been in a closet even if he had wanted to be. Isaac had also designed costumes for famed choreographers Twyla Tharp, Bill T. Jones, and Mark Morris. The thought of the equally demonstrative and energetic Mizrahi and Mark Morris in the same room together is slightly scary. In 1980, Isaac even had a part in the hit film *Fame* and in 1993 had played a fashion designer in the film *For Love or Money*. He would be a fun and very deserving choice, and a popular one too after our semicontroversial choice of Calvin Klein. Isaac's more outré designs would also provide a sharp contrast with the sedate ecru and beige CK collection. So it was enthusiastically settled: Isaac Mizrahi would be our 1994 honoree.

Isaac Mizrahi is a library-card-carrying New Yorker, born and bred in Brooklyn. Isaac credits his father, a children's wear manufac-

Janet Gretzky and her husband, NHL star Wayne Gretzky, stood by Isaac in 1994.

Isaac's tribute to those men, women and children who have died and will die from AIDS.

the Inuit fashions he saw in the classic 1922 Robert Flaherty documentary *Nanook of the North*. Further inspiration for the collection came from the 1935 *very* loose Hollywood adaptation of Jack London's *Call of the Wild* in which Clark Gable finds Loretta Young nearly dead after days alone on the frozen tundra. With his postmodern sense of irony and delicious love of camp absurdity, Isaac delighted in the nonsense that Young looked sensational, with a perfectly made-up face framed by elegant fur, even after giving birth in an igloo and fighting with sled dogs. To further illustrate the gulf between Hollywood and fashion Eskimo life and the real thing, the actual Nanook starved to death at about the same time audiences around the world were applauding this man who could smile so infectiously despite his cold and hostile environment. The documentary had been financed by the wealthy fur merchants Revillon Frères. I never did think to ask Isaac if he had recognized another amazing coincidence—the actor playing poker with Gable in *Call of the Wild* is Sid Grauman, the man who built Grauman's Chinese Theater.

Isaac and pals.

Isaac has a conversation with himself in the movie *Unzipped* that is very illustrative of the pressures a designer faces. He wonders if his idea for a collection of Eskimo-inspired designs is worth doing, then concludes, "Yes, because it is the only idea I have." I cannot imagine the anxiety of having to stay a step

Awesome chairwoman of the evening, author Linda Bruckheimer, with Mrs. Marvin (Babs) Davis.

Director Rob Reiner with his wife enjoy a night out on the town.

Linda Evangelista perches on the lap of her date for the evening.

Dan Aykroyd and wife, Donna Dixon.

Johnny Depp, Ellen Barkin, Linda Evangelista, and friend.

ahead of the fashion climate of the moment, offering designs each season that the power players of the fashion media didn't know they wanted until they saw it strut down the cat-walk. You must, in an instant, win the stamp of approval of the cognoscenti and then every-one else will follow. If you garner these taste makers' derision instead, you fear the loss of your company. The fashion world is like Hollywood in that you're only as bankable as the success of your last show. No wonder these designers are so high-strung, self-absorbed, and obsessive about every detail. Perhaps one needs to be slightly mad to dream of creating "banana-split jumpsuits in beast fur with hush puppy boots to walk the dog in." But Isaac also knew what Seventh Avenue's reaction would be if he used real ani-mal pelts instead of synthetic fibers. He'd "be stoned like some wanton heretic." Even the frivolous can be overwhelming. How does Isaac escape the stress? Marlboro cigarettes, doughnuts, playing bridge, and playing Bach on his piano.

So we had Isaac, his *Nanook of the North* flashy fake-fur fait accompli, and we would also preview the short documentary *Unzipped*, which fashion photographer Douglas Keeve was creating about a wild season in the life of his fashion designer former lover. Now all we

needed was the Chinese Theater. The Chinese is the most famous and most visited landmark in Hollywood, with millions each year approaching the foot and hand prints as if they were religious relics, fitting their hands or feet to match those of their favorite Hollywood god or goddess. It's as close as Hollywood will ever have to a holy shrine. Its jade green bronze pagoda roof rises 70 feet into the air, and the interior of the theater is filled with exotic art from China. It was the last and most extravagant creation of film the-ater impresario Sid Grauman, the man who also devised the lavish Hollywood movie pre-miere. The first movie premiere occurred on October 18, 1922, when Grauman opened his Egyptian Theater, a few blocks west of the later Chinese. As a battery of klieg lights swept the skies over Hollywood Boulevard, stars stepped from limousines for the Douglas Fairbanks movie *Robin Hood*. The Egyptian had already been under construction to resem-ble a Spanish hacienda when the sensational discovery of King Tut's Tomb captivated the world. Ignoring the Spanish tile roof, Grauman shifted to an Egyptian motif, with hieroglyphics on the walls and bulrushes and lotus emblems. Other Grauman movie palaces were the Mayan and Million Dollar theaters in downtown L.A. But the Chinese is no doubt the most famous movie theater in the world because of the Forecourt of the Stars where nearly 200 film idols, including three horses and two robots, have cast their prints in cement. According to Hollywood lore, the idea struck Grauman when silent film star Norma Talmadge visited his yet-to-open Chinese Theater and accidentally stepped into a slab of wet cement. Many guests to our fashion galas, plus Adrian's wife, Janet Gaynor, have been immortalized in the forecourt: Myrna Loy, Tony Martin, Jane Withers, Elizabeth Taylor, Ali MacGraw, Sylvester Stallone, and Steven Seagal. That one sees Steven Seagal but not Claudette Colbert or Audrey Hepburn illustrates the arbitrariness of the honor. It has always helped to have a movie premiering at the Chinese.

Our first order of business was to secure permission to use the building. This actually proved far easier than I could have hoped. Although managed by the Mann Theater Corporation, the Chinese Theater is owned jointly by Paramount and Warner Bros. stu-

Allana Hamilton Stewart and former husband George Hamilton. Their 1995 talk show lasted less than one season.

dios. They help cover the enormous costs of maintenance and upkeep of the designated historical landmark. (Changing the name of the theater from Grauman's Chinese to Mann's Chinese has always struck me as crazy, like renaming Mount Rushmore.) In the fall of 1993, I picked up the phone and called Barry Reardon, the longtime distribution chief at Warners. Reardon is a legend inside the film industry, both for his revolutionary changes in the business and art of film distribution and for being one of the last great gentlemen in Hollywood. In the higher echelons of Hollywood, the butterfly is usually protected by a cocoon of people who keep everyone from getting through to him or her. To my surprise, I was put right through to Barry Reardon himself. The only other time I remember this happening during my Hollywood fund-raising career was when my call to David Geffen was put through to him on his private jet, no questions asked. My second delightful surprise was that Reardon almost immediately okayed my request. Warners only needed it in writing; they asked for nothing in return. Not even free tickets or free advertising—nothing. Convincing Mann Theaters was equally simple. Their only question was how long did we needed the theater. "Three days," I said, flinching. "You've got it." The only restriction was that we not interfere with operation of the three smaller movie screens, added during the 1970s in an innocuous building just east of the main auditorium. That certainly was no problem and could I kiss someone thank you? Wow!

While I was trying to secure the Chinese Theater, Isaac on the East Coast was in hot pursuit of k.d. lang to perform at the aftershow dinner. She was on hiatus from performing and recording and was in New York, where Isaac repeatedly ran into her at many of

Comedian Sandra Bernhard arrives wearing an Isaac Mizrahi jacket made out of Coke cans.

Golden Girls creator/writer Susan Harris, a co-chair for the evening, arrives Mizrahi-style, complete with a backpack.

Actress Tia Carrera with an unidentified friend.

"Bound" by her commitment to AIDS causes, Jennifer Tilly was a regular guest at our shows.

the spring fashion shows (which are held in the fall). Isaac kept asking lang, pleading with her actually, until, once again with the help of unseen hands, Isaac found himself seated right next to lang at a party hosted by *Vogue* magazine. Cornered and subjected to a full evening of Isaac's hilarious wit and impish charm, the generous songstress agreed to be our featured performer. It would take some doing, though, to pull her band together because they were spread all over, some in Canada and others working around the United States.

Now, where was k.d. lang going to perform? Not to mention where were our 1,800 guests going to dine? Hollywood Boulevard, though undergoing a gradual renaissance, had progressively lost most of its glamour in the decades following World War II. The main reason the Chamber of Commerce has put 2,000 bronze star-shaped plaques honoring celebrities of film, radio, recording, and TV into a glittery sidewalk, beginning in 1960, is to make the Boulevard less of a disappointment to the millions of visitors who arrive

expecting Hollywood and Vine to still be the center of the entertainment world. Instead, they find a street that looks like any past-its-prime main street. Except for the lavender art deco Frederick's of Hollywood building, all of the legendary nightclubs, restaurants, and clothing stores have left and been replaced, for the most part, by immigrant businesses selling teen clothing, Hollywood souvenirs, and low-cost electronics. The grand Egyptian Theater had been shuttered, the Brown Derby had gone, and Max Factor's had become a museum. We had only three options in close proximity to the Chinese where we might hold the second part of our million-dollar fund-raiser. One was the Blossom Ballroom of the restored Roosevelt Hotel. This was just across the street from the theater and had been the venue for the very first Academy Awards dinner in 1929, but it would only accommodate 500 people for dinner. There was the roof of the Holiday Inn, assuming Isaac didn't dynamite it. Our third option was the AVCO parking lot adjoining and directly behind the theater. The brass at AVCO were eager to be part of this historic evening and that's the site Isaac chose. It would take a full week to remove, transport, and store the hundreds of heavy concrete parking blocks that populated the lot. They would all, of course, have to be returned and remounted after the event. But this was Hollywood, the big-time, real Hollywood where anything was possible. As part of the deal with AVCO, we gave them four tickets to the gala and contracted with them to manage the valet parking for guests. They would park the cars across the street at the Bank of Hollywood, a bizarre little banking institution with just 1,000 depositors but, fortunately, 2,000 parking spaces. The bank charged us for the use of their parking spaces but became indignant when I refused their president's request for a free table.

My most unpleasant surprise came when I approached Johnny Grant, the honorary mayor of Hollywood for as long as most people can remember. Hollywood is not really a city, but is part of the city of Los Angeles, so I must assume Grant's title was self-proclaimed. Most natives of Southern California and I grew up seeing Grant officiating each year at the Hollywood Santa Claus Lane Parade and mugging for the camera whenever a new bronze star was added to the Hollywood Walk of Fame. Grant even has his footprints at the Chinese Theater, but no one I've ever met could tell me what Grant's ever done besides being an honorary mayor. I assumed that Grant would be eager to help smooth the way for any event that would bring some old-style glamour and positive publicity to his favorite street. Sure he would help, for a big fat fee. We declined the honorary mayor's offer.

No self-serving mayor was going to get in the way of Isaac, a bad-assed Seventh Avenue designer from Brooklyn and two-pack-a-day Marlboro-smoking gay man who counts wild-woman Sandra Bernhard as his best friend. We got on the phone to the Los Angeles City Council member who represents Hollywood, Jackie Goldberg. Jackie is an openly gay woman who cut her political teeth as one of

Jackie Collins. Like "Old Faithful," she attended all ten fashion events.

Kate Moss.

Producer Jon Peters and his then-girlfriend, model Vendela.

Christy Turlington with actor Wesley Snipes. Isaac brought out the most stars of any of our honored designers.

A colorful tribute to our fight against AIDS.

the leaders of the Berkeley Free Speech Movement in 1964—the opening shot and template for much of the student radicalism of the subsequent decade. In just one afternoon, Jackie helped us obtain the many permits we needed to put on such a mammoth event. We even got permission to close down Hollywood Boulevard from Vine Street on the east to La Brea Boulevard on the west, which is unheard of in Los Angeles on a weekday at rush hour. Sure, the Boulevard closed for the L.A. Marathon and the Christmas Parade, but those were on Sunday. Jackie was a great help to us. George Christy, famed columnist for the *Hollywood Reporter*, later remarked that despite attending 40 years of premieres at the Chinese, "I've never seen anything like this evening" in the numbers of guests, press, celebrities, spectators, and fans lining the streets. We even had off-duty L.A. Police who donated their time to help with crowd control.

For each event, with the direction of the designer, we would put together an Honorary Committee for the dinner. It would be mostly composed of people who had recognizable names and who could lend their support to the event by getting their companies, business associates, and friends to buy tickets, tables, and advertising in the evening's commemorative program. In 1994, a single ticket to our event began at $350 and went as high as $5,000. A table of 10 started at $3,500 and went up to $50,000. My biggest thrill in my 10 years of fund-raising for HIV was when I sold two tickets for the Calvin Klein evening for the unbelievable price of $25,000 each! The event had long been sold out when, a couple of days before the gala, I got a call from the secretary of the head of a major studio. She wanted to know how her boss and his wife could get tickets. "I'm sorry, but we've been all sold out for weeks now," I apologized. There was a long pause, then in a condescending tone, "Well, s*ir*, how much would it take to dig up two tickets?" Irritated by her haughtiness, I shot back, "$50,000." "Can we send a messenger?" she said, without hesitation. "Uh, yeah, sure … send a messenger, that'll be fine," I muttered, all my irritation vaporized. I had only been calling her bluff

and threw out the figure of $50,000 to get the woman off my back. Now I was wishing I'd said, "$100,000." But the deal was made and I ended up putting the studio head and his wife in my box at the Hollywood Bowl, right next to other moguls Barry Diller, David Geffen, Revlon billionaire Ron Perlman, and manager of superstars Sandy Gallin.

Our 1994 Honorary Dinner Committee was the most impressive collection of Hollywood heavyweights we'd ever had for one of our events. It included Linda Bruckheimer (whose husband, Jerry, along with his partner, the late Don Simpson, produced a string of Hollywood blockbusters such as *Top Gun* and *Beverly Hills Cop*); Wendy Finerman, the producer of that year's *Forrest Gump* and wife of Columbia Pictures head Mark Canton; Susan Harris, the creator of TV's *Golden Girls* and a partner in TV producton powerhouse Witt-Thomas-Harris Productions; and Jeff Berg, chairman of ICM (International Creative Management), one of the industry's big three talent agencies.

k.d. lang crooned to help us raise money for AIDS services. But wore a Richard Tyler tuxedo.

Shortly after the Northridge earthquake, Isaac bravely arrived in Los Angeles to work out the production details for the show. Isaac, a few members of his staff, and I dropped by the offices of ICM to meet with our liaison to ICM Chairman Jeff Berg, and PR director Ellen Gilbert. We were put in a conference room and told Ellen would be right with us. An hour and a quarter later, Isaac, again in a black Joseph Aboud suit with his blue bandana headband, was fuming and the rest of us were plain bored. Finally, Ellen's assistant showed up and escorted us into her boss's office, where we cooled our heels for another quarter hour. As we waited in the windowless

Kate Moss pays homage to
Anjelica Huston.

office, we began to examine the many pictures of Miss Gilbert, which she had displayed. One that particularly caught Isaac's eye showed our absent PR director with Donna Karan and Barbra Streisand. The photo had been taken at one of the Clinton Inaugural Balls in D.C. The door opened and in wallked Ellen right in the middle of Isaac's critique of the various inaugural wardrobe mistakes. "I'm not sure who you people are or what you're here for," were the first words out of her mouth. Isaac took charge and explained, using the word *madam* as often as possible. (He later told me that women in their thirties hate to be addressed as madam. "It ages them," he explained, with a wicked wink.) "I've never heard of you," Gilbert told Isaac, adding that she only wore Donna Karan, one of her best friends; the other, Barbra Streisand. Now it was Isaac who wasn't impressed. What we had was, to quote Strother Martin in *Cool Hand Luke,* "a failure to communicate."

Isaac clarified that he had personally asked Jeff Berg to be a chair for the evening at the Chinese and Jeff had agreed. Isaac even produced a letter to that effect on ICM stationery signed by über-agent Berg himself. After a brief visit to her boss's office, Gilbert returned to inform us that ICM had no money for tickets, but they would be happy to help with celebrities, provided they were comped free tickets, herself included, of course. "ICM has no money?" I said incredulously as I looked around at their grand office building. As for celebrities, I always made it a policy that they should pay for their tickets

unless they were working in the show. "Who are we talking about?" I asked out of a perverse curiosity. "Julia Roberts, Barbra Streisand, maybe even my friend Hillary Clinton if she's available," was Ellen's defensive reply. How many times had I heard lame promises to deliver those very same big three? We stood up as a group and Isaac informed Ellen, "We'll get back to you." Jeff Berg's name, along with ICM's, was added to the top of our invitation and we forged on.

Our impressive Honorary Dinner Committee was, to put it kindly, dysfunctional. Only one member, the wonderful Linda Bruckheimer (also a writer whose debut novel, *Dreaming Southern,* had garnered raves), put her time, talent, and money behind her commitment to the event. She opened doors for us, got others to put their money where their promises were, and single-handedly sold most of the major, and most expensive, tables. Linda was always available for support, for lunch or to talk to, even if she was at her farm in Kentucky or in Aspen, New York, or any-

Lauren Bacall wanted to know where the cheese was.

Melrose Place star Daphne
Zuniga.

Mizrahi was clever and fun with
his designs in 1994.

even an ad in the evening's program. ICM
had also done nothing to recruit any celebrities for the show or even for the audience.
One big fat nada. Well, who should show up
the night of the event with a dozen friends
and no reservations to our sold-out event but
the honorary chair himself, Jeff Berg. I did
what I had learned to do brilliantly, if I do say
so myself—create space where there was none
before, a bit like the edge of our expanding
universe. I put up an additional table in the
dinner tent and put folding chairs at the end
of each row of theater seats for the show. But
not before I asked for his credit card.

"You asked Jeff Berg for his Visa card?"
chuckled a very amused Christina Applegate,
star of TV's *Married . . . With Children* and
Jessie. I was working in the Chinese Theater's
actual ticket booth, handing out tickets and
accepting late payments. Christina had just
given me her credit card, insisting on paying
for her own tickets. Berg's PR person, Ellen
Gilbert, gasped, "You must be kidding. We'll
send you a check," she promised. "I'll need a
Visa or a Mastercard. We don't accept
American Express," I flatly explained behind
my suppressed glee. Next thing I knew, I was
holding Jeff Berg's Visa card. I ran it through
and got approval. See how easy that was?

where else. She was always there for me and
for the good of the event. On the night of the
gala, Linda introduced me to her husband,
Jerry. I told him how special his wife is, and
he agreed. Then he paused for a second, and
put his arm around Linda to tell me that she
was "his wife." "You're a very lucky man," I
reassured him. They're a dynamite couple.

The other members of our Dinner
Committee ran the gamut from barely helpful
to worse than useless. One of them, rich from
her own work and married to lots more,
reserved a $15,000 table for herself and eight
of her friends and colleagues. She arrived the
night of the show wearing Mizrahi and was
given second-row theater seats. Later, we seated her and her guests at one of the best-
located tables in our tent. What, her $15,000
check never materialized? Was I shocked?
Well, not really. This was my eighth year and
I'd seen many rich people who don't pay their
debts, particularly to charity. After all, we
couldn't green light their next movie.

I was not prepared for ICM on the night
of the show. Neither Jeff Berg, despite being
an honorary chairman for the evening, nor
ICM had bought any tickets, any tables, or

Goddesses Raquel Welch and
Vendela.

It was summer in L.A., but this model in her faux leopard jacket and Eskimo snow boots didn't seem to notice.

Eskimo chic.

Nanook of the North inspired tulle and faux fur—worn by one of our 35 volunteer models.

A winter ball gown designed by Isaac Mizrahi.

As our guests entered the theater lobby that evening they came upon the regular concession stand, which was now a champagne station. Lines of young men in short white dinner jackets stood at attention holding trays of fluted crystal filled with champagne glasses. Other waiters handed each guest a white Chinese restaurant carryout container of red popcorn.

Our design for the inside of the Chinese Theater had to be simple for two reasons. The primary reason was that the theater interior is already extraordinarily ornate, with walls and ceiling covered with hard-carved Chinese images. The dominant personality of the whole auditorium is set by its Chinese red and gold colors. The seats, carpeting, curtain, and padded wall paneling are Chinese red, as magnificent in 1994 as the day the theater opened. We received permission to temporarily remove more than 60 seats and built a runway that jutted out into the dead center of the audience. Because of the steep bank of the floor, the final incarnation of our runway had the models trekking uphill, looking like they were on a nature hike in their Mizrahi splendor. Even Naomi would have had a tough

time oozing attitude on this catwalk. But it worked.

The second reason the set had to be minimal was that we would be using the movie screen. First, we would project the arrival of the guests onto the screen for those who had already been seated. It would be like the coverage of an old-fashioned grand Hollywood premiere, with Isaac's name on the two big marquees that framed the entrance. Later, we'd be using the movie screen to unveil the 20-minute documentary about Isaac, *Unzipped*.

Isaac's fashion show at the Chinese was magnificent. Isaac had wanted to do the same show he had done in New York, the one that was documented in *Unzipped*. There was one crucial design element that Isaac had used in his New York Nanook show that we would have to abandon in L.A. A few weeks before Isaac's collection was to be shown in New York's Bryant Park, the cover of *Women's Wear Daily* trumpeted the "Eskimo chic" collection by Jean-Paul Gaultier. Isaac had been Nanooked and frantically scrambled for an idea to save his show. He ended up showing the collection in front of a full-stage sheer scrim behind which one could see the models,

Makeup artist and author Kevin Aucoin, who had his hands full during the show, embraces Isaac following it.

It was a fun show as this model demonstrates in her sequined camisole and Indian boots.

Imagine faux fur in hot pink.

Tulle and faux fur cover Linda Evangelista in 1994.

makeup artists, Isaac, and the dressers preparing the show. The nuts-and-bolts view of the backstage drama was a hit, and Isaac's New York show was a huge success. The problem in L.A. was that there isn't really any backstage area at the Chinese—it's a movie theater and always has been. At most other venues, including the Los Angeles Ballroom at the Century Plaza, Isaac's scrim show could have been duplicated. But Isaac wanted the Chinese Theater more than he wanted the scrim.

His Nanook collection, however, was identical to the collection he showed in New York. It was tulle and taffeta, faux furs, and colors galore. Hooded parkas over taffeta ball gowns. Sophisticated evening clothes that were not really functional but fun to look at. His models included Christy Turlington, Kate Moss, Tyra Banks, Vendela, and more than 30 others. Isaac paid tribute to his friends and colleagues who had died of AIDS in a fantasy sequence of male models in white tights wearing huge feathered angel wings. The stage was filled with angel-winged men, one of whom held a two-year-old baby, representing the thousands of children who had died of AIDS. As the angels descended into the audience,

silence fell over the audience. Then, in a dazzlingly brilliant idea, Isaac again presented the entire collection, but this time, each garment was recreated entirely in a ghostly white. As the ethereal models in white walked the runway and down into the audience, coming from the rear of the auditorium as well as the from the stage, it suddenly began to snow in the theater! Only in Hollywood could such a marvelous effect be created, though, in its seven decades, it had never before snowed in the Chinese Theater. The stunningly beautiful moment, however, was quickly touched by absurdity as one of the snow machines malfunctioned and abruptly started blasting out fake snow like a cannon. The first *BOOM* startled us all, followed by laughter. Cheers arose from the crowd as the snow machine continued to blast its snow sideways across the auditorium like some burlesque "1812 Overture." Then to majestic music, Isaac himself made the traditional walk, or should I say, climb, up the runway in the official state color of New York—black.

With the fashion show and the screening of *Unzipped* completed, a mere three-quarters of an hour total, our guests made their way outside and into the huge red dinner tent. I didn't know you could rent a tent as large as we had on the parking lot behind the theater—35,000 square feet! The tent looked like a scene from *Mulan*. The ceiling of the tent was covered with hundreds of white Chinese lanterns in a dozen sizes, all lit red from within. The tables were covered in red, green, purple, cherry, black, and gold Chinese silk embroidered with landscapes, cherry blossoms, and dragons. Sixty thousand yards of silk were flown in from China to cover the two hundred 90-inch round tables. The place settings were simple oversized white china with black chopsticks, crystal stemware, and huge bouquets of pink, white, red, and fuchsia melon-sized feathery peonies (Isaac's favorite flower) in round crystal bowls. After a decade of these events, I can look back without hesitation to say that the Mizrahi dinner tent was the most magnificent setting we ever created, maybe the most magnificent I've ever seen. Our guests, not an easy bunch to impress, gasped as they walked into the tent. "Is this a movie set?" asked Academy Award–winner Anjelica Huston in astonishment as she reached to see if the enormous peonies were real or silk. Model Christy Turlington assured Anjelica it was not a movie set and the flowers were real. "And it all matches *my* lipstick," chirped the giddy Christy as she headed off to her A-list table to join photographer Herb Ritts, k.d. lang, model Kate Moss, and actors Johnny Depp and Ellen Barkin.

A heavenly body.

Faux fur and fun at Mizrahi.

"I want to sit at *that* table," moaned a poker-faced Sandra Bernhard. Sandra was wearing a short red skirt and a red and white jacket that Isaac had fashioned for her. It was covered in quarter-sized spangles cut from Coke cans. "But you're at Isaac's table, Sandra, the best table in the house … uh, tent." "But the popular kids are all at *that* table," she whined. Wow, was Sandra having a flashback from high school? I looked around the tent, though, and instantly understood her rationale … sort of. If you blinked three times and squinted, there was the lunchroom table with the most popular kids: the cheerleaders, Christy Turlington and Kate Moss; the cutest boy in school, Johnny Depp; the bad girl who broke all the rules, and how neat she was, Ellen Barkin; the girl everybody liked even though she played by her own rules, k.d. lang; and the good-looking gay guy who hung out with all the best-looking girls, but was never a threat, Herb Ritts.

Lost in my own fantasy for a moment, I scanned the room and squinted again and saw the Honor Society Kids, the power table: über-agent Jeff Berg; A-list director and California politico Rob Reiner; Columbia studio chief Mark Canton; and dominant producers Susan Harris, Tony Thomas, Wendy Finerman, Jon Peters, and Jerry Bruckheimer.

Looking to my right, I saw the older girls, the seniors, who had never made cheerleader, but were on the drill team. They were candy stripers, debate captains, members of the marching band or on the yearbook committee: Evelyn Ostin, wife of Warner Bros. Chairman Mo Ostin; Mrs. Sidney Poitier; Mrs. David (Linda) Foster; and Babs Davis (Mrs. Marvin).

I even saw the jock table: hockey great Wayne Gretzky and his wife, Janet; Mrs. Bruce Jenner; golf pro Gary McCord; Ivy League football star turned Superman Dean Cain; and a recognizable collection of personal trainers from Gold's Gym, World Gym, and the posh L.A. Sports Club.

Yes, Sandra had a point, even if she didn't recognize it. It was Hollywood High and you weren't anyone unless you were a part of a clique. I shuddered with the shock of amazed recognition. Were all these glamorous celebrities and fashion and Hollywood power players nothing more than the shallow, dim-witted super kids we had all known in twelfth grade? No, most of those A-list high school kids are probably stuck somewhere in dead-end jobs, living off memories of past glories. This crowd (with the possible exception of the jocks), from what I've learned over the years, were more likely the high school nerds, loners, social outcasts, the last to be picked for the baseball team and those who stayed home on prom night. These were the kids who used their discomfort and their different drummer to drive themselves to positions of fame, money, and envy. Was this overcompensation to the ultimate degree? Was I looking at "The Revenge of the Nerds"?

I shook myself from my reverie and yelled at Sandra, "Get over it, girl. Your best friend, Isaac, wants you at his table on his big night. So stop whining and sit down." Amazingly, Sandra did as I instructed. Maybe I should try that approach with more of these difficult celebrities. But she didn't stay put for long. Shortly, Sandra was dragging a chair up to the popular table, seating herself next to Christy Turlington. Christy, in turn, spent much of the party sitting on the lap of a very handsome boy model. k.d. wasn't interested, nor were Herb, Ellen, Johnny, or Kate. Well, Sandra was at the popular table, but no one seemed to care, or even notice.

Most people were content with their table, but others searched for me in hopes of upgrading. I was prepared. I once again had my therapist in tow, and this year I added my lawyer and my parish priest for further protection. Also seated at my table was the imposing presence of the late Chris Farley. I don't know if he could be a bouncer, but he looked like he could. Now if I could just keep Chris and my priest from drinking each other under the table. My walkie-talkie kept squawking for me: "Michael, can you read me? Michael, what is your position? Michael, come in." With that, my therapist grabbed the walkie-talkie and dropped it right into a pitcher of Evian water. I like his school of therapy—I'm glad he wasn't a Freudian.

We had done our customary food tasting weeks before, and the super chef and restaurateur Tommy Tang had won the contract. Tang is one of L.A.'s best-known celebrity chefs. He is a creator of the modern Thai and Pacific Rim cuisine movement, a best-selling cookbook author, and star of his own PBS cooking series. His entertainment industry hot spot on trendy Melrose Avenue in West Hollywood is famous for sushi, crispy duck, tiger prawns, and lovely Asian waitresses who are all transvestites. Isaac fell in love with Tang's signature crispy Long Island duck with honey ginger sauce. Tang also served grilled yams, steamed rice, wild mushroom salad, egg rolls, and mango and berry crème brulé for dessert. Plus, there were fortune cookies with off-beat fortunes such as, "You are pregnant and don't know it" and "Steve Tisch [a powerful movie producer] wants to make a deal with you."

The guests all seemed delighted with the food, though there was one prominent exception—k.d. lang. k.d. is an animal rights

Mizrahi, Fall Collection 1994.

activist, an antifur crusader, and an outspoken vegetarian. She was grieving at the sight of so much duck carnage. In retaliation, k.d. put aside the specially designed tuxedo that Isaac had created for her to wear that evening. (I imagine lang must have a closet full of tuxedos.) The fashion mavens, press, and Isaac all shrieked in unison as k.d. appeared on stage. The rest of us didn't have a clue what was going on or why tongues were wagging. When designer Richard Tyler and his table started to cheer and applaud, I innocently asked actress Jennifer Tilly, "Why is he so happy?" Jennifer clued me in, "Because k.d. is wearing a Richard Tyler tux."

Over the years, I looked forward to seeing Jennifer at our events. She always bought tons of things at our silent auctions and never asked for a free ticket. Jennifer once told me what a clothes freak she is. "I love clothes. I have closets full of vintage stuff. I have dresses from the 1940s, pants from the 1960s and famous clothes too. I keep everything from the movies I do and the clothes the other actors wear as well." Jennifer adored being photographed so she was a real asset. She could actually talk intelligently and passionately about AIDS to the press.

There were others who probably should have remained quiet on the subject of AIDS that night. We were interviewing the arriving stars and feeding the live footage onto the big movie screen inside the auditorium. When actress Donna Dixon told the camera, "I'm here tonight to support AIDS," her husband, Dan Aykroyd, quickly corrected her misstep, "She means she's here tonight to support the fight *against* AIDS." Donna still seemed unclear about the distinction and said, "Sure, that's why I'm here." When sneering, tousle-haired comedian and actor Denis Leary was asked why he was there, he replied, "Because my publicist told me to go and because there's free booze, food, and beautiful broads."

All in all, it was a cool crowd that night: singer Natalie Cole; movie director Barry Levinson; actresses Sofia Coppola, Linda Gray, and Raquel Welch; legendary model Lauren Hutton; the designer Valentino; and Warner Bros. Chief Terry Semel and wife Jane. I overheard a conversation between Ellen Barkin and Johnny Depp as they were sneaking some smokes (in this no-smoking town) out back by the porta-potties. They were discussing the outfits of the male models who were still in tights and oversized wings. "You wear those little jockstraps?" Ellen playfully asked Johnny. "I've got one on right now," he teased. "But those wings, they're strictly for the bedroom."

As the *Los Angeles Times* later reported, the only sore spot of the evening was "an insensitive, well, OK, just plain rude contingent who walked out early on k.d. lang's concert, prompting her to cut short her show in retaliation." Or maybe just in self-defense. Who was this "rude contingent"? Believe it or not, it was a group of celebrities (not all of them) eager to get to the after-gala party and upstairs to the VIP lounge.

Tickets to the after-dinner party were in greater demand than tickets for the event itself. The reason? It was free. The House of

We loved this model's Princess Leia hairdo.

Blues is a now famous nightspot on the Sunset Strip in West Hollywood, with an incongruous fake backwoods Tobacco Road exterior. The music club had contacted Isaac himself to offer their premises for the after-event party. It would be a place to unwind and compare notes, to see and be seen, and the party might even raise a bit more money. Isaac struck an agreement with the House of Blues to open the club, with no cover charge, only to those who had attended the event at the Chinese—models, volunteers, and people living with AIDS, those clients of the organizations for which we were raising money.

When I arrived at the House of Blues, about an hour after the dinner tent had emptied, I was surprised to see a line of people stretching around the corner. What appalled me, though, was to see that the House of Blues was charging a $10 cover to get in. When I talked to the doorman, he knew nothing of Isaac's agreement with the club, though he did understand this was the Mizrahi party. As I headed to the back of the line, I was intercepted by Linda and Jerry Bruckheimer, who whisked me into the club with them. The club was padded with people I'd never seen before. I followed the Bruckheimers, upstairs to the secure VIP room. I swear it was New York's notorious Studio 54 risen again. There was more snow in the VIP lounge than we'd had at the Chinese.

The award for the most disgusting behavior of the evening, though, must go to actor Mickey Rourke, the poor man's Bruce Willis. Isaac arrived at the House of Blues, making a flamboyant entrance. As Isaac struggled through the throngs of people, he accidentally bumped into Mickey Rourke, which prompted Rourke to call our honoree a "fag." All within hearing distance were stunned. Isaac smiled daggers at Rourke and calmly asked, "Beat up any women lately?", then walked away. Most knew that Mickey's career and reputation were on the skids after several terrible movies and his well-publicized beatings of model Carrie Otis. When last I heard anything about Rourke, he was taking up professional boxing.

Isaac never made it upstairs to the VIP lounge. It's just as well he didn't stay long at the House of Blues. He'd had his evening already, and this wasn't part of it. He was exhausted and eager to relax with his boyfriend Doug Keeve. Isaac happily headed across the street to the Chateau Marmont, where the two New Yorkers celebrated their brief reign in Hollywood with room service and a warm bath. Isaac's buddy Sandra had summed it up simply, "This was the best night in Hollywood ever." As I waited earlier at the Chinese Theater for my car to be brought by the valets, I overheard another waiting guest's summary of the evening: "It was the Oscars of tall chicks. They can say it's for AIDS and I hope they raise a lot of money. But it was a spectacle and that's what people were here for." As for Isaac, he simply wondered in amazed delight, "How can I ever top this?" It'll be a tough act to follow, but Isaac is young and, knowing his wacky creativity, his seductive charm, and his boundless zeal, I wouldn't bet against him.

A year after our Mizrahi event, I saw Isaac again when he was in Los Angeles for the theatrical premiere of the documentary *Unzipped*. The original twenty-minute film that we had screened at our event had been financed by Haschette-Filipacci Inc., the publisher of *Elle* magazine and other periodicals, who had also provided much of the corporate underwriting for the Mizrahi gala. Haschette had been eager to premiere *Unzipped* in Hollywood in hope of finding a distributor for the film among the industry heavyweights in attendance that night. To the delight of Hachette, the audience reaction to the film had been so wildly positive that Hachette decided to invest more money so that Douglas Keeve could turn his footage into an eighty-

Actor-cum-boxer Mickey Rourke would call our guest of honor a "fag" at the House of Blues after-party.

minute feature film. *Unzipped* would later win the Audience Award at the Sundance Film Festival, win kudos at Cannes, and do unusually well for a documentary during its theatrical release. It was definitely the best reviewed of the fashion-film trilogy released by Miramax—the other two being *À la Mode* (the original French title is *Fausto*) and Robert Altman's all-star *Prêt-à-Porter*. The feature-length *Unzipped* had its L.A. premiere in Westwood. Later, I saw Isaac at the after-screening party held at Barneys New York in Beverly Hills. Isaac pulled me close, kissed me on the cheek, and whispered into my ear that "none of this would have happened" without our event the previous year. He was in heaven.

9

Gianfranco Ferré

—They Are Not Long,
The Days of Wine and Roses

"If Hollywood breeding could be compared to **royalty**, then she would certainly be our Crown Princess."

—Liza Minnelli, on how she'd like to be introduced

In the audience at the Chinese Theater on the night of the Isaac Mizrahi show were representatives from three of the world's major fashion houses—Valentino, Donna Karan, and Gianfranco Ferré. Back in my home office were more than a dozen press packets and videotapes from other world-class designers, including Prada, Dolce & Gabana, Chanel, Armani, Gucci, Tommy Hilfiger, and Ralph Lauren. All were seeking meetings with me to discuss becoming the honorees for 1995 and for the subsequent years into the next millennium. I had made a personal decision by that time that I would serve as chairman for just two more events, 1995 and 1996, though I would continue to volunteer my services in securing future honorees. By the time Isaac's first model arrived on the runway, the annual event's steering committee and I had already given the nod to Gianfranco Ferré. Not only had Ferré been designing his own women's prêt-à-porter and couture collections and a men's collection, but since 1989, he had also been designing for the House of Christian Dior. Dior is to French couture what Levi-Strauss is to American fashion; it is hard to

remember a time when it didn't exist. Just as one can go almost anywhere in the world and the term *blue jeans* will be understood, Dior is a name also known worldwide, even by people who know no other name associated with high fashion.

As the guests at the Mizrahi dinner were about to be entertained by singer k.d. lang, powerful movie producer Steve Tisch (soon to be a Best Picture Oscar winner for *Forrest Gump*) announced to the assembled guests that Gianfranco Ferré would be our honored designer in 1995. The audience enthusiastically applauded its approval and within minutes, I was approached by people who wanted to make reservations a year in advance. Sure, some wanted to make sure they'd have first pick at the best seats for our next show, but they were also letting us know they liked our choice and felt we were doing a great job.

The personal representative for Ferré in the audience that night was Lynne Koester, the famous cover girl and runway model. At 6'2", with jet black hair and dark coffee eyes, Lynne was stunningly beautiful, even as she neared 40 years of age. To this day, she continues to be a house model for Ferré and Dior as well as Mr. Ferré's inspirational muse and close friend. Lynne had been a favorite of European designers for years and was well known in this country for her Herb Ritts photos in *Vogue, Vanity Fair, Bazaar*, and *Italian Vogue*. Interestingly, Lynne had also been used as a model of men's clothes by Thierry Mugler and had appeared as a man in a book of Herb Ritts photographs. Lynne, who has an Italian husband and two small sons, had semiretired to Montecito, California, a beach community about five miles outside Santa Barbara. Lynne also had a home on Lake Como in Italy and an apartment in Milan, but she was now accepting only modeling work that particularly interested her or manifested loyalty to old friends such as Thierry Mugler and Gianfranco Ferré.

Lynne and I hit it off amazingly well from our first meeting at the Century Plaza Hotel. Very quickly, I sensed that we would become friends. I would later invite her to join our event's small steering committee. I soon learned that her dedication to finding a cure

Handsome Patrick Dempsey modeled for his first time in the Gianfranco Ferré show. Here he is backstage.

Jaye Davidson and model Carol
Alt backstage.

for AIDS and to seeking compassionate care
and meaningful assistance for those living
with HIV went deep and was part of who she
was as a human being. She wasn't just another
celebrity with a cause of the moment, but a
sister who a few years earlier had lost a
beloved brother and his life partner to AIDS.

I explained to Lynne that the steering
committee hoped that she and Mr. Ferré
would seriously consider returning the event
to the Los Angeles Ballroom of the Century
Plaza. I told her the history of Calvin Klein's
desire to make a sensational impression, which
had moved our event to the Hollywood Bowl,
followed by Isaac Mizrahi's desire to compete
with Klein, which had moved the event the
following year to the Chinese Theater. These
had certainly been exciting shows and stunning venues, but the sites had drastically esca-
lated production costs, plus greater costs for
the rentals, food, lighting and sound equip-
ment, transportation, stagehands, and on and
on. With the need for AIDS services on the

Mr. Ferré and our favorite,
Leonardo DiCaprio—a really
nice guy.

Jennifer Flavin, Mr. Ferré, and model/limo joyrider Carol Alt.

Models Janice Dickenson, Paula Barbieri, and Veronica Webb. We loved Janice's new chest—compliments of Sly Stallone.

rise, the steering committee felt that by returning the event to the Century Plaza, we could once again rein in our production costs and return more money for services and HIV research.

Lynne totally understood and supported our rationale, but also made it clear that it would be Mr. Ferré who would have to make that decision. His niece Rita Airaghi would be visiting Los Angeles in the early winter months of 1995, and she would be the liaison

between Mr. Ferré and Lynne. Lynne and I would be working together here in California on an almost daily basis. Lynne intuitively understood the Ferré philosophy, knew him and his preferences intimately, spoke fluent Italian, and could get any questions answered with just a telephone call. Amen. The situation was wonderful and she was a joy to work with. It was a match made by our sometimes capricious guardian angels.

On February 1, 1995, as the Ferré staff was literally in the air on their way to Los Angeles from Milan for our first official meeting, Brandon Stephen Scott MacNeal, my beloved and best friend for 15 years, quietly slipped into a coma and died after an intense three-week battle with AIDS. Brandon wasn't too tall, 5' 10", with blond hair, and blue eyes that caught you by surprise. They were a color I'd never seen before, a heavenly shade I once tried to duplicate at a paint store that guaranteed they could match any color—but they couldn't match his blue eyes. Brandon was smart, sharp-tongued, a talented artist and a great baseball player. I had the most fun with him that I've ever had in my life, starting with our midnight skinny dip in the Pacific Ocean on the evening we met. Brandon loved Dalmatians, tuberoses, Christmas, babies, the colors blue and yellow, and, for some strange reason, me. He was the best friend I've ever had.

I was immobilized, numb, almost dead myself—less than empty. I wanted to lie down for six months. Brandon died at 6:33 P.M. The Ferré people were due in Los Angeles in a matter of hours, and I was supposed to meet with them the following morning. I couldn't cancel my meeting, because they had come so far. With an ache in my stomach, a weight on my chest, and tears in my eyes, all I could do was put one foot in front of the other. I called Lynne to tell her what had happened. I said I would be at the Century Plaza in the morning. I didn't sleep that night. I arrived at the hotel an hour early, with Lynne already waiting in the lobby. We had coffee and we cried. Then Rita Airaghi arrived. This handsome, professional, middle-aged woman, impeccably dressed in Christian Dior, made her way across the travertine lobby to where we were

Supermodel and Ferré
muse Lynne Koester
accompanies the great
designer.

Carol Alt interviews Mr. Ferré for
Entertainment Tonight.

had whispered into my ear so Lynne could translate it for me: "You have loved and have been loved. How lucky you have been in your young life and your friend in his. God loves you very much."

The following day, I received the largest bouquet of Casablanca lilies I had ever seen, with a card that read: "God bless you, Michael and Brandon. Gianfranco Ferré and Staff." Later that afternoon, I took half the lilies, made a dozen small bouquets, and dropped them off at the AIDS ward of County Hospital. In a sad contrast, not one individual with whom I had been working alongside at the charities we were raising money for thought to even call or send a note. Sometimes these charities can become so big that they forget what they are doing, or even why.

Considering the circumstances, my meetings with the Ferré staff on that second day of February were surprisingly productive. They were understanding when at times, I had to temporarily excuse myself. Lynne and I showed Rita the ballroom and discussed our reasons for wanting to bring back the event to

seated. I stood up, smiled, and offered my hand as Lynne made the introductions. Rita took my hand and held it, pulled me close to her and whispered into my ear something in Italian. Lynne had obviously told Rita what had happened. Rita later told Lynne what she

Kelly LeBrock and two male
models.

O. J. Simpson's ex-girlfriend,
Paula Barbieri.

Faxing With Gianfranco Ferré, June 1998

• **Mr. Ferré, why did you get involved with our AIDS fashion event?** Because it seemed to me to be a marvelous opportunity for making a contribution to the most important and demanding challenge of our time, a challenge in the face of which nobody can turn away. Among other things, the Los Angeles event allowed me to make a contribution to the fight against AIDS through my work, showing people what I do and that in which I most believe, my interpretations of life. • **Has AIDS affected you personally?** As is the case for everybody, I believe, AIDS has robbed me of some very dear friends whose affection, advice, and trust I now miss.

• **What, for you, was the most memorable moment of the 1995 Gianfranco Ferré AIDS Benefit?** More than a moment, it was a sensation that has stuck in my memory with particular force. It was the dedication and efficiency with which each volunteer worked, even those dealing with the humblest tasks. And the smiles on their lips even after hours and hours of toil. • **Is AIDS still an important issue in your life?** It is a fact of our times that cannot be ignored, nor should it be demonized, but which cannot be allowed to overwhelm us. It is an illness over which man is, however, gaining some advantage, even if the final step still has to be made. • **Is any color your favorite?** Red, for passion, energy, sensuality, strength, and temperament. Red is life. • **Do you have a favorite film or director?** I am very fond of Visconti. He is refined, an aesthete, decadent to the right extent. I love almost all of his films, from *Senso* [released in cut version as *Summer Hurricane* in the United States] to *Ludwig* to *Il Gattopardo* [*The Leopard*] to *Death in Venice*. • **Who is your favorite artist?** I think Pablo Picasso above all. His art expresses all the energy and tension of our age. • **Is there a period in history with which you have an affinity?** I love the Renaissance, an age of great men and women. However, it was also the age of the Sun King and Maria Theresa of Austria. The age of grandeur and that of reason. • **If you could sit down and have a conversation with any**

Mr. Ferré.

famous person, dead or alive, who would that person be? I would have liked to have met Gandhi. And also Picasso and Caterina d' Medici. Among my contemporaries, possibly Gorbachev. • **Which celebrities have you most enjoyed dressing?** It is rare that I do something I don't like and about which I'm not convinced. I have enjoyed dressing almost all the celebrities who have asked me, from the Princess of Kent to Oprah Winfrey to Whitney Houston, Isabelle Adjani, and Jessye Norman. • **Is there any celebrity you refuse to work with?** No. However, working with any celebrity means for me getting to know the real person. If this does not happen, then I prefer to give up. • **If you were not a designer, what do you think you would like to do for a living?** When I was little, I wanted to be a pharmacist as I was enchanted by the vials and alembics which were found in the pharmacies of that time. According to family tradition, I should have been an engineer. I studied architecture, then I became a fashion designer. I don't think I would want to do anything else. • **Are there other designers whose work you like?** I consider the work of Christian Dior, Coco Chanel, and Cristobal Balenciaga to be outstanding. Among today's designers, I admire Lagerfeld, Armani, and Yamamoto. • **What qualities do you look for when selecting a model?** Basically, the most important quality is that which was once called *comportment*. This means the ability to move on the catwalk and inside the dress in order to interpret it and capture its spirit. • **What qualities do think are sexy in a man and in a woman?** I consider the way a man moves, the tone of his voice, the shape of his hands to be sexy. In a woman, the way she moves, her expressions, her eyes, the way she smiles. • **What is the most commonly made fashion mistake?** Many people still lack self-confidence in deciding what to wear. Others do not look in the mirror after having decided what to wear. • **What about yourself would most surprise people who don't know you well?** Many people find it difficult to imagine that behind my seriousness and inflexibility, there is a considerable amount of passion. • **What brings you passion in your life?** Life itself, friendships, love, and work … the pleasure of self expression through my work.

Virginia Madsen and Antonio Sabato Jr. Antonio volunteered as a model.

Fran Drescher and Mr. Ferré backstage. We had a hard time convincing Mr. Ferré that Fran was a celebrity. He had never heard of her.

its birthplace at the Century Plaza. Rita had no problems with that and we moved forward in our planning. The ballroom was to be transformed into an Italian garden. There would be a 25-foot by 25-foot scrim onto which the fashions on the runway would be rear projected in real time with the show. Mr. Ferré's production designer would create blue-prints of the ballroom and design the set and runway. The collections to be shown would be Ferré's Fall 1995 men's and women's collections. At about 5:30 in the evening, as our meetings were winding down, I excused myself, explaining that I had Brandon's family, the hospital, and funeral plans to attend to. I was glad we'd accomplished so much. At such times, it can help to stay busy. And working with such decent people to make plans for creating something beautiful was also a comfort. As Gianfranco Ferré later wrote in our program for his show: "Beauty, elegance, and clarity instill life with harmony, imprint on the mind the vibrancy of a person or moment. They are the expression of deep human need."

In a fashion world pulled this way and that each year by the latest rummage through the fashion decades for some style to appropriate and dust off, as the newest postmodern doohickeys are presented on the runways with the hippest shock, titillation, or dark irony, Gianfranco Ferré stands guard and avant garde as the conservator of classic well-designed and well-made chic. He believes that one "can upset tradition only if we maintain the charm of tradition intact." Mr. Ferré wrote in our program that "Fashion is fickle, fleeting, thus has a profound need for professional integrity. Not for signatures without substance, for appearance devoid of meaning, for clamor over nothing. But for effective work, true invention, pinpoint solidity."

Of all the designers I worked with over the decade, Gianfranco Ferré is the only one who I always, automatically and compulsively, refer to with the title "mister." It was and still is always "Mr. Ferré," which was so natural that I didn't even notice I was using that title until friends told me. Mr. Ferré didn't demand or even suggest that formality; he just naturally earns it with his seriousness of purpose, the ethical dimension that permeates his work and life, and the old-world class with which he carries himself and treats others. On the other hand, at times he can seem as informal and lovable as a teddy bear.

Gianfranco Ferré graduated in 1969 with a degree in architecture from the Polytechnic Institute of Milan. At the age of 25, he turned his energies and interests to fashion. A period

Mr. Ferré surrounded by beauty.

living in the Far East further developed his taste for essential forms. In 1974, he met Franco Mattioli and began designing for his Baila label. The Bologna entrepreneur became his business partner, and together they founded the Gianfranco Ferré label in 1978, the same year Mr. Ferré presented his first prêt-à-porter collection. Mr. Ferré introduced a men's collection in 1982, a couture collection in 1986, and a fur collection in 1989. In May of 1989, Gianfranco Ferré was nominated Artistic Director of the House of Christian Dior for the Haute Couture, Prêt-à-Porter Feminin, Haute Fourrure, and Prêt-à-Porter Fourrure lines.

As a trained architect, Mr. Ferré is adamant that one must understand the structure of fashion before adding ornamentation. He says that one must create from the basement and design logically. You must know "why you want it, in which way you will do it, and in which way to wear it" and not be overtaken by the dream. It was written about Ferré in 1982 at the Massachusetts Institute of Technology's first fashion exhibition that "he conceives and assembles a garment as a three-dimensional entity, not as a facade for frontal display. As an architect considers how a pediment will cast a shadow over a facade, Ferré considers the defining properties of light. He uses a stiff oblong collar to throw a dramatic shadow on the front of a jacket. He uses a round, white fanlike collar to frame and light the face. His forms appear to be chiseled, not just cut. He relies on forms that are deliberately distinguished from the organic curves of the human anatomy." Once more, from our Ferré commemorative program, he sums up his approach to fashion: "I am a fashion designer, I create clothes, give shape to

Jennifer Tilly–looking delicious.

Mr. Ferré's Fall Men's Collection
1995.

Mr. Ferré and Liza. Notice I don't
show her feet.

dreams, satisfy a desire for beauty. But since I
have studied architecture, I am aware of what
designing entails on a concrete level, am able
to elaborate a method, transform an idea into
volumes and lines. Yes, creativity is inspiration. Nevertheless, for me it also involves
impulses of ingenuity, a capacity for applica-
tion and precision … So that Form becomes
magnificent Substance."

In a rare personal and candid interview, I
asked Mr. Ferré about his interests and why
he gives so much of himself, his time, and his
money to help people living with HIV in a
community so far away from the runways of
Paris and Milan.

The Gianfranco Ferré gala was scheduled
for May 10, 1995. This date is particularly
memorable to me because it fell three days
after Mother's Day and this arbitrary coincidence would create one of the toughest chal-
lenges I faced in nine years of producing this
event. In keeping with the Ferré Italian garden motif, the blueprints for the ballroom
included three floor-to-ceiling forty-foot-wide
walls, each wall to be covered in live pink
roses, 175,000 roses on each wall, more than
half a million pink roses in all! The walls
would have to be constructed outside the ballroom, and the roses would all need to be
attached no more than 24 hours before the
event so they would be fresh and fragrant. We
had two big problems. One became apparent
as I checked with California rose growers and
discovered that their entire crop was already
spoken for by wholesalers preparing for the
Mother's Day weekend. Mother's Day each
year marked the biggest occasion for flower
sales in the United States—by a long shot. I
could only reserve a paltry 10,000 roses in all
of California. My other dilemma was who
would build the walls, where, and how would
we transport them covered with roses, I
hoped, to the ballroom?

This was Hollywood. Hadn't we just
made it snow in the Chinese Theater? I called
Carol Ward, a friend of mine and a set
designer for the movies, and she agreed to
coordinate the construction and transport of
the walls. The walls would be built and decorated in a high school's football stadium and
would then be transferred on flatbed trucks to

Fran Drescher in her pink
evening gown—trust me.

the hotel on the day of the event. The roses,
well, that was another story. We went on a
worldwide search using the still-fledgling
capabilities of the Internet. Finally, we located
a grower in Argentina—where fortunately,
they do not celebrate Mother's Day—who
could fill our need for pink roses. A big plus
was that his price for 525,000 roses was far
less than the bid for 10,000 roses that we had
received from our local grower. The roses
would be shipped by airfreight and would
arrive in Los Angeles on Monday, May 8.

Now, the tension of "Can we get the
roses?" was replaced by the tension of "Will
we have enough time to assemble the rose-
covered walls?" Carol kept assuring me that
we could, that "this ain't no Rose Parade,"
referring to the annual rite of the New Year
when thousands of volunteers spend days glu-
ing billions of single flower petals to huge
floats. In comparison with that massive annual
undertaking, all we had to do was attach half
a million whole flowers to three walls—a
piece of cake compared to a Rose Parade float,
at least according to Carol. Still, each rose
would have to be cut, de-thorned, stripped of
its leaves, and then placed into a small plastic
vial of water to keep it fresh. Then the vials
would need to be attached to the walls. The
project was so complex, not to mention odd

"Mama" Michelle Phillips in her white tuxedo suit looked gorgeous.

and colorful, that it drew attention in the *Los Angeles Times*, which ran a story about us under a headline that read, "Everything's Coming Up Roses for Local AIDS Charities." After the article ran in the *Times*, I was besieged with offers from people wanting to volunteer their time and labor to help make this event happen. Maybe this was going to be more like the Rose Parade after all—only in May. Along with staff, we used dozens of volunteers around the clock. They were people with HIV and AIDS, straight guys with their cute girlfriends, retired people, neighbors of the high school, and even a few gang members who had been ordered by the courts to do community service in lieu of receiving fines or jail time. It was a delightful conglomeration, all working together with purpose and palpable joy. On the night of the show, all these volunteers were invited to enjoy standing room at the rear of the ballroom to share in the glorious fruits of their donated labor.

The ballroom tables were draped in an embellished white-on-white linen fabric, with chair covers to match. The tablecloths bunched at the floor and the chairs were tied with large bows in the back. The fabric was designed and donated by an Italian manufacturer (friends of Mr. Ferré) and was cut, sewn, and pressed by our many volunteers in Los

Angeles's garment district. Each place setting included white china, sterling silverware, cut crystal wine and water goblets, and even a crystal knife rest. The centerpieces were round bouquets of pink, red, and white roses in crystal bowls. Candlelight from votive candles flickered through cut crystal, and each table was pin-spotted with a soft pink gel. It was an Italian garden, serene, fragrant, and enchanting.

Sandwiched as it was between the hair-raising and hair-losing experiences of working with Klein, Mizrahi, and Oldham, all slightly mad geniuses and egomanical American designers, it was vividly apparent in contrast how relatively effortless the Gianfranco Ferré event was to produce. Mr. Ferré had a gentle Italian spirit. He was generous, and his word was more binding than a written contract. His sense of ethics and fairness was startling. When the bills began to roll in for the roses and staff to build and assemble the walls, Mr. Ferré quickly ordered that those bills be paid for out of his own pocket. It reminded me of working with Gianni Versace and his insistence that he pay for any of the extravagant expenses incurred to present his image in the precise way he desired. "Those Italians," I thought to myself, "you just got to love 'em." But Mr. Ferré's sense of propriety took him even further than just paying the expenses for the three walls. Afraid that such extravagance for a half million roses might appear unseemly or might overshadow our purpose of raising money to help people living with HIV, Mr. Ferré made a contribution of an equal amount to AIDS services and research. I'd never seen such a complex awareness of levels of perception mixed with an old-style gentleman's sense of rightness. Such class took my breath away. In the end, the Ferré event would be our most successful ever, giving to the charity nearly 90 percent of every dollar raised.

The casting of models for the show began in April. Mr. Ferré preferred a touch of Hollywood, mixed with an assortment of international models, and flavored with a light twist of controversy. One of our Hollywood contingent was actor Antonio Sabato Jr., whose former wife is model Tulley Jensen. Sabato would shortly appear on a huge Times Square billboard in Calvin Klein briefs as the

The "Flight Jacket" was back in 1995.

Jackie Collins and Sandy Gallin at
the Ferré event.

new CK undie-boy. When that contract ended in 1998, Sabato became the spokesman for Durex condoms, though that position did not include a Times Square billboard. Before all this corporate exploitation of the midarea of Antonio's anatomy, however, Mr. Ferré had seen the young actor and asked him to model in his show, fully clothed—first in a suit and overcoat and then in black velvet trousers and a white shirt with a jacket draped over his shoulder.

Another actor tapped by Mr. Ferré to model in his show was the talented Patrick Dempsey, whose boyish Irish-American good looks have kept him steadily employed in movies and TV since he stumbled into an acting career through his early success as a world-class juggler. He has played many quirky and charming young men, often irresistible to older women as in *Loverboy* and *In the Mood*. Into the mix, he has thrown a tough guy dramatic portrayal in *Mobsters* and a convincing portrayal of the young John Kennedy in the TV miniseries *JFK: Reckless Youth*. That evening, Dempsey looked like a hunky Shirley Temple, with golden curls that fell against his shoulders and framed his boy-next-door face as he modeled Ferré overcoats and bulky oversized sweaters.

Looking slightly out of place among the other young male actors was the more androgynous Jaye Davidson. Davidson's electrifying film debut as the English hairdresser Dil in *The Crying Game* spawned a highly successful advertising campaign for the movie, which pleaded with filmgoers not to reveal the secret of his character's gender to those who hadn't yet seen the film. Although this was far from a new advertising gimmick in Hollywood—Hitchcock had successfully used it to promote *Psycho* three decades earlier—it

helped turn the low-budget *Crying Game* into a big hit. As Jaye walked the runway that night, he playfully twirled a red and black cape over his head. The cape knocked off one of his earrings, which was quickly grabbed off the catwalk by a starstruck fan. As the fan showed the earring to his buddies, Jaye committed the unpardonable sin for a runway model and broke out of his model persona and demanded that his earring be returned. The fan petulantly threw the earring at him, which hit Jaye in the chest. This unscripted scene was causing a backup on the runway, and the show's producer cut the lights into a

Volunteers Dana Estrada and
Margaret Foutz in front of one of
our rose walls.

One of the massive Ferré rose walls and table settings. There were 175,000 pink roses in each wall.

Mr. Ferré with Liza. After her recent hip-replacement surgery, she needed a (rhinestone-covered) cane.

full blackout. When the lights came back on, Jaye was gone, not to be seen again until the finale. The earring was still on the runway.

Fran Drescher, the TV star of the hit sit-com *The Nanny*, had contacted me weeks before the show through her publicist. She offered her services if Mr. Ferré would like to use her in the show. I faxed her offer to Italy and received a fax back that gave an unequiv-ocal, "Who?" No one at Ferré in Italy or Dior in France had ever heard of Fran. I explained

who she was and informed them that with her long shapely legs, svelte curvaceous body, and thick black hair cascading around her lovely face, Fran would look great in a Ferré any-thing. I didn't mention that as a comedienne, she's hailed by some as the new Lucille Ball because of the startling contrast between her movie queen looks and the goose-with-a-head-cold cacophony of nasal sounds she makes through her thick Queens accent. Fran not only starred in *The Nanny*, but produced it

One of Mr. Ferré's couture ball gowns—black velvet and matching tulle.

Mr. Ferré's 1995 Fall Collection.

with her then-husband of two decades, Peter Marc Jacobson, and she also wrote scripts for it. The word from Italy was to hold off any commitment until Mr. Ferré had a chance to meet her. We needed celebrities to make introductions and presentations at the ceremonial part of the evening. Therefore, being a big fan of Fran's TV and movie work, I invited her to introduce another speaker and me. She quickly accepted the invitation. Now I had to figure out a way to have the Ferré people dress her for the evening.

When Mr. Ferré finally arrived in Los Angeles and met Fran, he agreed to have her

in the show, but still balked at using her as a model in the fashion show. He still wondered, "Who is this woman?" Fran looked sensationally sexy in her floor-length pink satin Ferré evening gown, with a four-foot train stretching out behind her caboose. With her Rita Hayworth hairdo, Fran looked like a film goddess from the late 1940s. Still, even some Hollywood icons weren't recognizing Fran. One Oscar-nominee with her prints in cement at the Chinese asked me the same question Mr. Ferré had asked, "Who is this woman?" I explained, "You know, *The Nanny*." "Oh, she's a nanny. How nice," said the still confused screen legend. I just let it ride, figuring that when Fran was introduced later, the story would sort itself out. The dress that the Beverly Hills Ferré Boutique on Rodeo Drive had lent Fran to wear for the evening ended up being given to her because the train had been stepped on by so many people that the dress could never be sold. It turned out to be good publicity for Ferré, as Fran would be widely photographed wearing it a few days later at the Cannes Film Festival. The Italian press would later dub the dress the "Traveling Chinese Theater" because it had so many stars' footprints on it.

The controversial model in our show was the beautiful model and actress Paula Barbieri, who had become famous as the ex-girlfriend of O. J. Simpson. During the notorious O. J. trial, capturing the world's prurient attention at that time, the prosecution was suggesting that it was Paula breaking off her relationship with Simpson that had emotionally pushed him over the edge into a murderous rage.

Paula called us to ask if she could model in the show. My first reaction was "Sure, why not?" She was gorgeous, famous, and sweet on the phone. Some thought it would be a bad idea. I faxed Paula's photo to the Ferré camp in Milan, with an explanation of the controversy. The reply was quick. Mr. Ferré had not heard of Paula either, but as long as she hadn't murdered anyone herself, he was willing to meet her.

Because of the ongoing O. J. trial and its wall-to-wall exploitation by the media, we did have legitimate concerns that using Paula in the show would distort the press coverage by making her appearance the whole story. If we did use her, it would have to be a closely guarded secret before the event. After meeting with Paula, we all, including Mr. Ferré, fell in love with the woman we had known only from the tabloids. She was going to be in the show, but in all pre-show publicity, she would be known simply as "Pauline." On the night of the show, there were more than 150

Actress Kelly LeBrock backstage before the Gianfranco Ferré show. She volunteered to help us out on two shows.

Ferré's Fall Collection enabled us to raise more than $650,000!

Mr. Ferré's 1995 Fall Collection.

photographers gathered outside the ballroom, lining the runway. With Paula's makeup and hairdo done differently, she was basically unrecognized by the paparazzi—just another attractive model donating her services to help a worthy cause. One major exception was the crew for the *National Enquirer* who had been tailing Paula, night and day, for months. Because they had followed her from her home to the hotel, they knew exactly who she was, though they sure weren't going to tell that to their competition. The story that later appeared in the *Enquirer* unfortunately didn't even mention the AIDS fund-raiser, but ran under a typically misleading *Enquirer* headline, "O. J.'s Girlfriend Runs-Away."

Our star supermodel for the evening was Beverly Peele, a tall African American beauty who was nearing the end of an illustrious career. She had graced the cover of every fashion magazine on the planet. Accompanying Beverly down the runway that evening was her baby girl, who was adorned in that earliest and most classic of fashion looks, her birthday suit.

Another famous model of the 1980s had donated her modeling services as a favor to Lynne Koester. Or so we thought until she showed up backstage with a film crew from the *Entertainment Tonight* TV show. It turned out that *E.T.* was paying this model handsomely as a correspondent covering our celebrity-filled soireé. Despite this, we were picking up her four-day hotel bill at the Peninsula, an expensive and posh little Beverly Hills hotel. About a week after the event, you can imagine my surprise and outrage when a limousine bill for this model arrived at my office. It was a bill of nearly $2,000 for her four-day, 24-hour-a-day limousine service. This model had somehow known which limousine service we had a good working relationship with. They donated service to us (for instance, picking up Mr. Ferré at the airport), and we gave them publicity or a few tickets in exchange. That is why I couldn't just toss the bill in the trashcan. I sent the bill to the model's manager and she returned it. I sent it to *E.T.* and they returned it. Finally, as a favor to us, the bill was covered by the one corpora-

tion who had supported us since the very first show, the Robinson-May Department Stores.

There was one famous model, a household name, who had such an impressive résumé and reputation that, sight unseen, she was immediately approved by Mr. Ferré. On show day, this fabulously famous runway model arrived in the ballroom adjacent to the grand Los Angeles Ballroom. We had once again transformed this secondary ballroom into a massive dressing room and makeup and hair salon. To the surprise of Mr. Ferré and everyone else, our famous model was … well, huge. She was, in fact, too big to fit into any of the clothes that had been prepared for the show. Not wanting to hurt her feelings or send her into an anorexic tailspin, Mr. Ferré found a men's robe, then stripped her naked and dressed her in that. That was our famous model's only appearance in the show. It was a bit nerve-racking for everyone, but was clearly the right thing to do. By the Todd Oldham show a year later, this lovely woman had slimmed down again and looked great in a see-through Oldham gown.

Other famous models in the Ferré show included Jennifer Flavin (who a few years later would receive worldwide tabloid attention when Sophia Rose, her daughter with now-husband Sylvester Stallone, was born with a dangerous, and since surgically corrected, heart defect); Janice Dickenson; Rachel Hunter; Irena, a Siberian beauty who would skyrocket to supermodel status by 1997; and actress Kelly LeBrock. One of our fair-maiden models for the evening got caught red-handed as she left the ballroom that evening wearing a $10,000 Ferré beaded gown. She claimed it was compensation for her services. The following day, the Ferré people pleaded with our naughty hottie to please return the gown, but with no success. The plot, however, thickens. It appears that our bad girl, who had recently married a mutlimillionaire many years her senior, had evidently not endeared herself to her husband's longtime valet. One might even say that this valet despised the woman he perceived as a gold-digging interloper. When our kleptomaniacal beauty checked herself into the hospital for a much-publicized tit and ass lift, the trusty valet slipped into her closet, removed the Ferré gown, and messengered it back to the Ferré production staff. The newly lifted shoplifter was later divorced. Despite the personal excesses and wild escapades of this notorious model, and to the surprise of many, she keeps on going like the Energizer Bunny in her two-decade modeling career. The whole incident does suggest a play on the title of a classic John Ford movie that starred our friend Roddy McDowall, *How Green (with Envy) Was My Valet.*

Oprah Winfrey was set to present Mr. Ferré with his official proclamation from the city of Los Angeles and his Crystal Apple Award. Ferré had dressed Oprah in her famous emerald green gown with a train for the 1994 Academy Awards, and they had become fast friends. Oprah, however, had to bow out because of scheduling conflicts. I was pleasantly surprised to receive a handwritten note on her personal stationery along with a large five-figure check for the charity. She asked that I read her note to the guests on the night of the show. Oprah's note read: "Dear Michael, Unfortunately, due to scheduling conflicts and the demands of my television show, I will be unable to be there to present Mr. Ferré with his award. Please accept this donation. I wish you good luck and send my love to all involved. Would you please read my note to your guests so they know that I feel bad that I am unable to join them and Mr. Ferré. Oprah Winfrey."

With Oprah unable to be in Los Angeles for the show, we had to scurry to find a big star to present Mr. Ferré's award. Once again, I called upon the infinitely helpful friend of our event, manager and film producer Barry Krost. Among the stars whom Barry represented was Liza Minnelli, and Barry asked Liza if she would be willing. Liza had a long history of working hard to help raise money for AIDS causes. According to Barry, Liza would travel around the country to places where other stars would not think of going for a charity event—cities in Texas, Ohio, Florida, Colorado, and elsewhere that would normally go begging for any celebrity to help promote their events or to help raise awareness. Also, Liza's first husband, Australian singer and songwriter Peter Allen, had died of

AIDS in 1992. Liza and Mr. Ferré had been friends for some time, as had Liza's stepmother Denise Hale, a San Francisco socialite who had once been married to Liza's father, Vincente Minnelli, the legendary director of MGM musicals. Denise Hale was now married to a wealthy, elderly founder of the huge retail conglomerate Carter, Hawley, Hale, which owned the California-based Broadway department stores and which had purchased Neiman-Marcus in the 1980s. *Women's Wear Daily* reported that when Mr. Ferré created an original dress for Denise Hale, the buttons weren't made with rhinestones but were covered with real diamonds. Whenever Gianfranco Ferré was in San Francisco he would either stay with the Hales or at the home of the queen of the romance novel, Danielle Steel.

As for getting a big star for our show, who else might we find who had won an Oscar, an Emmy, a Golden Globe and three Tony Awards? Barry assured us that Liza would be happy to help us out. Liza was living in Los Angeles in 1995, recovering from hip replacement surgery. She requested that we find her a rhinestone-covered cane to match her purple-beaded Ferré outfit for the evening. Unlike the other designers we had worked with over the years, Mr. Ferré had a steadfast rule against giving celebrities free clothes. It was his feeling that if they were making all that money, they could pay for their own clothes (which, interestingly enough, are also tax-deductible business expenses). Liza was an exception because her stepmom was one of Mr. Ferré's best clients. On the afternoon of the Ferré show, I knew that Liza Minnelli was in the hotel for rehearsals, but I had not met her or even seen her. I was out front overseeing the setup of the ballroom when my walkie-talkie asked that I report to the green room, which is the large room where celebrities hang out while waiting for their time to appear onstage. What I didn't know until a few minutes later is that our green room had been commandeered as a private dressing room.

I knocked on the door of the green room and a familiar voice said, "Come in." I walked in on a bizarro Hollywood moment that shall forever be branded on my brain like a Cher tattoo on my cerebral cortex. Inside the dreary, fluorescent-lit room was Mr. Ferré averting his eyes from the sight in front of him—Liza Minnelli totally naked, stretched out on a green velvet sofa. I instantly turned my back and began to get out of there fast. "Who are you?" asked Liza sweetly before I escaped. "I'm Michael. Someone just asked for me," I said as I grabbed the door to exit. "Stop. Are you the director?" she wanted to know. "No, I'm the chairman and producer," I mumbled. "Well, get back in here and shut that door." Her tone had changed from sweet and now seemed angry. "Come over here," I was ordered. I walked over to the sofa where a seamstress sat on the floor sewing the hem on her purple gown. I tried to avert my eyes from Liza's nakedness without appearing totally stupid. I had not before encountered this celebrity situation and was unclear how best to handle it. Miss Minnelli commenced to explain to me how she wished to be introduced that evening: "If Hollywood breeding can be compared to royalty, then she would certainly be our Crown Princess." Then, "Did you get all that? Now read it back to me." We still hadn't been formally introduced (though I admit there was not much formal about this meeting), so I paused, stuck out my hand, and introduced myself. She made no attempt to shake my hand and instead rolled over to one side, showing me the impressive scar from her recent surgery. Mr. Ferré, still averting his eyes, seized this moment for his escape, with a parting "Ciao" as he headed out the door. Suddenly, it was just me, the seamstress, and a naked Liza. Uncomfortable does not begin to suggest what I was feeling. I asked Miss Minnelli if she needed anything else before I left (some clothes maybe?). "Yes," she instructed, "I need the hotel to send a manicurist." That was just the opening I needed to head for the door. "I'll have one sent immediately," I gasped to her as I quickly shut the door behind me. Ah yes, there's no business like show business. I was beginning to see that I shouldn't bring my therapist only to the show and the dinner, but also to the rehearsal.

That evening, minutes before Liza Minnelli was to go onstage to introduce Mr.

Ferré, she emerged from the hijacked green room dressed in the glorious Ferré beaded gown. She looked beautiful in the purple gown, with her trademark makeup of inch-long eyelashes. But as Fran Drescher and I, waiting backstage to take our places at the podium, looked down, we shrieked with laughter to see Liza wearing purple bedroom slippers. They were the fuzzy kind that looked as though they had been used to dust the entire hotel! Because of her Italian father, Liza spoke Italian and understood when Mr. Ferré came over to speak with her, no doubt telling her that she needed to wear the shoes he'd picked out for the dress. "No," she yelled back at him in English. "I'm wearing these slippers or I'm not going out there." Mr. Ferré started to scold her in Italian as his hands waved and he got red in the face. With the audience waiting out front to cheer their favorite fashion maestro, one of Mr. Ferré's aides asked me if we had an alternative star to make the introduction. Fran Drescher immediately, and loudly, volunteered. When Liza heard this, she instantly kicked off her slippers and yelled for her assistant to grab those goddamned shoes. Properly attired now, Liza made her entrance and the audience loved her.

Later, after our stints at the podium, Fran in her skintight pink gown with the four-foot train and I were returning to our respective tables in the ballroom when I accidentally stepped on her dress, stopping the actress dead in her tracks. As Fran struggled to regain her balance, her arms swung out and hit a waiter who was standing directly behind Liza. Food flew off the waiter's tray and hit Liza, her stepmother, and even Mr. Ferré. "Quick, let's get out of here," commanded Fran in her finest Nanny Fein voice. "Liza's going to think I threw food at her." With that, we scattered in opposite directions.

The show was glamorous, visually stunning, with a decidedly Russian feeling to it. I kept thinking *Doctor Zhivago*, because the clothes were dark, powerful, and suitable for a czar or a czarina. In retrospect, it does seem a bit odd that during the last two shows, we had presented *Nanook* and *Zhivago* clothing to an audience in balmy springtime Southern California. The music was a mix of opera, rock, and Italian and Russian classics. The finale was Beverly Peele holding her naked baby daughter (had Liza been auditioning for this part?) as the other models lined the runway to the song "What the World Needs Now Is Love." The male models, each with a bottle of Stoli vodka in one hand and a crystal goblet in the other, saluted Mr. Ferré as he walked onstage with Liza and her rhinestoned cane. Among the cheering audience that night were Leonardo DiCaprio, rocker Rod Stewart, Sophia Loren, Julianne Moore, Meg Ryan, actor-brothers Dennis and Randy Quaid, tap-dancing legend Ann Miller, Jennifer Tilly, Julie Newmar, Jane Seymour, and the openly gay director of film classics such as *Midnight Cowboy*, John Schlesinger. I was busy snapping photos near the runway as the audience rose in a standing ovation to Ferré and the models. Suddenly, one of the male models reached down and pulled me up onto the stage. He handed me a glass of Stoli, and then the entire ensemble on the stage toasted me! It was a surprise that Lynne Koester had planned without my knowledge. I began to tear up as I was handed the microphone. I said simply, "Ladies and gentlemen, tonight's evening is dedicated to my friend Brandon MacNeal, who died of AIDS on February first. I miss you, Kiddo." Then I raised my glass as did everyone in the room.

10
Todd
Oldham
—Todd's Coronation

"My approach to **creativity** is to be able to create something that only can exist in **this moment** and can reinforce a hope for the future on what's been done in the past and bringing the sum of this in the present for the **future.**"

—Todd Oldham

Fran Drescher arrives in a sweet
pea colored pink evening gown.

In a glamorous kingdom of model perfection, where imperious designers clamor for absolute power—and sometimes Absolut vodka—as subservient scribes dictate fashion law and shower hyperbole on the heads of the chosen, a most recent and most beguiling prince destined for fashion importance came of age to ascend the Throne of Shmatte. Rising from the provinces of Manhattan, young Prince Todd of Oldham heard the fashionistic cries of the village people and the tapping of their street-smart susceptibilities. Prince Todd proclaimed death to the insipid minimalism of the reigning Seventh Avenue courtiers and heralded a new age of exuberant wit and pricey irreverence. As the trend-eager villagers cheered and the savvy scribes cooed common kudos, old Sir Ralph and the smug Duchess Donna and the rest of the self-contented court cringed. Youthful, sexy, and disarmingly charming, young Prince Todd,

Lea Thompson arrives. Later that
evening she was held up at gunpoint.

though wearing the emperor's new clothes, sought to be crowned the new King of Fashion.

Having captured the adulation of the MTV nation as host of "Todd Time" on MTV's *House of Style*, Todd Oldham embodied the audacious quirkiness and down-to-earth brazen zeal that would catapult our AIDS fund-raising efforts into the style of the next millennium, or so we thought. A young Texan who had lived four years in Iran as a child, with no formal fashion training, Todd Oldham was then at the zenith of his thirty minutes of fame. His incarnation of high couture mixed Dalmatian, red velvet, crocodile, and wood-paneling prints with 1970s upholstery, Scotch Tape plaid, laminated denim, quasi-fuzzy leopard pieces, and botanically imaged silk dresses cut close to the body. He was definitely making a statement, but no one seemed quite sure if he was having fun or making fun. There definitely seemed to be some Dadaist-type deflation of fashion going on. But can you really debunk fashion and still sell dresses for $8,000? Todd could. Could trashy, bad-girl clothes be considered both high fashion and attacks on the tyranny of good taste? Todd was making it all look so effortless. He was affable, laid-back, and blissed out. All the while, paparazzi pushed, flashes popped, and Hollywood stars elbowed their way into the best seats. Ugly antiglamour had become the most glamorous look in town, and high fashion, at least for now, appeared to have stumbled into a parallel universe. After all, if we had moved into a mirror world where supermodels could also be role models, then why shouldn't Todd Oldham be Crown Prince?

In 1995, a request for a royal audience with the new heir apparent was dispatched to the province of Manhattan with the now-coveted invitation to be our tenth-year honoree. With glad tidings and good cheer, Todd agreed to accept, in early 1996, the newest laurels to be laid at his sandaled feet. Todd arrived in the L.A. fashion hinterlands complete with his own royal court. Accompanied by his longtime consort and a pompous court jester and his sorceress sidekick (who could magically morph from distressed damsel to fire-spewing dragon lady)

More than 1,700 people jammed the 1,200-seat Todd Oldham show tent. Event publicist Katy Sweet (forefront) chats on her cell phone.

and various ladies-in-waiting, Todd met with me to begin preparations for what would become an unprecedented and glorious fund-raiser/coronation. Todd and his advisers searched for an appropriate arena in which to stage his West Coast ascension. They rejected out of hand our preferred site, the Los Angeles Ballroom at the Century Plaza Hotel. "No hotels!" we were instructed with promises that "we can raise the money to go outside." But, then, it was a hotel, one that had been boarded up since 1990, which first caught Todd's eye.

The famed Ambassador Hotel had opened in 1921 on a former 24-acre dairy farm facing a dirt road that did not even connect with downtown—a road now called Wilshire Boulevard. The hotel had been the location of early Academy Awards banquets and Jean Harlow's wedding reception. The hotel also figured in political history as the site where Richard Nixon composed his famous televised Checkers speech, which convinced Eisenhower to keep him on as his 1952 vice-presidential running mate despite a Nixon financial scandal. And it was in the Ambassador that Robert Kennedy was assassinated after celebrating his 1968 victory in the California presidential primary. The hotel was now used occasionally as a location site for bad TV movies.

On a warm September afternoon in 1995, Todd, his female sidekick whom we'll call Red (because of her very red hair), and I drove through the gates and onto the enormous grounds of the old Ambassador. The landscaping had all gone to seed, and every inch of land was overrun by weeds except where covered by cracked and buckled blacktop and concrete. Hundreds of feral house cats scampered for cover as we parked our SUV near the main entrance and headed into the abandoned hotel. Inside, the air reeked of stale Johnny Cat, as we were met at the door by a Hollywood old-timer who had spent his adult life working as a waiter at the hotel. His job now was to escort location scouts through this inner-city relic as he pointed out the parts of the hotel that could safely be used and the parts that had been condemned after the 1994

Baywatch's David Hasselhoff with his wife on shore leave.

Ouch! Sandra Bernhard wears a
gold lamé Isaac Mizrahi to the
Todd Oldham event in 1996.

Brendan Fraser and Downtown
Julie Brown, wearing Escada.

Lori Petty arrives all decked out
in Oldham.

Northridge earthquake. The first stop on our
tour, gruesomely enough, was the ballroom
kitchen where Robert Kennedy had been shot
in the head. Our host enthusiastically pointed
out the exact location on the floor where the
slain senator had fallen. It was certainly
intriguing to see the historic location I'd seen
dozens of times before in the news footage,
with 6'6" former football lineman for the L.A.
Rams Rosey Grier tackling assassin Sirhan
Sirhan as Grier screamed out to others, "Grab
the gun! Break his fingers if you have to!" It
gave me the chills. A bad omen.

"Perfect," announced Todd as we climbed
the enormous staircase leading to the formerly
posh Coconut Grove ballroom from which all
the big bands of the 1920s and 1930s had
broadcast radio performances. Todd loved the
hotel's history and Red loved whatever Todd
loved. The property had been used for other
AIDS fund-raisers. I'd heard stories about the
roof leaking and guests being robbed and their
cars vandalized in this now run-down and

blighted neighborhood. When Todd discovered that the property was then owned by
New York and Atlantic City real estate mag-
nate Donald Trump, he said, "I'll call Ivana
[Trump]. She's a good friend. Maybe she'll
donate it for the evening." Luckily for all of
us, but especially the 1,700 guests who would
end up attending the event, the property management company who handled the
Ambassador gave us a firm "No." They didn't
want to risk the potential liability of having
that many people in an unsafe building.
"Thank God," I thought to myself as I called
Todd with the splendid news.

In late November, a location called
Bergamot Station came to our attention as a
possible venue for the Oldham show. Nestled
in the southeast corner of the upscale beach
community of Santa Monica, the station was
an old railroad yard cluttered with ramshackle
warehouses and factories. These buildings had
been converted into a compound that housed
a cluster of 22 chic art galleries showing the

best of L.A.'s contemporary artists. The buildings themselves were stark and minimal, many with corrugated steel roofs and walls, concrete floors, and huge sliding doors that opened to a view of the Santa Monica Mountains. When Todd finally made it back to L.A., he loved the Bergamot Station site with its rawness and sheer scale.

Our venue was set. It was a huge 27,000-square-foot building with two adjacent warehouses, each an additional 14,000 square feet in size. In its original incarnation, the building had been a factory and warehouse for a manufacturer of water heaters. The space was enormous and wide-open; it was like standing inside an airplane hangar. The building's corrugated metal roof and walls had long ago been rusted by the salt air, and the concrete floors were stained with grease and oil. Pigeons flew in and out of the barn-sized

doors as they tended their nests and fed their squabs in the rafters above.

The transformation from dilapidated warehouse to a tent fit for a prince was as clever and shocking as any sorcerer's spell. The 27,000 square feet would be divided into two big rooms—a dining tent and a show tent. The show tent would be bleacher seating, a first for our fashion shows but successfully used in shows for the New York fashion press. The floors would be carpeted, and the walls and ceiling upholstered with the six colors of the Lambda Gay Pride rainbow flag—red, orange, yellow, green, blue, purple. The colored material to be used was thin plastic sheeting that was light and could be easily draped and hung. This design was somewhat surprising to me as I had assumed the reason Todd had liked the deserted warehouse was for its stark, postindustrial, dilapidated, crude look. Now all that was to be covered up with

The *Hollywood Reporter's* George Christy arrives at the Oldham event in 1996.

cheery, bright colors. It was my tenth event and I still was not any closer to understanding how a fashion designer's mind worked than when I had started with my first event. The end result suggested a Felliniesque medieval circus tent, imposing and strangely beautiful. The whole look worked, though not quite as well as the Isaac Mizrahi Chinese Theater tent, which had made such an impact on everyone in 1994. The Oldham venue, although playful, bordered on kitsch. It was such a kaleidoscope of brilliant colors that it eventually wore on the nerves of one of our famous guests on the night of the show. "There's too much going on here," remarked the leading lady movie icon of the 1970s as she made her way through the throngs of other celebrities, journalists, and guests. "What on earth was *she*

Three of the biggest names in Hollywood arrive at Oldham: Sandy Gallin, Jackie Collins, and Barry Krost.

Leggy Naomi Campbell was a
handful at the Oldham event.

Model Janice Dickenson works
the Oldham runway and her hair.

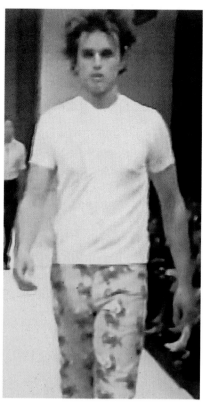

'60s a-go-go. The audience loved
their Oldham.

thinking, or was it the drugs? A flashback,
maybe?" Oh, well, you can't please everyone
all of the time. But she did have a point; it
was a big-top psychedelic experience.

Most of our 1,700 guests loved the venue,
the look, and the whole occasion. The
Oldham audience tended to be young
Hollywood—agents, managers, publicists,
attorneys, and starlets, studs, and directors in
waiting—the next generation of L.A. philanthropists. Raised on MTV and postmodern
irony by parents who had once been hippies
searching for meaning with LSD and free
love, this audience seemed to really get
Oldham; they understood the camp and fun
of the moment. The event didn't seem so
much about the fight against AIDS anymore,
as most of our guests had missed the beginning shock wave of the epidemic. They were
seizing the evening, eager to rub elbows with
the stars in attendance: actors Angela Bassett,
Ali MacGraw, Leonard Nimoy, Elizabeth
Berkley, Sandra Bernhard, Brendan Fraser,
Lori Petty, Lea Thompson, Tippi Hedren,

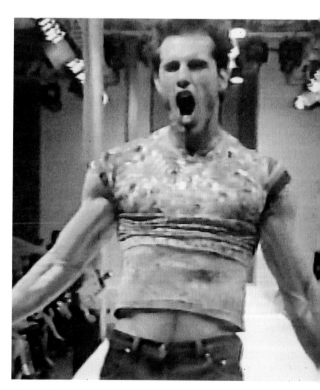

Down, boy!

Gay pride at the Oldham show.

Model Lynne Koester.

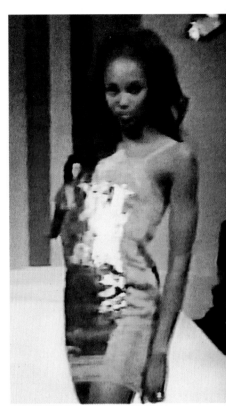

Naomi Campbell.

All grown up from her Saturday
morning stint on *Saved by the Bell,*
Elizabeth Berkley knocked us out.

Julie Newmar, Peter Berg, Fran Drescher, and
Cameron Diaz; and singers Rod Stewart,
Sheryl Crow, and Paula Abdul.

Trying to seat all these celebrities with
their peculiar needs and the other guests who
wanted to be near them made the creation of
my seating chart, once again, a never-ending
danse macabre. Two weeks before the event,
the phone began ringing off the hook with
special requests. One of the more peculiar
came through the PR representative of the
large, successful German fashion house
Escada, which had underwritten a sizable part
of the evening's expenses because of their relationship with Oldham (Todd had been hired
as a design consultant). The PR rep, calling
from New York City, wanted me to find the
president of Escada a date for the evening.
And not just any date, but a "glamorous and
powerful" date, presumably thin enough to
wear clothes from his label. The president
would be flying in from Germany and expected to garner a fair amount of free publicity for
his high-profile empire in exchange for the six

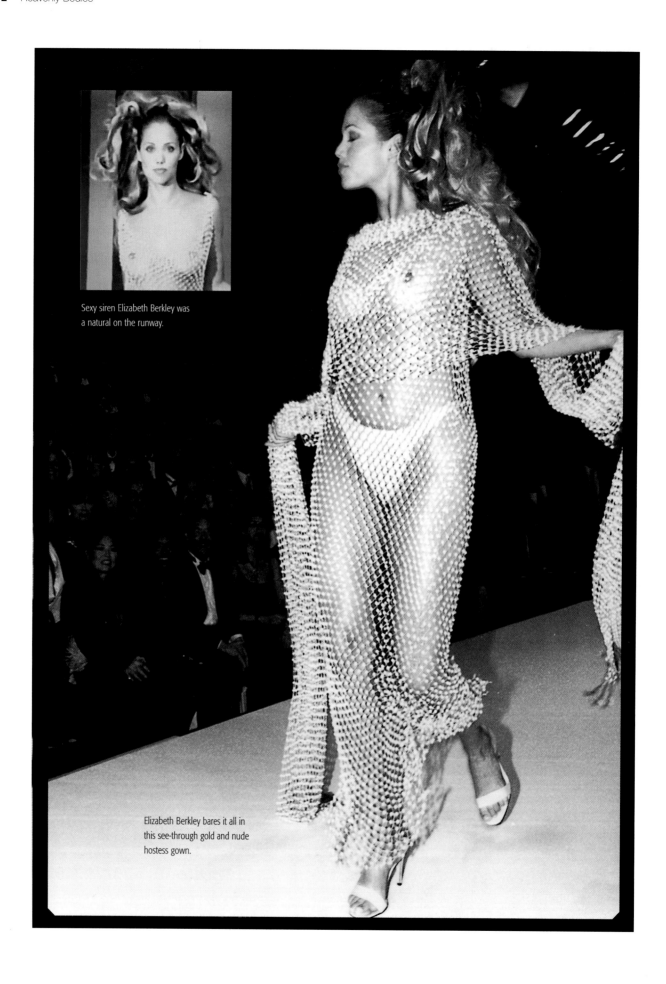

Sexy siren Elizabeth Berkley was
a natural on the runway.

Elizabeth Berkley bares it all in
this see-through gold and nude
hostess gown.

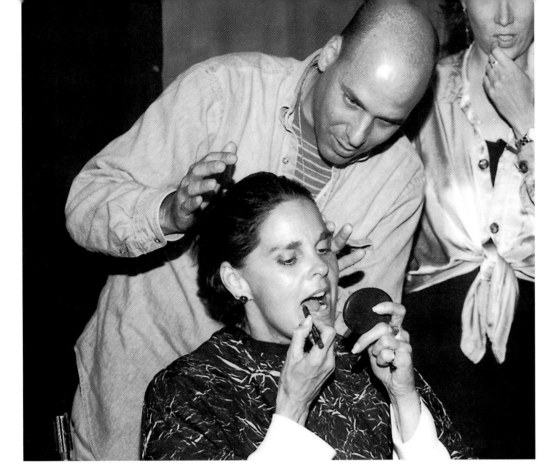

figures he had contributed to underwrite the evening. The PR rep informed me that the president "would like Sherry Lansing if she's available." Mind you, Sherry Lansing is not some eager young starlet; she's the chair and CEO of Paramount Pictures Motion Pictures Group. I tried hard not to laugh into the phone as I explained to him that Sherry Lansing is married to Academy Award–winning director William Friedkin. "Well," he shot back, "this isn't supposed to be a *sex* date." "No, you're not hearing what I'm saying; she's married, she doesn't date, her husband wouldn't like it." I guess part of being a PR rep is being optimistically bullheaded, because he immediately came back with, "Can you get Cher? Or Goldie?" By now I could no longer hide my laughter. In fact, I was in hysterics. I knew he was only doing his job, but he might as well have asked me to fix the California state lottery so that his boss could win the jackpot. Finally, I suggested that he might try inviting some celebrity clients from the Escada store in Beverly Hills. I wished him luck, told him I had other matters to attend to, then hung up the phone, and fell into a fit

of uncontrollable laughter. Could I fix his boss up with Goldie? Yeah, like I was some kind of gentile Dolly Levi for celebrities.

A different sort of problem, one I truly wanted to help with, was posed when a famous character actress called me. Having made a name for herself in prominent supporting roles in two Whoopi Goldberg hit films, this actress hadn't worked much lately. I'd seen her name many times before in connection with fund-raising events for different AIDS charities. I knew she had worked hard donating her time and efforts, and I told her I hoped I would

The beautiful Rachel Hunter, one of the nicest models I worked with.

A model reveals herself at the Todd Oldham show.

An Oldham model in a peek-a-boo top.

meet her at the show. "I'd like that, but I haven't been invited," she said. Her call was shortly after Todd had arrived in Los Angeles and she wanted to know where she could get in touch with him, as they were old friends. I gladly told her that he was staying at the Four Seasons Hotel in Beverly Hills. My next call was from Todd telling me not to give out his whereabouts to anyone. He told me there was no room at any of his three reserved tables for this actress and to look elsewhere—"I really don't care whether she attends or not." I then called the representatives at Escada who had been begging for stars they could seat at their tables. Their reply was a swift decline of the offer, saying this star was not hot enough or thin enough for their clothes. I called the actress back and offered her seats at my table. I told her my guests included Tippi Hedren, Ali MacGraw, the director of that year's hit *Happy Gilmore* and 1999's *Big Daddy*. Dennis Dugan and his wife Sharon, my therapist Chris, and several other friends. She seemed hurt by Todd's no-room-at-the-inn excuse and thanked me but declined my invitation. Damn, to be out of work for 10 minutes in

Hollywood! Fortunately, this actress is hot again because of a featured role on a successful TV sitcom and a 1999 Golden Globe nomination. Today she's back on top, with invitations pouring in asking for her presence at the biggest parties in Hollywood and from fashion designers everywhere begging her to wear their clothes.

One delightful surprise on the day of the show was a call from the publicist of the sexy young lap-dancing star of the previous year's *Showgirls*, Elizabeth Berkley. Elizabeth was the only actress whom Todd had asked to model in the show, and she wanted to know where she could buy a ticket for her mother to attend. It was the only call that day where I hadn't been begged by a manager or a publicist to comp their clients. There was one aging rocker whose biggest hits were in the early 1970s who wanted complimentary tickets not only for himself and a guest, but for his entire entourage. After all, reasoned his manager, this rocker's lovely young wife was a model in the show. Satisfying this request turned out to be easy as one call to Escada, still eager for stars, found seats for the gravel-voiced rocker and his pack of pals.

The requests for placement at A-tables reached an unprecedented fevered pitch in 1996. It seemed as though everyone with a name or money thought they had a God-given right to approve the seating chart prior to the event. Messengers would be sent to pick up a photocopy of the master plan of the dining room and would always leave my office empty-handed. After the messengers would report back from their failed missions, I would get a desperate phone call and all sorts of drama would ensue. In ten years of handling the seating at these events, I'd heard it all. "I've got Princess Diana coming as my guest, so I'll need a good table." "Do you realize who I am?" Or my least favorite, "If I don't like my table, I'm taking yours!" Once at an earlier event, a very large-busted woman with red-orange hair and a lime-green sequined evening gown actually carried through on the threat to take my seats. She moved herself and several of her friends to my table and refused to get up as my guests arrived. I quickly had four additional place settings added and everyone was happy, friendly, and very, very

On friendlier terms—Todd and
Naomi share a moment backstage. He would later be quoted
as saying about Naomi—"We
have a no-asshole clause at
TO…we don't hire her."

snug. The woman was so pleased with her
evening that she came back every year there-
after, donating more than $50,000. She could
have sat in my lap for that!

Year after year, though, the thorniest seating problems were posed by the major magazines and their guests. Magazines such as *Elle,
Vogue, Bazaar, In Style,* the *New Yorker* and
Vanity Fair always made sure that their tables
not be placed near each other. The guests of
these magazines were primarily major or
prospective advertisers, celebrities they were
wooing, and members of the New York power
elite. After a few drinks, people often began
to table-hop and mingle. The last thing any of
these magazines wanted was for one of their
advertisers, lubricated and relaxed, to be introduced to their competitors. I also had to be
keenly aware and careful that *Vogue,* for

instance, did not get a better table than
Bazaar or *Bazaar's* coverage of our event
would be severely scaled back. Simply put, the
better the table, the more editorial coverage
we would get, and therefore more awareness
of the events and the causes. This was a tricky
job and you could easily get run over even if
you were on the right track. Still, it was not
impossible. You just had to understand the
players and move accordingly. It was like a
chess game that required skill, knowledge,
nerve, and some luck—not to mention a high
tolerance for abuse. I guess growing up with
dysfunctional parents taught me some handy
life skills after all.

Big fashion retailers could be equally as
fussy, not just about their tables but about
their corporate sponsorship of events. During
the summer of 1995, shortly after Todd had

The 1960s ruled at the Oldham event.

Naomi Campbell shakes hands with Fran Drescher while Todd looks on.

agreed to our event, a bidding war broke out between Saks Fifth Avenue and Neiman-Marcus, each wanting to be the sole retail underwriter of the Oldham event. We had come a long way from our early years when the May Department Stores Company chain was our sole, brave retail sponsor. Now we had all of them, Saks, Neiman-Marcus, Macys (which would start their own San Francisco fashion event called Passport and later bring it to L.A.), and Robinson-May, vying for the top spot. They understood the publicity and prestige that our fashion gala could bring them. It brought out the biggest stars in Hollywood and the fashion world, and the chief retail sponsor could garner worldwide publicity and goodwill. With all of these department stores trying to top each other in their philanthropy, I was beginning to feel like I was in a scene from *Miracle on 34th Street* with Macys and Gimbels each competing for more Christmas spirit than the other. In early 1996, the competition had been narrowed down to just two remaining players, Saks Fifth Avenue and Neiman-Marcus—each retailer coming to the table with a six-figure offer to help defray the ever-growing produc-

tion costs of the event. Each offer was conditional on that retailer being the sole retail sponsor. Saks had just completed a $15 million renovation of their Beverly Hills store and wanted us to have cocktails and dinner in the store and the fashion show in a tent in their rear parking lot. They felt that the show would be a perfect way to introduce the new SFA to Los Angeles and the world. In the end, though, because of their higher offer and their past support of our event, and also because Oldham wanted to do the show at Bergamot Station, not in a parking lot, Neiman-Marcus won the star billing.

Oldham's Court Jester and his ever-present sidekick, Red, continued to amaze us with their outrageous and expensive behavior. As was typical, the cuisine for the evening was of extreme importance to the designer. Todd, an animal rights and antifur activist, and a vegan himself, insisted that the dinner for all guests be vegetarian. He held his ground that no animal would lose its life for an event that was honoring him. I certainly respected Todd's deep convictions, but this meant I needed to find a caterer who could create a gourmet vegetarian menu that would be enjoyed by nonvegetarians and who could handle such a large event. The usual bid sheets were faxed out to the best caterers and restaurants in Los Angeles, with added instructions that "no fish, fowl or meat or any animal products" be used. After the proposed menus and bids were received, we began the tasting process—a series of lunches where Court Jester, sidekick Red, and a few others would sample the bill of fare from each candidate. Jester cut the tastings short by suddenly hiring, in a moment of purple passion or, more likely, wishful fantasy, the caterer who had prepared the most expensive bid. Jester's decision appeared not to be based on the quality of the food or the proposed menu, but on the caterer's blond hair, blue eyes, muscular chest, big biceps, and firm bubble butt. So a lucrative contract was signed by Jester with apparently no motive other than a distant hope to sample something that could never have made it onto our vegan menu—beefcake.

I don't know if the caterer ever did kickback any sugar to Jester, but in his defense, I must admit that the dinner was memorable:

asparagus vinaigrette, potato and roasted pepper pancakes, ragout of wild mushroom, artichokes, roasted vegetables, and a mixed berry napoleon. Everything was beautifully prepared and served, though apparently not sufficiently filling for many of our guests. A parade of people came over to my table to ask me when the main course was being served. "You just ate it," I informed them. I tried to become less visible behind the elaborate table arrangement—a royal crown (Oldham's insignia trademark) filled with a garden of wheat grass, hyacinths, freesia, tulips, and ranunculus, complete with a candlabra of jeweled bark topped with faux leopard lampshades. Despite this centerpiece, clearly inspired by Liberace and Martha Stewart with help from Seigfried & Roy, the bellyachers still found my table. Fortunately for me, I was seated between my friend Ali MacGraw and my therapist (a must-have guest for any event where one is perceived to be in charge despite having little real power). Most of the complainers became tongue-tied and meek as soon as they recognized Ali and they'd wander off. For the grumblers who persisted, my therapist offered free psychological personality evaluations that inevitably persuaded each of them to journey on.

Another visitor to my table during dinner was Todd himself. He came over and whispered into my ear that he would like to be introduced to my table guest, actress Tippi Hedren. Alfred Hitchcock had discovered the New York model Tippi Hedren when he viewed her in a commercial on NBC's *Today Show* in 1962. Hitch was looking for a replacement for his

A ravishing Rachel Hunter in black velvet.

A leopard print "Little House on the Prairie" sundress with spaghetti straps.

Veronica Webb in a colorful "everything goes" Oldham.

Naomi Campbell in a mini Oldham.

favorite icy blond leading lady, Grace Kelly, who according to him was now "off in Monaco playing a Princess." Hitchcock immediately cast Tippi in her two most famous roles, as bird feed in *The Birds* and as a frigid kleptomaniac who goes bonkers when she sees the color red in *Marnie*. Hedren's *Marnie* costar was Sean Connery, trying to break away from his James Bond typecasting, as the psychiatrist eager to cure Marnie's frigidity, though he finds her thievery a bit of a turn-on. When I introduced Todd and Tippi, Todd gushed extravagantly that the only reason he was there that evening was "to meet Tippi Hedren." Tippi seemed taken aback, even a bit annoyed, by Todd's effusive hyperbole. "Honey, you're here tonight to raise money for AIDS," Tippi reminded him. Then, as if to keep Todd in his place, she continued, "I've never heard of you, but then I'm not really into fashion." The correction having been made, Tippi proceeded to let Todd off the hook by telling him how impressed she

was that he had chosen to serve an all-vegetarian dinner. Tippi has herself been an animal rights and environmental activist for more than three decades and is founder and president of the Roar Foundation, which runs the Shambala Preserve, an 80-acre wildlife habitat perched on the edge of the Mojave Desert, forty miles northeast of Los Angeles. Tippi lives at the game preserve and awakens each morning to the sounds of lions, tigers, leopards, servals, panthers, cheetahs, cougars, and two African elephants. The high desert game preserve had originally been an African-type location for her 1982 motion picture *Roar*, an eleven-year labor of love directed by Tippi's then-husband Noel Marshall and costarring her actress-daughter Melanie Griffith. (It was while working in 1973 as an extra on her mother's film *The Harrad Experiment* that Griffith met her twice ex-husband Don Johnson.) Tippi is also a vegetarian, so with this and animal rights causes in common, she and Todd ended up hitting it off very well and parted with a big hug.

As the candlelight flickered warmly at our table and I relaxed into the pleasant company of my tablemates, my walkie-talkie suddenly blared an urgent request. I was needed out front. The new problem turned out to be Naomi Campbell, our star superstar model for the evening. I recalled how touched I had been at our Versace evening when Naomi had insisted on donating to the event even though she was already donating her invaluable presence on the runway. But that had been in 1991 and an extra five years of life in the supermodel netherworld can do a lot to change a person. The other models were already backstage preparing for the show; Naomi was still out front. With no previous notice, she had brought along a large entourage, which included her publicist, L.A. agent, boyfriend, trainer, and a couple others, and Naomi was demanding that they not only be allowed in for free, but that they be given the best table in the house. When our staff had tried to explain to her that the event was sold out and there was no table to seat her guests, she became outraged and threatened to leave with her friends and not model at all that evening. (Three years later, I was not surprised when I heard that Donatella Versace had quit using Campbell, the model most identified with the Versace shows, and read that Todd Oldham had said about Naomi, "I don't use her—I have a no-assholes clause.")

So our star model for the evening was threatening to walk unless I could seat her friends in our bursting-at-the-seams dining tent. And I was supposed to solve this problem. No wonder this would be my last year as event chairman. I frantically scanned the room, desperately straining my panicked mind for any solution. Then my eyes fell on the very table that many of our female and gay male dinner guests had been eyeballing since we first sat down—a table of adorably handsome Italian soccer players. One of the soccer players was married to another of our famous models, and the entire team had been flown over, compliments of *L'Uomo Vogue*, the Italian men's fashion magazine. They were clearly having a great time right where they were.

Fortunately, the teammates were so hammered, happy, and easy-going that they loved my idea of moving their whole party backstage, where, I'm embarrassed to quote myself, they could be "where the real action is" with naked women and an abundance of Cristal champagne.

Faster than one could shout, *Volare!*, our soccer team was happily ensconced backstage and our high-fashion extortionist had a table—and agreed to stay and do the show, bless her heart. It had been the right call; Naomi was phenomenal later on the catwalk. She has the most amazing runway walk. Her feet seem to attack the tarmac, almost as if she were driving the heel in, drilling for oil, every time she puts a foot down. She was definitely the most memorable part of the show. As for our soccer team, they had a great time being bad boys, naughtily flirting with the models who enjoyed egging them on. They all had a grand time turning the backstage into total pandemonium. It may also explain why the models exuded such hot sex appeal onstage that evening. I think some of them undoubtedly helped themselves to some Italian dessert that night, even before leaving Bergamot Station. Later at the after-party, some of the soccer players could be seen drunkenly dancing, wearing the exaggerated and snarled wigs worn by the models in the show. Some of the guys even had female panties on top of their wigs or twirled them around on their index fingers as they danced. "It got pretty wild backstage," remembers model Lynne Koester. "Those guys loosened up everyone. It was like passing out Spanish fly."

Lynne Koester had surprised and delighted me a few days earlier when she unexpectedly called up and volunteered to help out with the last-minute pre-event grunt work in my home office. We had become close friends the previous year working together on the Gianfranco Ferré gala. I was touched by her offer and immediately put her to work answering the phones, which were ringing off the hook.

When the dinner and brief speeches concluded, our guests were ushered into the second half of the warehouse, which had been

Snappy Rachel Hunter.

Photographer Herb Ritts, Naomi
Campbell, and Todd backstage.

transformed into a show tent. Jewel-colored
stadium cushions, sixteen to a row, were
affixed to the bleachers. The cushions, in
cranberry red, royal blue, imperial purple, deep
gold, and emerald green, each adorned with
the trademark Oldham crown, had been made
and donated by the Karen Kane Company, a
national sportswear company based in Los
Angeles. There were, however, 500 not-so-
fortunate behinds that had to do without one
of these spectacular cushions. Because of all
the free tickets comped by the Oldham crew,
and all the frantic last-minute additions, we
ended up with 1,700 people cramming into
bleachers planned for 1,200 people. True to
the festive spirit of the evening, people made
the best of the tight situation, sharing cushions, sitting on laps, or opting to stand as they
settled in to view the show. As I escorted a
well-known actress and former fashion model
to her seat on the bleachers, I suddenly heard
a loud whoopee cushion sound, followed by a
loud bellow, "Who cut the cheese?" Then
another loud rumble as someone again broke

wind. I turned around just in time to see sexually ambiguous comedienne and provocateur
of all media Sandra Bernhard loudly exclaim
to her publicist, "It must have been all of
those vegetables at dinner." Then she stood up
and ferociously fanned her famous fanny. The
actress I was seating, the height of grace and
old-style good manners, discreetly asked a
young man several cushions away if she could
change places with him—apologizing that she
was not the one with the gas problem. The
young man was entranced by her and happy
to oblige. I kept recalling Sandra Bernhard as
the wonderfully psychotic groupie tormenting
Jerry Lewis in *The King of Comedy* as she kept
squirming and crossing and recrossing her legs
throughout the fashion show. I kept hoping
that Bernhard would go stand by an exit
where her flatulence could go unfettered, but
the news cameras were rolling and the photographers were snapping pictures and this
was a major photo-op. What was a girl to do?
I saw a reference to Bernhard's poison gas
attack in one of the tabloids a couple days

later and wondered who spilled the beans. Maybe it was her own publicist, whose job it was to keep her name in the press. It's not like the incident would tarnish her pristine girl-next-door image.

The show was late to start and the crowd out front was getting anxious. Even more anxious backstage was Naomi Campbell. She was scheduled to be the first model out on the runway and she had important after-show plans with her table of guests. She wasn't going to let the Cheech and Chong management style of Todd and Jester make her alter her social calendar. As she wasn't being paid and was doing a favor for Todd, she insisted that the show start NOW! Next thing I knew, we had two volatile women, Naomi and the Jester's sidekick Red, spewing venom at each other. With Naomi and her fellow Brit, Red, going toe to toe, the insults being hurled got very creative. With my headset on, I was hearing adjectives and nouns I was not familiar with, though I did catch their drift. "Wow," I said to the fashion editor sitting next to me, "listen to this." She put on the headset and her face lit up like a Broadway marquee. I asked her to save my seat as I headed backstage to see what I could do to help. Actually, I didn't have any idea how I could help, I mostly wanted to see this performance live. What a scene! The soccer players were taking bets. Red was now even redder with bulging veins and Naomi was yet again threatening to walk. Just in time, though, the lineup was ready, the music began, and Red gave Naomi a good shove out onto the runway. Naomi instantly transformed from a screaming harpy into supermodel of the world and the audience went mad for her. The photographers went crazy too. Naomi made sure they all got their fill. No one else that evening created anything like the excitement Naomi did—even the surprise stroll of sexy Elizabeth Berkley in a see-through haremish outfit that exposed her bare breasts and thong-clad bottom. Besides my friend Lynne Koester, other famous models that evening included Beverly Peele, Rachel Hunter, Tyra Banks, and Janice Dickenson. The second the show finished, Naomi was whisked off into the night in her midnight blue limo, her good deed for charity

Julie Newmar takes a break backstage. She attended most of our events—a real activist.

done. The next day's *Women's Wear Daily* would sport a glamorous photo of Naomi and Todd—cheek to cheek for charity.

One model was back for another year, sans the $10,000 Ferré gown she had forgotten to return the previous year. A huge model in the '80s and a major tabloid target in the 1990s for her rumored pregnancy by an action-movie superstar, she was once again up to her whack-a-doodle behavior. High on something, she had quite a buzz going by the time she hit the catwalk. With the photographers and TV cameras at the end of the runway, our toasted mannequin disregarded all directions and played to the cameras, causing the models behind her to back up like cars behind a rush hour accident on the Hollywood Freeway. Each time this pickled poser approached the end of the runway, she carried on like some exhibitionistic amateur. She blew Marilyn Monroe kisses, shimmied like a stripper, licked her lips lasciviously and tossed her hair like some unknown starlet on the beach at Cannes. As a topper, she gave Naomi the finger—yes, on stage. Backstage, after the show, I went up to thank her for

Rachel Hunter enjoys a toast
backstage.

floral print suit designed by Anna Sui!
Despite having insisted on an after-party to
follow the show, Todd and his boyfriend quietly sneaked out the back of Bergamot Station
and didn't attend their own party.

Little more than two years later, Todd
Oldham would pull the plug on his high-end
collection, just three weeks after Isaac Mizrahi
had also shuttered his company. Someone
must have finally kissed the Prince because he
had suddenly turned into a toad. He licensed
his name to The Limited, a chain of ordinary
clothing outlets and announced that filmmaking "was actually the only thing I knew I
wanted to do from the very beginning. I'm
still debating whether to be involved in
clothes or not, but I always knew I wanted to
work with movies." In fact, Todd confessed to
me, shortly after I first met him, that "I
became a designer so I could meet people in
the movie business who can help me become a
director." Oldham had arrived, hit it big, and
was gone in a mere eight years. And he wasn't
even sure he likes clothes—he wants to direct!
Oldham was like the Abbie Hoffman of the
fashion world; he instinctively knew how to
manipulate the media. I wonder if the New
York fashion press has realized that their
hunger for novelty, for whatever is new even if
it isn't good, has made them fair game for
each naked emperor in new clothes.

This too marked the finale of my participation as chairman of these fashion events. I
had at least lasted longer than Oldham, a
decade and then some, and it had been quite a
ride. During that decade, Mackie, Oldham,
and Mizrahi's companies had gone belly up.
Mizrahi and Oldham were trying to get into
movies, and Mackie is doing Barbie dolls.
Versace had been assassinated and Adrian was
still dead. It had been a decade in which we
started with the undeniable timeless genius of
Adrian's designs and ended with the flavor of
the moment, postmodern kitsch of Oldham.
We had started as a committed band who created a joyful evening, all with volunteer effort
and donations and against all odds. And we
had seen, year by year, a progressive takeover
of the event by corporate publicity machines,
grandiose egos, and big-time charity power
politics. By the end of our wild decade, the

donating her time as she was shoving several
bottles of very expensive Cristal champagne
into her Prada shoulder bag. "Right!" she said
to me as she checked the hang on one of the
soccer players, then headed for the exit, still
dressed in a Todd Oldham original. When a
security guard stopped her, reminding her to
return the Oldham dress, she simply reversed
direction and headed out front into the pandemonium of the crowd inching its way into
the after-party. She was quickly out another
exit—wig, dress, champagne, and soccer player, all gone.

Despite all the drama and trauma sur-
rounding it, the fashion show had been a huge
hit with the audience and the media. The
finale was the traditional fashion show last
gown—Naomi Campbell pranced down the
runway in an Oldham thrift store–chic wedding dress, wearing a dog collar and a rhinestone-studded S&M bondage face cover. The
young bride should never forget to properly
accessorize. When Todd Oldham took his
bow on the runway, he wore a powder blue,

Janice Dickenson shares a
moment backstage with actress
Ali MacGraw.

original purpose of the event, to help people
with HIV and AIDS live with care and dignity, seemed to have become lost underneath
layer upon layer of self-interest and hubris. To
some degree, this book may chart what happens to charity events that become too big
and too successful, that end up spending too
much to do too little. How homemade and
humble, unselfish and naive beginnings can
turn into a media-glitzed showbiz publicity
circus. Or maybe it's only about what happens
in New York and Hollywood, where news has
been replaced by publicity and where talent
has been replaced by fame. I don't mean to
sound disillusioned; the trip was fascinating as
hell and an interesting sociological study. It
was Mr. Toad's Wild Ride and *Love Story*. It

was Dorothy looking behind the curtain to see
that the Wizard of Oz was only a medicine-
show man. It was the *Roman Spring of Mrs.
Stone* and the winter of my discontent. It was
a dramatic and fascinating study of the human
spirit.

During that decade, a couple hundred
thousand more Americans succumbed to
AIDS, including my best friend, Brandon
MacNeal, as did several million more around
the world. Now it appears that HIV infections
may be about to increase again, striking
minority communities, young heterosexual
men and women, and again the new crop of
gay men who have not yet buried their
friends. So was it all worth doing? Of course
it was—we could not have done nothing.

Todd Oldham receiving his
Crystal Apple Award from
"Nanny Fein," Fran Drescher.

Index